THE
DEER HUNTER'S
BIBLE

FOURTH EDITION

George Laycock

Broadway Books
New York

BROADWAY

The Library of Congress Cataloging-in-Publication Data has
cataloged the previous edition as:
Laycock, George.
  The deer hunter's bible.

  1. Deer hunting. I. Title.
SK301.L3   1986   799.2'77357   85-29215
ISBN 0-385-19985-6

22 21 20 19 18 17 16 15 14

CONTENTS

THE DEER HUNTER'S BIBLE

ONE
KNOW YOUR DEER

When I first saw the large buck through my binoculars, he was within one hundred yards of another hunter, a fact that neither of them realized. The hunter turned slowly and faced the direction from which the buck was approaching.

Through the naked branches of the hardwoods, I could look down on the scene as the drama unfolded in the gray morning light. I had spent most of the previous day studying the deer of the neighborhood and thought I had their habits figured out nicely. The buck should have fed down along the creek and come back up the hill to bed in the thickets near which I waited. Instead of angling toward me, however, he was about to come within range of the man waiting beside the trail with his back against a large oak tree.

The buck stopped often and lifted his head to test the air, then moved on. He was not feeding now, but instead was moving steadily through the woods as if overdue at home. From my angle it seemed that, by now, the hunter must have him in view. Then the sound of a single shot rolled up the mountainside.

The hunter's companion, whom I hadn't seen before, came over from the far side of the hill. He shook hands with his friend and clapped him on the back. They stood looking down on the splendid buck for a few minutes before beginning to gut him and drag him from the woods.

In varying forms, this scene is repeated for more than a million successful deer hunters in this country every year. North American hunters come to

On opening morning of the new season, a hunter waits silently in his tree stand as a trophy buck steps into range.

the deer season nowadays to pursue millions of deer. From this storehouse hunters may, in a single season, take several times the number of deer that existed in the country in the early 1900s. This is the golden age of deer hunting, and it is little wonder that every year thousands of new deer hunters are

2

THE DEER HUNTER'S BIBLE

out in the woods and fields, pursuing whitetails, mule deer, and blacktails.

Deer hunting is an old and honored pastime. People have hunted deer since stones were the latest thing in weapons. For hundreds of years the ancestors of those among us who trace their family history to Europe knew that the pursuit of deer was the sport of noblemen with horses and buckhounds. But in America, deer quickly became everybody's big game.

Deer hunting on the American frontier was a necessity as well as a sport. Where legal, deer hunting today employs a few beagles or mixed-up potlickers, but mostly is practiced with no dogs at all. Instead of outrunning your deer, you outwit it, outwait it, or outguess it. How you hunt deer is limited only by the law, your imagination, strength, and knowledge of the woods and fields.

Native American hunters took deer in traps, drove them into water off the tips of peninsulas, used fire, snares, bow and arrow, atlatl, and any other tool or method they could devise. The odds were against them and their primitive methods, and in spite of what General Custer might have thought, there never were great numbers of Indians. The wild game and the Indians continued from year to year in a kind of balanced economy until the time that Europeans began establishing settlements along the East Coast.

While explorers, adventurers, mountain men, professional hunters, and settlers pushed deeper into the West, cities in the East and South grew. The demand for food and leather sent the professional hunters scouring the country for salable game. They hunted the animals down with a relentlessness and efficiency that must have shocked the Indians, who could recall more orderly times. One hunter in New York State is said to have killed more than 2,500 deer before he died in 1850. Maryland hunter Meshach Browning, who was at his prime in the early 1800s, reported in a book of his frontier adventures that among the game he killed were more than 1,800 deer. Overhunting and destruction of the native forests, however, soon reduced the large wildlife populations that had made such records possible. In 1862, following passage of the Homestead Act, settlers moved westward in growing numbers, drawing on the herds of wild game they encountered.

Out of the western plains and hills came wagonloads of deer and elk and there were years when venison was a drug on the market. When there was little market for the meat, the hunters continued to kill deer because they could sell the hides. We need to view their acts in the framework of their time. The meat hunters' methods were acceptable in their day because the nation had not yet matured in its thinking about its wildlife resources or come to understand the principles of game management.

By 1900, deer had been eliminated from much of their former range and many states moved to protect them by declaring closed seasons. For some this protection came too late. At the beginning of this century, the deer herds in state after state were down to a few hundred or none at all. Older citizens of my native Ohio went through their youth without ever seeing a wild deer because the deer were gone.

Then timber began to return to the hills, second-growth forest vegetation that favors deer. Given better sources of food, as well as the protection of wildlife laws, the deer started to recover. State game agencies began shifting deer around and rein-

By live-trapping and transplanting deer, biologists have helped reestablish them in many areas where they had once disappeared. *American Forest Products Industries*

troducing them to regions from which they had vanished. Missouri, for example, completed a twenty-year program of live-trapping and transplanting that returned the whitetail to its former Missouri range in abundance.

The result has been the rapid return of the whitetail wherever habitat would support it. The deer also extended their range northward in Canada with the advance of forestry and agriculture. Most parts of the continent where they can live are now saturated with them. The whitetail is also highly adaptable and can live near people and their developments.

The state with the largest number of whitetails today is undoubtedly Texas, with a deer population calculated in 1982 at 3.6 million, the state's highest known level ever.

Abundant deer bring increasingly liberal hunting seasons as game managers attempt to keep deer populations in line with available food supplies. Most states limit a deer hunter to one animal per year, but some have so many deer that they are relaxing the regulations in an effort to limit damage to yards, gardens, orchards, and field crops. In Alabama, where hunters take about 200,000 whitetails annually, and deer damage to farm crops is frequently a serious problem, bow hunters are allowed one deer per day throughout the three-and-a-half-month season. Gun hunters also are limited to a deer a day, although extra permits are issued in some areas in efforts to keep the herd down to manageable size. Theoretically, an Alabama hunter could legally take dozens of deer every year.

In some areas the whitetail herd is still vigorous and expanding. Elsewhere, the deer have reached their saturation point, having grown to the level permitted by the food supply. Blacktail and mule deer, perhaps because of competition by livestock, have suffered setbacks in some years.

The expanding deer herd was certain eventually to lead to conflicts with the growing human population. There are deer living in the suburbs of our cities. Long Island residents complain about deer eating their expensive hydrangeas. Farmers know that deer help themselves to grain crops and sometimes trample and eat garden plants. An apple grower told me that the only way he can get young trees started, now that deer are superabundant, is to fence them and, as an added measure, spread a ring of human hair, collected from local barbershops,

around each seedling. The hair apparently loses its power over deer and has to be replaced every few weeks. He gladly permits hunting on his property in the legal season.

Deer frequently get into so much trouble when they venture into town that the incidents make the papers. A drygoods store owner in Racine, Wisconsin, looked up in time to see a deer dashing through the rear door. There was a wild chase up and down the aisles. Eventually, with the help of city police, the confused deer was cornered over among the unmentionables and carted back to the woods uninjured.

In northern Ohio, one family was comfortably seated at the dinner table when an adult deer came leaping through the picture window. Forty-five minutes later, after a room-to-room chase made a shambles of the house, the deer escaped by crashing through another large window. Damage was computed at $2,500.

Late one evening a jetliner was roaring down the runway for takeoff at the Greater Pittsburgh International Airport when an eight-point buck wandered onto the runway in front of it. There was little that the pilot could do. The passengers felt a bump. The plane lifted off, then circled, and returned to land again. None of the ninety-five passengers was injured but some nerves were badly shaken as they transferred to another plane to complete their journey.

In another town, a buck came down Main Street, became confused in the traffic, and ended up being tied to a parking meter by police until the Humane Society came to rescue him. Hundreds of thousands of deer have run into the paths of passing vehicles, and generally caused enough problems to make everyone well aware of the fact that the deer herd is prospering.

Deer of various species are native to much of the world, except Australia and most of Africa. They are thought to have arrived on this continent from Asia some twenty-five million years ago. They have since survived ice-age glaciers, changing climates, natural predators in wide variety, and the coming of man, both ancient and modern. They have outlived Smilodon, the giant sabertooth cat, mammoths, mastodons, and numerous other mammals now extinct, all of which argues well for the deer's ability to adapt to changing conditions.

The three deer normally considered by deer

As autumn comes to western mountains, mule deer bucks are often seen in the high-country meadows.

Mule deer numbers fluctuate mysteriously at times, and one factor may be the changes wrought by people on their habitat. *Oregon Game Commission*

hunters are the white-tailed, black-tailed, and mule deer. Other North American members of the deer family include the elk, moose, and caribou.

Telling Them Apart

In some western states more than one species of deer are hunted. Even so, the hunter wants to know what species he is looking at, and telling them apart is not too difficult.

To determine whether the animal you are observing is a whitetail, mule deer, or blacktail, take special notice of the antlers, tail, ears, metatarsals, his behavior, and the way he runs.

Often you can distinguish white-tailed from black-tailed deer by their antlers alone. Adult buck whitetails have antlers with unbranched tines extending from the main beam. But in the mature mule or black-tailed buck the antlers branch and branch again. The antlers of the whitetail are also carried farther forward over the face, while those of the mule deer extend upward more directly. Where you may run into difficulty separating the bucks by antlers alone is in the case of spike or forkhorn bucks. Often these antlers will look much alike on all three species.

Should you see whitetail and blacktail side by side you can immediately spot the difference in the ears. The mule or blacktail has ears nearly twice as large as those of the whitetail. The ears, of course, account for this deer's name. Captain Meriwether Lewis first described the mule deer in 1804 when he killed a couple of them near the mouth of the White River in South Dakota.

Often the tail is the best indicator of all as to the kind of deer you are seeing. The tail of the whitetail is big; it is pure white on its undersurface. As the whitetail flees, its tail flips up and flags back and forth. While the Columbian blacktail may sometimes run with the tail elevated, it is less inclined to flip it around. The mule deer has a smaller, less conspicuous tail and carries it down when running. Look at the coloring on the tail. Only the tip of the mule deer's tail is black, while the blacktail's tail is black on all of the outer surface. The whitetail shows no black on the tail.

Another distinguishing feature is the metatarsal gland identified by a tuft of hair on the outside of the hind legs of all three species of deer. There are also tarsal glands on the inside of each hind leg at the hocks. Deer urinate on these areas and can track each other by the scent trail they leave. Metatarsal size differs with the kind of deer. Whitetails have metatarsals about an inch long while those of

These typical mule deer bucks, in their Wyoming home, are favorites of western deer hunters.
U.S. Forest Service

the blacktail may be as much as three inches long and mule deer metatarsals are more likely five inches long.

As a deer runs away notice how he travels. The whitetail gallops off in graceful style, and when thoroughly startled doesn't leap but travels close to the ground. If only slightly alarmed, he may take only a few bounding leaps and stop to satisfy his curiosity about whatever disturbed him.

The mule deer, however, bounces along on stiff legs as though each leap should carry him higher and give him a better look at the open countryside in which he lives. All four feet hit the ground at once with such a jolt that each landing forces air from his lungs in a "whoosh" readily heard for some distance.

The Whitetail

The whitetail occupies vast areas of timberland and farm borders from mountaintop to sea level. His fate has always been tied to that of the wooded areas, whether pinewoods of the South, oak-hickory of the Midwest, aspen and cottonwoods of the Rocky Mountain streambeds, or the white cedar and hemlock of the North.

In primitive times, from the northern limits of Canadian timberlands south all the way into Mexico and the Florida Keys, the whitetails roamed the woods. They lived from the Atlantic Coast, where the earliest settlers saw them, to the slopes of the Rockies. There are subspecies of white-tailed deer in Bolivia and Peru.

How many deer the land can support within this wide range depends largely on how man uses the land. Among the most productive states for white-tail deer are the north central-northeastern states from Minnesota to Maine. This includes Michigan, Wisconsin, New York, and Pennsylvania. Then add Texas because this state, with some three million deer, ranks at the top in whitetail production. Some southeastern states have exceptional deer populations also, permitting hunters to take several legal deer each year.

No big-game animal has been studied more than the white-tailed deer. Hunters, of course, have studied their game for centuries: how the deer live, move, act under every impulse and pressure. In more recent years many wildlife biologists have approached the subject with scientific techniques and cool objectivity. Little by little, they have put together what is known of the story of the whitetail, his foods, habitat needs, seasonal activities, and the troubles that beset him.

Subspecies

The people who spend their lives studying such things find a lot of difference between the whitetails of one section of the country and those of another. There are, for example, the little Coues deer of the Southwest and the big whitetails of the Upper Mississippi Valley. There are at least thirty known subspecies of whitetail. You have to get out the calipers and the charts and keys to tell many of the subspecies apart.

Our Littlest Deer

Smallest of all the whitetails is the endangered Key deer, which in recent years has faced extinction on a few islands off the coast of Florida. The average doe stands little higher at the shoulders than twice the height of this book. The bucks weigh about seventy-five pounds.

Surrounded as they are by orchids and evergreen tropical vegetation, the Key deer never know the winter food shortages that kill off so many deer in the woodlands of the north country. These island deer have their own enemies, however.

Old-timers said the Key deer once were numerous. But by 1949 biologists searching the palmettos for the little Key deer decided that their numbers were down to about thirty. What had killed the deer? Poachers, mostly.

The Key Deer National Wildlife Refuge was authorized by Congress in 1953. The Florida Game and Fresh Water Fish Commission set in motion a careful study of the Key deer and gave assistance in insuring them protection from further poaching. Only two years later, in 1955, the herd was up to 130 animals. Now they've spread back to some of the islands they hadn't lived on for many years.

Only slightly larger than the Key deer is the little

The whitetail buck, often considered America's number one big-game animal, is distinguished from the mule deer and blacktail by his tail, ears, antlers, and habitat. *Erwin and Peggy Bauer*

The branched antlers of this trophy-sized mule deer help set him apart from his cousin the whitetail. *Erwin and Peggy Bauer*

The alert whitetail, always sensitive to the actions of people, has learned to survive around human population centers. *Ohio Division of Wildlife*

The whitetail lives in a wide variety of habitats ranging from mountain valleys and farmland to the Southern swamps where this sleek doe takes refuge in dense vegetation.

Coues deer, or Arizona whitetail. It inhabits the rugged mountain slopes in southern Arizona, southwestern New Mexico, and the west coast of old Mexico.

Other sections have their own subspecies of the whitetail. Those found on Blackbeard Island and Sapelo Island off the Georgia coast have, through the centuries, developed into a distinct subspecies. Also, the fine big whitetails of the Dakotas have developed into a separate subspecies.

The Virginia whitetail was called *virginianus* by Catesby, who saw them, supposedly in "great numbers," when he sailed into the James River in tidewater Virginia in 1712. Unlike the whitetail which, in many parts of the country, has become a mixture of strains from trapping and transplanting, those in the swampy lowlands of Virginia are still of the pure strain. The deer have maintained their numbers through the years in Dismal Swamp and the swamps of Surry County.

The hunter, however, is seldom concerned with the exact subspecies of whitetail existing in the region he is hunting. It's enough that all the whitetails have spread into a wide variety of territories from mountains to sea level. From the timbered mountains of Vermont and the wilderness of northern Maine south to the swamps of the Everglades the whitetail is legal game. Whether you pursue him on the edge of an Iowa cornfield or waylay him in the South Carolina tidelands, he is still one of the finest of all big-game animals, alert, tricky, and vigorous.

Mule Deer

The mule deer ranges from the western edge of Minnesota to northern Alberta and into British Columbia. His range extends southward along the slopes of the Rockies through eastern Colorado and into Mexico through western Texas, west to Washington and Oregon, and down the Pacific Coast through most of California.

The mule deer is a clumsier-looking animal than the whitetail. He lacks the grace of movement and the trim lines of body. His ears are big and his legs stout; these characteristics fit him well for the places in which he lives. Those large ears let him pick up the sound of a rolling pebble across the canyon, and the stout legs carry him in bounding leaps that make him a match for the fastest horse.

Whether or not the mule deer is as smart as the whitetail is often argued. They live in different types of territory. The mule deer is a deer of the big open spaces and the mountain meadows. He has speed and sharp senses of hearing and smell. His sight, like that of the whitetails, is fair.

Winter sometimes brings mule deer together in concentrations.
South Dakota Game, Fish and Parks Department

One reason I love to hunt the mule deer is the very country he inhabits. It's good for the soul and peace of mind to invade occasionally that big western country with its brilliant blue skies and distant horizons uncluttered by man's handiwork.

Black-tailed Deer

Through the forests and mountain slopes of the Pacific Coast, from California to Alaska, the coastal blacktail lives in the densely growing thickets. The blacktail looks considerably like a smaller edition of the mule deer. The two are close relatives, and sometimes they even hybridize. The blacktail has the jumping gait of the mule deer, and his coat, although a little darker, is much the same color. His rack is seldom anything to excite the trophy hunter.

These imported fallow deer are part of the small herd ranging the Land Between The Lakes, a 170,000-acre public recreation area in western Kentucky and Tennessee. *TVA*

Foreign Deer

We have on this continent as fine a native representation of the deer family as anyone might ask for, but there is still the tendency to look beyond the borders and import the deer of other lands. Moving deer from one part of the world to another is an old game. Transplanting wild animals, of course, is not limited to deer. Our everlasting urge to improve the native fauna brought us the starling,

house sparrow, and carp, as well as pigeons that foul the statues in our city parks.

The same restless search prompted the people of New Zealand to import and release in their hills the European red deer, first cousin of our elk. In the following years New Zealanders watched as the red deer flourished in their new home and destroyed native forests, causing serious soil erosion. Even a year-round open season on these big deer could not keep their numbers under control in New Zealand.

More recently, the red deer became domestic stock for New Zealand ranchers, who keep them to supply the remarkable demand from the Orient for antlers to be used in folk medicines. But serious problems can result when a foreign species is released where there are none of the natural forces that normally curb its population in its native habitat. The same thing has happened time and again with many animals in many lands, and the safest policy is to be satisfied with native wildlife and not introduce foreign species.

This country does have a few wild herds of foreign deer. Maryland has a herd of the little Sika deer native to Japan, eastern China, and other parts of eastern Asia. These small spotted deer of the thick brush are hunted in parts of Maryland. Observations and experiments indicate that the sika deer has the potential to become a serious competitor of the native whitetail.

There are also a few small herds of European fallow deer in this country. These deer bear little resemblance to any native American deer. Fallow deer stand about three feet high at the shoulder and have broad palmated antlers. A small herd of fallow deer has long been established in western Kentucky in the Land Between The Lakes National Recreation Area managed by the TVA. Another remnant herd persists in Alabama, a residue of an earlier transplanting experiment. The state wildlife agency largely ignores them and few would care if they disappeared.

A large share of the foreign deer in this country is kept on game farms, primarily to supply exotic trophies. Texas is the major center for such ranches. Providing fenced-in deer and other animals for visiting hunters has become a sizable industry in that state. A much larger Texas business, however, is catering to hunters who prefer pursuing the native whitetails which the Lone Star State has in abundance.

TWO
HOW DEER LIVE

On opening morning I drove out of the county seat
and down the river to the road which turns off
straight as a string toward the hills a mile to the
east. After two decades, names on the mailboxes
were still familiar. The old two-room schoolhouse
had been turned into a dwelling. Aside from that,
the countryside was much as I remembered it.

I drove into Ralph Shipp's barnyard and after
catching up on neighborhood news asked him
about the deer. "Hunt wherever you want to,"
Ralph boomed. "There's plenty of deer back there.
See out there by the old hickory tree where the hill
and the woods come down to the creek? There's a
path across the creek six inches deep where deer
come down into the fields to feed at night. I've seen
'em there in summer. I wouldn't know where they
are now. You'll just have to go looking."

A quarter mile up the road, right at the foot of
the hill, tall, slender Warren Fluharty gave me
about the same story.

There's a half mile of rutted, grass-choked lane
from Warren's place up the hollow and around the
hill to where our place used to be. The coal mine
and the two houses up that road have all been abandoned. I had to walk the last half of the way.

The old house was falling in and the barn was
already down. Fences had disappeared and
cornfields had gone back to pastures and brush-
lands, a turn of events good for deer. For several
hours I hiked around those familiar hills looking
for tracks.

The snow had fallen three days previously, had

The immobile whitetail buck blends into his environment,
ready for instant escape when he senses danger. *Michigan
Department of Natural Resources*

partly melted in the afternoon sun, and had
refrozen in a crust that crunched underfoot like
crisp breakfast cereal. Any buck worthy of the
name could hear me clear over to Fred Sollar's.

But before noon I did come across one set of
tracks made by an animal I would have given a half
interest in my pickup truck just to see. Hunting,
however, at least still hunting, was hopeless on this
day. And there had been no sign of another hunter
back in these hills since the snow three days earlier.

By noon I was ready to give up and go down to
the south edge of the county, where there were cer-

tain to be hunters on the state-owned public hunting area. A few of them had deer out by the edge of the road, too. But the thought of those big tracks back on the old home place haunted me. There was nothing to do but go back there the next day.

Late in the afternoon, on the chance that someone would be abroad to move the deer on this day, I took my stand beside an aging beech tree well up on the hillside, just out of sight of the old house. From there I could see most of the valley below.

An hour passed slowly. Nothing moved. Finally the crows began coming in over the hill in a long line, returning to their roost from cornfield feeding grounds down along the river. For half an hour I amused myself trying to estimate their numbers. I had about given up hope of seeing a deer in what were now the closing moments of the season.

But, across the valley, along the edge of the woods I saw a movement. Through my binoculars I watched a deer move casually along the edge of the woods. He stopped frequently to check for acorns beneath the oaks and to take an unhurried look behind him. Then he stepped from the edge of the woods into a patch of light from the setting sun, and I had a look at one of the finest bucks that ever left his track in these hills. Almost certainly, he was working in my direction.

The air was still. I made no movement. Let him come, I thought, but make it a little faster, please, because the season is going to be over in another half hour. But this buck was in no hurry. He worked along the edge of the woods until he reached the little creek, walked along its brushy edge for a few yards, and stepped across it to my side.

He was no more than two hundred yards from me—perhaps three or four times as far as I could hope to shoot accurately with my shotgun and rifled slugs. At this moment the wind made itself heard in the limbs of the old tree above me and unfortunately, for me at least, the wind was on the back of my neck. A moment later the buck lifted his nose high and turned his head to one side. He lowered his head again but only for an instant; something had disturbed his peace. He was no longer relaxed. I moved no muscle now. But I sensed that it was hopeless. Of all a deer's senses, his sense of smell is probably the most highly developed. Man odor drifting down the evening breeze would certainly send any buck into action.

An instant later the old buck was off and trotting leisurely up the hill in the direction from which he had come. For all I know he lived on there for years, undisturbed.

I have often thought of the big buck since that day. Such thinking is more than idle speculation. The deer hunter needs an understanding of the day-to-day habits of the buck. This is the knowledge that gives a good deer hunter that little edge. Season after season there isn't any substitute for understanding your game.

Through the evenings of early autumn you work with your guns and get your equipment ready. You plan your hunting trip and study your maps. You figure out how you'll stage a drive better than the one last year. You try to figure out ahead of the season's opening all the angles that might help you outwit a deer. What you're really trying to do is solve in advance all the problems that might come up. It's fun that way. Much of the planning hinges on an understanding of the deer's habits. The daily life of that old home-place buck I missed can, for example, be pieced together into a fascinating series of events that must occur as the old buck lives out his life in that hill country. And the story of his life is the life story of a buck through much of our deer territory.

The story goes something like this.

Does and Fawns

About the first of June, does slip away to have a new crop of young. The fawn is usually dropped in a patch of thick cover, more because that is where the doe happens to be standing than because she searches out a good place for having her fawns. Many does, if they've had plenty to eat, have twin fawns.

In all the world of nature there are few creatures better protected against eyes and noses than the newborn fawn lying flat in a bed of Christmas ferns or hidden in the brush along the edge of a woodlot. Patches of sunlight on the forest floor match the white spots of his coat so well that it takes sharp eyes to spot his outline. And fawns, for the first few weeks of their lives, apparently have little if any odor. Dogs trailing adult deer have been known to leap right over fawns without discovering them.

Young fawns stay where their mothers hide them and have so little odor that most predators can't detect them. Rarely abandoned, they should be left where they are found. *U.S. Forest Service*

Winter is the difficult season for deer. Much of their food is covered by snow, and, as the season progresses, browse gets increasingly scarce. The more deer there are in an area the more difficult it is for them to find food. *South Dakota Game, Fish and Parks Department*

The doe at times may be out of range of the fawns' soft bleating. She returns every few hours to feed them, and shortly the fawns begin to follow her on short exploratory trips. Eventually they nibble at the green browse she eats.

Even after the doe weans her fawns, they stick together in a family group right into the autumn months. Sometimes the old doe may have a fawn or two with her from the previous year, and her current year's fawns as well.

The fawns lose their spotted outfits at about three and a half to four months of age and take on the color of the adults. Through most of their range, this is well ahead of the hunting season. Once in a long while you'll hear of a late-born spotted fawn seen in the woods during the hunting season. His male cousins, if they are well fed, will already weigh about seventy-five pounds.

By that first autumn the fawns have already learned a lot of the things a deer needs to know. Theirs is a life of restless watching. They may be bedded on a grassy knoll chewing their cud, but for all the peace and quiet around them their senses are alert to strange odors, sights, and sounds, because their best defense is instant flight.

When things are going well, they wander from place to place in lazy fashion, stopping here and there for a maple leaf or a soybean. If they grow suspicious, they may break into a trot, and if really upset they flip up their great white tails and clear out at speeds that may reach twenty-five miles an hour; as they mature, their top speeds will usually increase. Adult whitetails have been observed to high jump eight and a half feet and clear twenty-nine feet in a broad jump.

How long do deer live? One that is seven or eight years of age is an old-timer. In Missouri, a checking-station inspection showed that only 6.6 percent of the deer killed were more than four years old. The average age of legal deer taken in the West Virginia hunting season is between two and a half and three years. A few ear-tagged animals have been known to live fifteen or sixteen years. Only a small percentage of deer can look forward to old age whether hunters take them or not. But there are others to take their place.

Deer and Predators

Anytime the deer population in a favorite hunting area seems to be falling, predators may get the blame. Deer are prey at times for a wide variety of meat-eating animals other than man.

Historically, the major predators of deer were cougars and wolves. Where these large predators still survive, deer may be important to them. One authority on wolves estimates that a wolf will kill about fifteen deer annually. No North American predator eats deer exclusively. Deer and elk are important prey to mountain lions, but research has shown that lions do not depress the healthy deer population.

Other wild animals that consume deer include bobcats, coyotes, and bears, but much of the venison they eat may be carrion from deer that die of old age, sickness, or as hunting-season cripples. Any of these animals, plus foxes and a few other small predators, could take fawns and probably sometimes do.

These are all natural acts in the world of the deer, and the deer has evolved with excellent protection against them. It has exceptionally sharp senses of hearing and smell, plus the swiftness that helps it escape.

Large predators that depend on deer as a food source have become scarce or absent over most of their range because of the pressures put on them by people. Wolves are gone now from most of their former nationwide range. They survive in the lower forty-eight states only in sections of northern Minnesota and perhaps Wisconsin and are sometimes sighted in the northern Rocky Mountains in Idaho, northwestern Montana, and Wyoming. Wolves are so rare that the U.S. Fish and Wildlife Service placed them on the official lists of threatened and endangered wildlife. In northern Minnesota, however, some outdoorsmen are still quick to blame the wolf for destroying the deer. How much the few hundred remaining wolves there actually reduce the deer population in that northern country is a matter of considerable debate. Perhaps more important is whether or not we should deny any relict population of wolves their share of natural food from the store of deer. The wolf, as well as other predators, are all unique members of the wildlife communities they comprise, and there is a changing attitude that leans toward accommodating such predators and allowing them their natural foods. They have their role to play in the natural order and each of them is an interesting animal in its own right.

Predation, and its effect on wild populations, is a complex biological subject that we tend to oversimplify. Killing wild predators seldom produces impressive population increases of the prey species. Too often the killing of predators has been more an act of vengeance by one predator, man, against another than an effective game-management practice.

Deer can withstand natural predation and replace their losses. These are good times for deer, especially whitetails, throughout much of their range. The most effective predators of deer are the millions of hunters who pursue them each autumn. Nevertheless, the deer still flourish.

Dogs and Deer

Free-ranging dogs run deer the year around, and while there is considerable debate about the exact effect of these unnatural pedators on the deer, one thing is certain—being run by dogs can never do them much good.

On one of the many occasions I witnessed dogs running deer, I was canoeing a small woodland stream in late spring with a companion. For some time, we heard a pair of hounds on a hot trail along the ridge above us. Finally, they worked closer to the creek. We stopped paddling, drifted, and soon glimpsed a doe bounding through the woods.

A short time later the doe broke out of brushy cover at the edge of the stream and splashed into the water a short distance downstream from the canoe. Then two beagles came to the shore and began running up and down the bank in confusion. None of the animals noticed the canoe which drifted steadily closer.

As the hounds started into the water, we yelled at them and they turned and vanished into the brush. The doe stood panting for a moment. Then she too bounded back into the thick cover, and that was the last we heard of the chase.

Whether or not the hounds would have overtaken the doe, there is no way of knowing. But, at least in this season, when the does are heavy with fawns, they should not have to run for hours at a time to escape stray dogs.

Those of us who keep dogs have a responsibility to keep them under control. We owe it to both the dogs and the wild game they chase. Some states permit citizens to shoot free-running dogs caught running deer or other game. There is some question about the degree of harm these dogs actually do to the deer herd, but that is no excuse for letting dogs, including the well-groomed family pet, have the run of the woods.

What Deer Eat

In the cold of winter, when plants are dormant and food is scarce, northern deer get their most severe test. This is the season that separates the survivors from the less hardy. Deer adjust in several ways to the coming of winter.

Hunters know that deer get new coats. The whitetail exchanges its reddish summer color for a gray winter coat, while the Rocky Mountain mule deer changes its grayish-brown summer coat to one that is more reddish brown. The new coat provides superior insulation, both conserving body heat and absorbing heat from the environment.

Biologists also now know that as a deer changes into its winter coat, its body temperature drops. Its heartbeat slows in winter, and it becomes less active

than it is in warmer weather and may spend much time bedded in the shelter of dense evergreens. By lying down, perhaps sheltered by snow and by dense vegetation, the wintering deer loses less body heat than it does when standing and exposing more of its body to cold and wind.

In summer, when food is plentiful, male deer must feed heavily to maintain their vigor while growing new antlers. Deer bed during the day, feed mostly at night. *Canadian Pacific Railway*

One of the most important food plants for mule deer through much of the Western country is mountain mahogany. These deer are occupying typical mahogany country. *U.S. Forest Service*

In addition, as winter nears, the deer normally stores up energy in a layer of fat. Then, by conserving energy, the deer can get through the cold season with less food than it needs in warmer weather.

But real problems can arise for the deer as winter proceeds. The days become longer in late winter, and as the days lengthen, the deer's body begins to return to its earlier activity levels. By February and March, the deer needs more food to keep its body functioning, and this increased need comes well ahead of new spring growth in the plants that nourish deer.

For this reason, late winter is a highly critical time in the annual cycle of northern deer. Starving deer are often confined to the deer yards where snow may still be deep and food has been used up. This is the time when weak deer die.

Fawns of the previous spring are especially vulnerable to heavy winters, and some studies show these young deer comprising 80 to 90 percent of those lost to winter starvation. The starving deer loses the fat across his rump and back and his loose-fitting coat grows dull and shaggy-looking.

Bone-marrow color is also an indicator of the deer's condition. The well-nourished deer has white bone marrow that is mostly fat. This fat is the last to be utilized by the deer, and as it is consumed to supply the energy needs, the color of the marrow changes gradually. When the fat is mostly gone, the marrow is red. Red marrow in the femur, or upper leg bone, is a reliable indicator that tells biologists, or anyone who checks it, that the deer was starving.

If deer are starving, there simply are too many deer for the available winter food. Furthermore, deer struggling to survive the winter will perish all the faster if they are under stress from running dogs, snowmobiles, cross-country skiers or other forces that make them leave their winter beds and use their small stores of energy to escape.

Deer can starve to death with full stomachs if what they consume lacks sufficient nutritive value to keep their bodies going. This can happen when they are reduced to eating large twigs, which are mostly cellulose and a poor source of protein. Starving deer, however, will consume branches as long as they can reach them while standing on their hind feet and stretching. This hardship fare produces the browse line so evident in some northern woods. The presence of a browse line tells biologists, and others, that the area's wintering deer are either starving or soon may be.

What a deer eats, of course, depends on the part of the country in which it lives. There has been extensive study of deer food habits throughout the country. Biologists know which browse plants are the most heavily consumed, and hunters who want to understand deer and where they may be feeding should check these lists of favorite deer foods.

As spring comes on, living becomes good for deer. They feast on the succulent new green growth of a wide variety of plants. They like tender grasses, along with weeds, sedges, and the leaves and twigs of shrubs.

This is a season when deer seem to need a lot of salt. They frequently seek out salt licks from mid-March through May. As summer brings ripening fruits, deer add these to their diets.

In autumn, when you are scouting out deer feeding areas, do not overlook oak forests, especially in years when there is a good mast crop. In early autumn, through much of the country, the oak trees begin to drop their acorns and the deer are among the first to know it. They may move out of the bottomlands and away from the edges of farm fields, working their way up into the slopes to harvest the acorns. Whitetails, mule deer, and blacktails all consume acorns when available.

In one Missouri study, biologists examined stomachs from deer taken during the hunting season and identified the foods consumed by 440 deer from various parts of the state. This is one of the more reliable scientific methods of determining deer food. Statewide, 42.5 percent of the Missouri deers' food was mast from 11 species of oaks.

Ranked according to importance as deer foods, in this study, were acorns of the following oaks: black oak, white oak, post oak, scarlet oak, and blackjack oak. Acorns first became available in September and continued to appeal to deer into winter as long as the mast lasted.

After oaks, this Missouri study ranked these foods in descending importance: corn, buckbrush, sumacs, lespedeza, then grasses and sedges.

Winter whitetail foods have also been studied extensively in the northern forests where these deer live. Research in New York revealed that the following plants are favorites of wintering whitetails.

white cedar	striped maple
yew	dogwood
apple	staghorn sumac
mountain maple	red maple
wintergreen	

When deer could not find these favorites, they turned to a long list of alternates, including the following.

elderberry	arbutus
highbush cranberry	honeysuckle
hemlock	blueberry
mountain ash	willow
cucumber tree	

In the northern forest areas, deer thrive best in mixed stands of conifers and hardwoods, where there are trees in a wide variety of age classes. Especially good for deer are those woods that have conifers scattered through the hardwood stands, because the evergreens give the deer hiding places.

In many places during the hunting season, mule deer rely heavily on mountain mahogany, sagebrush, serviceberry, oaks, bearberry, and myrtle.

The blacktail deer in winter, depending on what part of the range he occupies, lives on such things as willow buds, evergreens, ferns, manzanita, and acorns.

At least 75 percent of the average winter diet of the deer in the Black Hills section of South Dakota is from eight kinds of plants. These include ponderosa pine, Oregon grape, kinnikinnick, common juniper, chokecherry, serviceberry, mountain mahogany, and weeds.

Deer, at some time or other, eat most things that grow within their reach, depending on how nearly they're starved. When the "candy" species are gone, they turn to what's left. Six hundred fourteen plants have been listed as consumed by whitetails in North America.

Deer Nutrition

There has been so much said about deer losses in "hard winters" that it comes as something of a surprise to find that deer populations can suffer from poor summertime range. This is true for both whitetails and mule deer herds. The losses are seen in the rate of reproduction, which reflects the quality of habitat. Deer have more young when they are well fed. One California researcher reported that blacktail deer there had 147 percent reproduction in a study of open brush cover with herbaceous plants growing in it, but that in mature brush cover with little herbaceous food beneath it, reproduction

Winter tests the deer's ability to survive. Food supplies reach their lowest point of the year, and deer on overpopulated range may perish. *Missouri Department of Conservation. Don Wooldridge*

dropped to 84.3 percent. In New York, two researchers using an eighty-six-acre deer enclosure found that when there were good deer foods each doe had 1.9 fawns per season. If food was poor the fawn crop fell to less than one fawn from every two does.

Researchers have many ways of digging out interesting and vitally important facts about the way deer live. One of these is collecting information at the deer-checking stations operated during the hunting season. If you've come through one of these checking stations and wondered what the information collected might lend to knowledge of the deer herd, you can get some idea from what one study revealed in Missouri. Biologists examined 4,529 deer brought through checking stations. They recorded weights, measurements, age, sex, antler development, foot length and girth, and whether or not the does were producing milk. From these bits of information they came up with some conclusions interesting to biologists and hunters alike.

Deer on fertile, uncrowded ranges, they found, are larger, have bigger antlers, and produce more young than deer on less fertile or more crowded range. On good range more than a third of the doe fawns breed in their first autumn and have their first fawns when they're a year old. The bulk of the legal kill is made up of young deer, fawns, yearlings, and two-and-a-half-year-olds. All this information helps set sensible deer seasons to keep deer and food supplies better balanced.

THREE
HOW TO LOOK FOR DEER

Through most of the year the old buck is a loner, but in fall he is deeply interested in where competing bucks and breeding-age females are. At all times, he is alert to signs of danger. *Michigan Department of Natural Resources*

There are at least two reasons why so many of the bucks killed by hunters are young animals, often spike bucks. One is the preponderance of younger bucks. The other, and to most deer hunters, more challenging reason is that old bucks are harder to catch up with. They didn't grow old by being careless. Expose a buck to enough gunners and he is likely to learn at least as much as the hunters who miss him.

There's good reason for thinking deer are harder to hunt today than they were when white men first discovered the whitetail. Deer alive today are descended from those which were best able to adapt themselves to new conditions rapidly. The less intelligent bucks, the strains with the least sensitive warning systems and the slowest reactions, are taken first, while the more able live to perpetuate their strains.

The old buck lives alone and prefers it that way. He wants no herd of does or careless fawns around him. Consequently about the only time of the year he's going to seek out company of his kind is when the mating urge comes on him. That accomplished, he goes right back to his hermit's life. These are the old-timers who often carry the finest racks.

Not that all old bucks have to be outwitted. Sometimes they can be outwaited instead. I recall one ten-pointer collected by a friend of mine who decided some years back that he would go forth and find out what this deer hunting was all about. And go forth he did, in new hunting coat and with a shiny new gun. He was filled with hunting lore collected in a couple of bull sessions.

I have nothing against his methods or his approach. It's only that luck might well be a little more selective about whom it favors. As this friend has since related on several occasions, his hunt proceeded somewhat as follows:

"I drove over to Dunham," he says, "and as far as I could go back on this forest road. Then I got out and leaned against the front of my car. Pretty soon there was some shooting down in the woods. First thing I knew something was crashing through the brush. I brought up my gun and then a big buck ran out of the woods and I shot him."

And that's what happened. The buck dropped almost beside his car, so he put it aboard and came out of the woods. The season had been open about an hour.

Well, that old buck might have been as wise as they come. He had already stayed alive through four or five hunting seasons. But usually the old buck has to be hunted out in his own territory. And

accomplishing this is the test of the true deer hunter.

If it's a big buck you're after you'll do well to study how he lives. Unless he's disturbed, he lives much the same life from day to day.

Catch Him in Bed

There was a fresh fifteen-inch snow on the ground some seasons back when my friend Walter Newsom, deer rifle in hand, went into the woods. For three hours he walked slowly through the woods alternately marveling at the beauty of the winter landscape and searching the snow for the footprints of sizable deer. This was good country and he knew it well. But the only track he crossed in those hours was one that might have been made by some inexperienced fawn, an animal smaller than he cared to trail.

Toward noon, driven by hunger and a growing weariness from breaking trail, Walter leaned back against a pine tree and slid to a squatting position. As he reached into the game pouch of his coat to extract the sandwich he carried there, he detected a movement beneath the low-hanging branches of a fir tree some forty feet away. Walter's hand stopped. Long seasons of roaming the woods and practically living with the deer had conditioned him. Gradually he turned his head. There was no more movement beneath the overhanging snow-weighted limbs.

But Walter was looking toward the first deer he had seen all day. "He knew I was there," said Walter, "but for some reason he didn't think I knew he was there in his bed." That was a mistake.

"I should have known where to look that morning," Walter said later. "After a heavy fresh snow like that the deer like to get right in under the low branches and bed down." If the snow gets deep enough, deer may bed down for two or three days. "On a morning such as this was," Walter concluded, "you gotta look in their bedrooms."

If you can tell where deer are likely to bed down, the knowledge can shorten the hunt. But it's not always easy. In general, however, look for the sunny spots in open weather in fall or winter. Sometimes the deer will get up and move if their bed becomes shaded. In addition to the sun they like a spot that is level, dry, and fairly smooth. In

The still hunter should move slowly, stop frequently, watch, listen, and wait. On cold, snowy days, search the thick cover where deer bed out of the wind.

wet areas they often choose a slight rise and escape the dampness. The old bucks often bed on a sunny slope just below the ridge of a hill where they are protected from the wind and where they have a good view of the countryside below.

Some years ago, at a time when I was off hunting in another state, a group of friends with whom I hunt in southern Ohio decided to vary their driving of deer with some still hunting. Half a dozen of them drove as far back on an old tote road as they could, then set out along a ridge expecting to turn into the woods, one at a time, as they found places that looked promising. The plan was to regroup at the car by noon and allow time for lunch, followed by a big drive of an area a few miles to the north.

Gene Knoder quickly sized up the situation as the rest of them started down the ridge. Instead of going along he worked his way down a side hollow to the left as rapidly as he could.

Preseason scouting pays off by revealing where deer feed and bed, and routes traveled between these areas. This much-traveled deer trail gives the hunter several choices for stands on opening morning.

Two does and three fawns got up well out of range ahead of the main group of hunters and slipped over the ridge to the right. What those hunters hadn't seen was the buck. He had slipped over the hill in Knoder's direction. In fact, they had forgotten about Knoder until they heard the sharp bark of his autoloading shotgun. They went down and helped him drag out a 265-pound buck they had routed out of bed and sent down in front of him.

My neighbor Wilson Masters invariably allows himself at least a full day in the woods ahead of the opening hour. Except for the deer, and a rare human being, he's there alone. He scouts the ridges and the creek bottoms and the abandoned farmlands. By evening he has a good idea of where deer are feeding, where they are bedding, what trails they follow back and forth, where the biggest tracks are, and where various deer trails cross. He knows that such crossings, if the signs are fresh, can become hot spots on opening morning once other hunters set the deer to moving. "I can't say," he admits, "that I get a deer every year, but I do know that I have more fun and get more shots over the years by scouting them out ahead of time."

An amazing amount of deer hunting is based less on such planning than on luck. You can be certain, however, that the old-timer who hangs up his deer every year has more than luck to thank.

I once met a farm boy turned contractor who became a millionaire. "Ben," one of his cousins said to him at a family reunion, "you sure are lucky."

"Did you ever stop to think," Ben answered, "that the harder I work the luckier I am?"

The same principle applies to deer hunting. The more you plan and think ahead, the more you study your game, and the harder you work at outwitting your deer, the "luckier" you're likely to be. But the challenges and puzzles you must contend with to outsmart the sharp old bucks provide half the fun of hunting them. Before you go deer hunting, learn as much as you can about the country you will hunt, your weapon, the habits of the deer, your companions, and the hunting methods that pay off.

Some deer hunters consider preseason planning so important that they regularly allot half as much time to it as they do to hunting.

One exception to the need for preseason scouting occurs when the hunter hires a guide. Presumably the guide already knows where the deer are most likely to be. Another exception might exist when you hunt only in drives and can rely on the captain of the drive to know where the deer are and what they will do.

There are several kinds of evidence that reveal the presence of deer. Watch for scrapes and for saplings where bucks have rubbed the bark off polishing their antlers. Keep an eye open for signs that deer have nipped off the tips of browse plants. If you know their favorite foods in the region, you can check these to see if deer have feasted on them. Some of these foods are listed in Chapter Two.

Deer form daily habits of feeding and bedding and are likely to stick to their routines unless they are disturbed or unless the sources of food give out. They feed on different plants at different seasons. In spring, for example, they feed heavily on grasses. But with the coming of autumn they move to the woods to gather acorns, beechnuts, and browse.

Watch for their footprints and droppings. With a little practice you can learn to tell the old evidence from the fresh. Fresh droppings are soft and shiny; old ones get dull and hard. Fresh tracks have distinct edges except in those places where dry earth or sand rolls into them. Even then, you can tell whether or not the sand has rolled into them recently, because weather and time erode the tracks and make them less distinct.

The three common ways in which deer are hunted are by still hunting, staging a drive, and hunting from a stand. There are variations, and a few less common techniques, that will bear explaining.

The small-game-hunting season is a good time to begin looking for deer sign. If you can locate the places in which they are feeding and moving at this time, you can quickly check out the area for fresh sign at the beginning of the deer season. This hunter is checking along the wooded edge of an Ohio cornfield.

The Still Hunter

Still hunting does not mean that you stand still all the time. It means that you slip along as quietly as possible to get within range of a deer. This is a style of hunting practiced by the best of woodsmen. You pit your stealth and knowledge against the instincts of the deer and if you succeed you get a sense of satisfaction found in few other kinds of hunting.

The deer has much better hearing than we do. Usually he hears you long before you ever know he is there. Nearly any hunter can be certain he is observed, smelled, and heard by far more wild game than he ever sees.

One study in Michigan showed clearly that it's

no easy matter to find a deer that wants to stay hidden. A deerproof fence was built around a square mile of forest land and thirty-four deer were turned loose inside. Seven average deer hunters tried to hunt them out. With does and bucks legal, these hunters needed fourteen hours of hunting for each deer bagged, and when they were limited to buck hunting they bagged one buck in every fifty-one hours of hunting.

Still hunting is best practiced individually or by only two or three companions. The aim is to locate your deer and not spook him before you can get a shot.

The still hunter must be constantly alert to the slightest movement or sound. He stops often and surveys the woods or brush around him. He studies the landscape for an antler or a flicking ear. If a fly lights on his nose he brushes it away slowly—unless he knows a deer is watching, in which case he doesn't brush it away at all.

If he is in a hurry to get to that next ridge, or to get back to camp, he may as well go ahead and forget about hunting.

Some still hunters move a couple of hundred

When studying the landscape for signs of deer, watch for movement or the distinctive outline of head or ears revealing the presence of this bedding mule deer.

yards and stop for a half hour before moving another two hundred yards. Others move short distances and stop for short periods of time. Some even move at a normal walking pace from one place to the next on the theory that deer aren't at ease when they see someone sneaking through their woods. When terrain and cover are suited to it, I like to stop for ten to twenty minutes every few hundred yards.

Some places look so promising you spend more time watching them. Sometimes it pays to wait a little longer when you come to a spot where you can watch some natural passage, such as a point where a lake and cliff force game to a narrow passage.

Some places are poorly suited to the still hunter's art. This method is a poor choice, for example, in an oak woods where each step crunches enough dry leaves to alert every animal within a quarter mile. In such places there is almost nothing you can do to keep quiet enough to slip up on a deer. You can step on rocks, logs, and moss beds part of the way, but seldom all of it. Even a recent rain seldom makes a hardwood forest quiet for walking during fall and early winter months. The answer, then, is to take up a stand or organize a drive. You face the same difficulties where the cover is thick and you flush game out far ahead as you push through the thicket.

Crusted snow also sends advance word to any deer in the neighborhood. But fresh snow is espe-

cially attractive to the still hunter because it muffles his footsteps and shows where the deer went. Don't get so fascinated with the tracking that you forget to look ahead for the deer, as one of my deer-hunting friends did. His eyes were riveted to the ground. He rounded a bend in the creek bed and was brought back to earth by the snort of a startled buck. The hunter, normally an expert shot, was so rattled he lodged the bullet from his .30-06 in an ironwood tree and the buck he had hunted so persistently for two and a half hours went untouched. Look ahead of you and pick your path for a dozen steps or so at a time, so that you aren't always looking at the ground under your feet.

The more you practice this brand of stealth, the more accomplished you become at it. You begin to notice things you never saw in the woods before—how small animals react to your presence, and the warning of the bluejays. Once you begin to fit into the woodland scene naturally and not stand out as a foreign object, you increase your chances of seeing deer and getting close enough for a shot.

Don't ignore a doe even if you're out for a buck. The doe may tip you off to where the buck is. She may keep looking back. And usually that's where the wary old buck will be.

What should you do if you spot the buck? It de-

In some areas all deer are legal game and, therefore, of special interest to hunters. Even if you are hunting for a buck only, study the movement of the does. The position of the tail, and how she watches her backtrail, are tips that a buck is coming.

pends, first of all, on whether or not he has also spotted you. If he suddenly looks at you, freeze. If you have one foot in the air keep it there if you can. If you must adjust your posture, by all means do so casually and slowly and do not even turn your eyes to look directly at the deer. After a moment or two there is a good chance the deer may move on undisturbed or put his head down for a bite of food. Some deer, out of plain foolhardy curiosity, will come toward a hunter who manages not to look menacing. If you're moving forward and the deer thinks you don't see him, he may stand still expecting you to pass. Then when you're in the clear, where bullet or arrow has a path to the target, make your move and make it fast. A deer that is tense and alert and certain he is discovered doesn't give you much margin in time.

If you spot a deer that is out of range and decide to stalk him, you have chosen for yourself a genuine challenge. Don't make the mistake of thinking that a deer pays no attention to the trail behind him. If he sees you slipping along behind, he'll not wait around to see if your intentions are honorable. A wise old buck may double back parallel to his trail for a short distance to make certain he is not followed.

Take advantage of trees and other bits of cover and always be ready to stop when the deer brings up his head to check the landscape. Then move forward again only when he relaxes. If the wind is blowing from you to the deer the odds are in his favor. His nose is one of his most sensitive aids. If the animal is on a regular trail, and you know where the trail leads, sometimes you can cut across and intercept him. Generalizations seldom apply here. As you come to understand your game and know how to move in the woods, you fashion every step of your hunt to the demands of the moment.

Just how nicely a hunter can put a knowledge of woods lore to work for him was demonstrated some years ago by Fred Bear, who told me the story of a memorable hunt he had in Schoolcraft County in Michigan's heavily timbered Upper Peninsula. I have hunted in that county and can easily visualize the episode as Fred described it to me.

"There were two of us," Fred said, "hunting in a hilly section of young hardwood timber. Snow began to fall and it looked as though it had settled in for all afternoon. We hunted along together for a while and finally decided to separate and try some

still hunting alone." At that moment they were standing on an old tote road. They simply turned back to back and walked off in opposite directions.

"Once we were several hundred yards apart," Fred explained, "we planned to leave the road and move off parallel to each other." There is always the possibility in such a hunt that a deer put out by one hunter will cross the other hunter's path and give the second man a shot.

Fred reached a point on the tote road where he was about to enter the timber. His companion was already off the road and some four hundred yards ahead of him in the woods. Then Fred spotted a movement through the brush and froze in his tracks. Within a few seconds he saw the animal again, a big whitetail buck bearing as fine a rack as he had seen in a long time.

Fred said he was afraid that the deer, moving in from the side as he was, would spot his hunting companion.

"It was the middle of November," said Fred, "and with all the leaves off the trees, the deer was almost certain to spot my friend first. I thought about it for a moment and tried to figure out what the buck would do then. I knew that a traveling deer running into trouble will invariably backtrack."

This gave Fred his clue. As soon as the buck was out of sight Fred hurried forward to where the deer's trail went through the woods. Fred had hardly gotten behind a tree when the buck came highballing back through the woods on the exact trail he had staked out in the opposite direction. "In a case like this," Fred said, "the buck thinks the route behind him is clear."

All Fred had to do was wait until the buck came within range, step out from behind his tree, and score. Fred, among the most famous of all bow hunters, stopped the running buck for one of the finest trophies he had ever taken.

Hunting from a Stand

Hunting from a stand is nothing more than parking yourself on the most promising spot you can locate and waiting for some unsuspecting deer to stumble into the scene. In some places the hunter utilizing a stand spots himself on a runway. Then

Good location, plus patience, can reward the hunter on stand, as the right animal moves into a downwind position.

he sits on a stool carried for the purpose and sometimes even outfits himself with a small stove and windbreak as weather protection.

Tree blinds are common for both gun and bow hunting.

If there's any cover at all to take advantage of, and there nearly always is in deer country, there is little reason for building or using a special blind for deer hunting. I much prefer to take advantage of the natural cover. You won't, of course, want to stand with the sky for a background or in a place where the outline of your body can be plainly spotted. But all you need to break up the man look is a stump beside which you can crouch, or some tall grass or a little shrubbery to protect you.

A deer's eyesight is not particularly good. Color means little to him. Motion is another matter. A deer may stand and stare at you, trying to figure out what you are and why you are there. But as much as blink an eye and you've answered his question.

What is much more likely is that he will detect you by sniffing the wind or hearing some sound you make. Those big ears flick up at the slightest excuse and funnel the strange sounds to the animal's brain. This is why, when choosing or preparing a blind or stand, you should be certain to remove all twigs and loose stones from beneath your feet.

The deer's nose can detect man odor carried to him while he is still well out of range or out of sight. And this also has to be considered in choosing your stand on a deer run. You need to be downwind from deer as they come along the trail. A crosswind on the trail is the next best bet.

When you survey the area, find where the deer are feeding and where they are bedding. The vegetation will be mashed down where they lie. Then try to find the trails they're using between these places. If you can't locate the bedding and feeding areas you may still be able to find the trails. The advantage of finding the feeding and bedding spots, of course, is that these help tell you where the deer may be at certain times of the day.

Deer normally bed down during the day and feed at night. Late in the day they get up from their beds and move off slowly toward the feeding area. About daylight they begin to move back to the bedding area. Remember that deer will often feed later in the morning and earlier in the evening on a cloudy day. Although they may bed down in some protected spot during a storm, they will often come out afterward to feed.

So, in lightly hunted areas the best times to wait on the trails are the first hour after daylight and the last hour before dark.

The rest of the day you may want to still hunt and try for a jump shot, or, as some hunters do in midday, go back to camp for a nap.

In heavily hunted regions, however, when deer have been disturbed, you may kill a deer from a stand anytime during the day. Bill Rom, founder of Canoe Country Outfitters at Ely, Minnesota, with more than forty deer to his credit, has taken at least two deer while eating lunch. Both times he looked up from a sandwich in time to see and shoot bucks.

One of my South Carolina friends tells the story of the deer hunter who really wanted to stay in the cabin but went out for the day only because the refreshments were depleted. He passed the day sleeping beneath a tree. He awakened to see, and shoot, a buck practically sniffing at his shoes. When his companions returned, without even sighting a deer, there he was sound asleep again.

This idea of staying on stand while others keep the deer moving is nothing more than a variation on deer driving. You're waiting for someone else to drive your deer to you. The only difference is that the other hunters don't know they're cooperating.

Instead of giving up and going back to camp for lunch, stay out through the noon hour. With the woods suddenly quieter, the wary bucks may try slipping back to heavy cover.

This, of course, is a plan that occurs to many hunters. Sometimes there seems to be a hunter behind every tree and the deer are off bedding down unmolested until somebody finally gets tired and wanders off his stand.

Choose your blind so that your scent doesn't drift across a deer trail near another hunter's stand, and don't move in on established hunters' territories. This is no more than good manners.

The Deer Drive

Among the most productive of all hunting methods is the deer drive. No matter what anyone says, staging a drive does not call for a great deal of skill. You need a leader who knows the territory and where the deer are likely to go, and beyond that all you need is the willingness of the rest of the party to follow his instructions. But a drive can be a lot of fun for a lot of people and it can put meat in the pot.

"A good drive depends on somebody who knows the country. Our drives in Pennsylvania," a hunting-camp leader once told me, "are usually along some hogback and the leader is in the center of the line of drivers. He walks along the ridge. That way he can keep the lines fairly straight and keep contact with both ends of it."

Most deer drives employ half of the hunt's members, in a line, to move the deer by walking noisily through the cover. The other half are standers waiting in a line at the end of the drive. Supposedly the standers get the shots but it doesn't always work that way. More than likely the deer double back and try to slip through the line or get out around the ends. If you use three or four men as drivers, have the end men make noise and the ones in the center move with stealth. The center men often get shots at deer trying to slip back through the quiet part of the line.

To stop escape around the ends of a line you can use flankers. A flanker on each end of the line moves forward well ahead of the rest of the line and has a good chance to get shots at deer trying to work out around the edges. Drivers and standers usually trade off with each new drive to equalize the opportunities for shooting.

Whether planning a deer drive or studying the nature of the terrain where you will hunt alone, topographic maps and compass can add to the safety, productivity, and fun of the hunt.

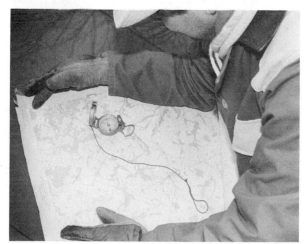

Obviously any such effort to move and shoot deer calls for a high degree of caution on the part of the hunters. The hunters on stand must be especially careful not to shoot a driver, and the driver makes enough noise to keep standers aware of his location. It is equally important for the drivers to do no wild shooting. Some groups don't permit the drivers to carry guns.

A stander should always stick to his station once he is placed there by the drive leader. To wander off through the brush would be pure folly and an unforgivable sin on a deer drive.

There is some question in the minds of seasoned deer hunters about how much noise is needed to drive deer. Some state regulations prohibit the use of special noisemakers. A driver carrying a stick can move the deer out ahead of him by simply banging it against a tree every few yards.

The best deer drives move slowly. The aim is not

The buck relies on his highly developed senses of hearing and smell to warn him of human presence in the woods, while the hunter practices stealth and studies the value of scents. *Michigan Department of Natural Resources*

to startle the deer into full speed. A running shot in thick cover is difficult and a thoroughly frightened deer may cross the county line before slowing down. The aim should be to make the deer slip along ahead of the line in the mistaken belief that he is staying out of danger.

The wind is important in all deer hunting. When a deer can tell by testing the breeze that he's heading straight for trouble, he is going to look for a way out. And nine chances out of ten he'll find it. He hates to be driven straight into a wind.

The captain of the drive has to take all such factors into consideration. He also wants to take full advantage of the features of the landscape. Lakes, streams, cliffs, and open fields are all barriers that in the right situation can help drivers put the deer where they want them to go. It's often possible to move the deer out of large wooded areas toward some constricted neck of land through which they must pass to another area. If the standers can locate themselves on a cliff where the deer may have to pass beneath them, this is all the better, because chances are good they will not be looking up and the wind isn't as likely to carry man scent down to them.

Most drive captains try not to bite off too much area for a single drive. On long drives there are many opportunities for deer to escape short of the standers. You can't pile up deer on a drive. A mile is a long drive and often a half-mile drive is a better one.

Drivers should maintain a fairly straight line when the terrain permits it. The captain should give new hands some idea of how fast they should move and the less experienced drivers can often be placed between the old-timers. How close together they should be in line depends on the cover. A hundred yards is close enough in open woods, but twenty-five yards may be too far apart in the swamps.

Hunting with Dogs

In most states law prohibits hunting deer with dogs. But in some southeastern states it is permitted. It is also legal in Ontario, where it has long been practiced.

Dogs are used as drivers. Their job is to bring the deer past hunters who are stationed at strategic

These Ontario hunters, and their permissible beagle, use a canoe to take them to productive deer habitat. *Ontario Department of Travel and Publicity*

crossings. In Arkansas there are special hunts in which beagles are the only legal dogs for deer. The hunters spread out on the ridge tops and the beagles can be heard moving deer from a distance. The big advantage of beagle-size dogs is that they move the deer slowly. Bigger hounds might run the deer at full speed. Deer moving slowly will usually stick close to their home territories and circle back without running more than a mile or so from where they were started, especially in heavy cover.

Most packs of deer dogs are of mixed ancestry. There is no breed of dogs in this country developed especially for deer.

A lot of hunters who drive deer with dogs simply tell a friend or two or a brother from the next hollow and turn the dogs loose. Some, however, organize regular drives just as they would when men are doing the driving. The captain plans the drive, says where to turn the dogs loose, and tells the standers where to wait. The advantage, of course, is that all the hunters can take up a stand and anyone has a good chance to get a shot.

Most of the states that permit hunting deer with

the aid of dogs do so because this style of hunting is traditional. Grandpa did it. From a practical view there are areas, especially in some Southern states, where lowlands are covered with heavy stands of palmetto or other dense vegetation that would make it extremely difficult to hunt without dogs.

In these swamplands, the Southern deer hunter who has hunted behind dogs all his life offers no apologies for the practice. "What else could you do," one of them asked me once, "when it's so dark in them swamps the alligators get lost and you wouldn't see a deer 'till you stepped right on him?"

States that do permit hunting with dogs often have heated debates about the wisdom of this brand of deer hunting. There has been a running argument in Arkansas for years over the law permitting hunting deer with dogs in the mountains. One hunter, writing to the editor of *Arkansas Game and Fish,* said, "I'm not a biologist, but I've got enough sense to know that deer won't move normally if dogs are running all over the woods with some turkey behind them whooping them on. Even the squirrels go in their holes."

Meanwhile, one Arkansas biologist speculates on why so many more deer are taken in nearby states than in adjoining parts of Arkansas. He sees the legal use of dogs as a highly important depressing factor and, speaking of the practice, says, "It has always been legal in Arkansas. It has always been illegal in Missouri and Oklahoma."

Several states, including Arkansas and Georgia, have conducted research to see what happens when dogs chase deer. In some areas there seems to be little effect, but research supports the belief that such hunting in mountainous regions puts the deer at a definite disadvantage. Arkansas is the last holdout retaining legal mountain deer hunting with dogs. In most places, it is limited to the lowlands.

Hunt the River Bends

In his Michigan countryside George Parks worked out a deer-hunting idea some years ago that helped him get a maximum of deer with a minimum of footwork. George made part of his annual income from taking care of dudes during the deer season each winter. He had a few tiny cabins where visiting deer hunters lived snugly, and Mrs. Parks would fix the meals. There wasn't a deer trail through his section of the Upper Peninsula that George didn't know. And he was considered one of the best deer-drive organizers for miles around.

But it was when the clients had gone home that George settled down to his favorite type of deer hunting. Where the rivers bend back on themselves in a graceful series of curves, as they often do up in that country, each hairpin curve creates a little peninsula. These were the places George Parks hunted after a fresh snow. He would walk across the base of the peninsula looking for deer tracks. If there were no fresh tracks George moved on to the next river bend. If there were fresh tracks he would go in to look for the deer.

If he was hunting alone George would catfoot down the center of the peninsula, eyes and ears alert for the slightest sign. He was meat hunting now, but he was also getting a real charge out of the adventure. If the deer broke for the open or tried to slip out past George, he might get a shot.

A little better plan, George always thought, was for two men to hunt these river bends. While one stood at the neck of land to try for a shot if a deer should bound out, the other one would move quietly around the peninsula until the wind carried his scent to the deer. The deer would more than likely try a sneak play at this juncture and one or the other of the hunters would get a shot. George liked it when a band of ice had started to freeze out from the river's edge. It's a rare deer that will try to escape across the river, especially when it is edged with ice.

Things have changed a little in northern Michigan since George Parks herded deer and dudes through the hemlock and spruce. Cabins such as he offered were then much in use. Today the hunters often come in trailers or make their own camp or stay in motels. But George Parks's method of hunting the river bends is as good today as when he first figured it out.

Float for Deer

Still another style of deer hunting is simply to float for deer along suitable streams. Waterways are attractions for deer, especially in early morning and late evening when the animals often come down to the streams to drink. If you've floated onto the scene quietly at the right moment you may bag your deer and not have far to drag him. You had better check the state laws first, however.

A close relative of this style of deer hunting is to drift, paddle, or scull along the wooded edges of lakes watching for deer near the shore.

Deer taken in these ways are not always right beside the water's edge. Keep a sharp eye on the underbrush back from the edge. Often deer will stand where they think they're hidden in the brushy streamside cover. If you spot a deer that sneaks off as you drift onto the scene, you may have to combine floating and still hunting to get close enough for a shot.

One major problem that crops up in much of our farming country for the floating deer hunter (who sometimes carries a bass or trout rod as well) is trespass. The best places to practice this hunting style are on large public holdings, such as national forest areas. There are also places in some of the commercially owned forest holdings that lend themselves to float hunting.

Hunting the Mule Deer

For long years there has been a running argument over whether or not the mule deer is smart. Some say he is, while others insist that there is nothing dumber.

Many an eastern hunter, fed on a diet of stories about this "dumb cousin" of the tricky whitetail, has gone West convinced that he could bag a trophy muley between smokes. If he's willing to settle for an unsophisticated yearling his hunt may be short and sweet. But if he's really after a trophy, and there are some magnificent ones, he may go through the season, and the next season too, without even sighting a rack he wants.

A mule deer's nose and ears are at least as well developed as those of a whitetail. He can pick up the faintest man odor on the breeze and his scoop-shovel ears collect sounds at amazing distances.

Instead of running or trotting like the whitetail, the mule deer leaps along in great bounds that carry him over rocks; in some places he is known as the "jumping deer." Hitting a muley on the run is, if anything, even more difficult than hitting a whitetail on the run.

The mule deer occupies a great variety of territories, ranging from mountain meadows to valleys in the lowlands. Early in the season the bucks, especially, are likely to be right up among the mountain peaks. Mule deer are migratory. For centuries, herds have followed the same trails from the mountains to the lowlands. The time of departure depends on the onset of winter and on the food supply. A sudden storm can bring them down early. A lot of mule deer hunting is done along these migration routes. The herds that migrate move from five to fifty miles and sometimes come down as far as seven thousand feet in elevation. There are mule deer territories outside the mountains where the animals are not migratory. And even where they do migrate, the fact is of little help to the hunter unless the time of the move coincides with the open season.

Many a hunter, failing to understand the habits of the mule deer, has hunted in the high meadows after the deer have moved down or in the lowlands before the deer have concentrated there. Those coming into mule deer country for a first-time hunt would do well to use a professional guide.

Sometimes it's difficult, even for hunters who practically live with the mule deer, to know where they are hanging out. Some years ago, while hunting muleys and antelope in northeastern Wyoming, Bill Glick and I were staying on the ranch of one-time homesteader Perry Wallace, a wiry, fast-moving outdoorsman of diminutive size who spent a lifetime studying game animals around his home country. For most of a week we looked for the deer. We saw a few does and some fawns but neither Perry nor anyone else could figure out where the big bucks had gone. It was all the more confusing to him because he had seen bucks around the place until shortly before the season opened. Then they had dropped from sight as though someone had tipped them off.

Near the end of the week we visited a ranch forty miles away and bagged a couple of fine bucks. On the final morning, when Perry drove us out to the airport, we crossed the creek at the edge of his ranch. There, down from the bridge in a meadow shaded by cottonwoods, was a whole herd of deer, among them two of the finest bucks I'd ever seen. Perry just shook his head and mumbled something about next year.

Milt Guymon, an Oregon Department of Fish and Wildlife employee, once had a rare opportunity to witness an interesting contest between five hunters and several buck mule deer. Guymon and his companion, perched on a rock outcropping, were able to look down on the whole affair less than five hundred yards from them.

Three of the hunters were on horseback. "For almost an hour and a half," wrote Guymon in the Department bulletin, "we were amazed at the ease with which buck deer outsmarted their adversaries." Three of the hunters failed to connect with fast-running bucks when they had shots. But more often they simply didn't realize how close they were to what they were looking for. The dry range conditions no doubt had something to do with the fact that the bucks were either sticking unusually tight in small pockets of brush, or moving out far ahead.

One of the horsemen rode up to a snowbush thicket no more than fifty feet in diameter, dismounted, shouted, and heaved rocks into the brush. Obviously any deer there would have come out, so the hunter took off through the sagebrush. But as he went, a fine four-pointer sneaked out of the brush in the opposite direction.

The observers watched two hunters work on foot through a small snowbush and wild cherry thicket. One stayed outside and the other beat the bushes.

When they left, the two bucks the observers had seen go into that thicket were still there hiding. Within thirty minutes after the hunter had thrown rocks into the patch of snowbush, several deer moved back into it, including one fine buck.

As the hunters worked higher, more deer moved out and down. In all, the observers saw twelve bucks play hide-and-seek with the five hunters working the brush and rimrock. The hunters had seen no more than five.

Obviously deer can get mighty tricky at staying out of sight.

The mule deer is ordinarily hunted in more open country than is the whitetail. Long sloping mountainsides spotted with sagebrush, juniper, and mahogany are his country. If he is routed from the thick cover of a canyon, he may make straight up the slope toward the ridge, where he drops from sight on the other side. While he's traveling he's often in the open. And this accounts for the fact that mule deer are often taken at considerable ranges—150, 200, and even 300 or more yards. Scope sights are called for, and lightweight bullets with long, flat trajectories such as the .270, the .30-06, and the .257 Roberts.

But if you haven't hunted the muley, don't get the impression that you'll have only running shots at your game. If anything, he has an even sharper curiosity than the whitetail. Even if you make no effort to stop him, he will often slam to a halt just before bounding out of sight and take a last, and sometimes costly, look back. There are times when the muley bounds in one direction and then in the other, as though he hasn't quite made up his mind. The smart old buck will sometimes top a ridge, cut sharply to the left or right, keep on his course for some distance, and then change again until he has so completely eluded his pursuers that he is the only unconfused creature on the mountainside.

Muleys are hunted in much the same way the whitetail is. Some mule deer hunters stage drives for them in spite of the open nature of the country and the difficulty of keeping these deer moving in the direction the hunters want them to go. Some drive the ranch roads and hunt from a pickup truck or jeep. Horseback hunting is a favorite method of many a mule deer hunter. Often a horse and rider can get much closer to a mule deer than the rider could on foot.

But the biggest challenge to the mule deer hunter is the still hunt that takes him out on foot to find and pursue his game, either alone or with a friend or two.

There are times when the deer seem to know they're out of range. I recall an evening in northeastern Wyoming when a line of seven deer walked single file along a mountain ridge a full half mile away; from where I stood, they were sharply silhouetted against the setting sun. But there was no trophy buck among them exposing himself. An old buck may occasionally be found with the does and fawns or hanging around within sight of the family herd. But he's quick to abandon them to their own defenses if he senses danger. During the rutting season he loses some of his caution.

When you set out to find deer, keep in mind their need for food. Check the ridges and valleys for fresh sign. Inspect the edges of meadows and those spots supporting a good cover of weeds or shrubs on which deer might feed. These are preferred to the open grasslands. Also check around water holes, springs, and livestock salting areas, and if none of these show fresh sign, look around the edges of the more thickly growing timbered slopes, especially the openings in timbered areas. If all this checking reveals no *fresh* sign, move on and check another region. There's no use waiting for the deer to show up in country they're avoiding.

The mule deer, like the whitetails, feed mostly at night, and the best times to spot them are the early morning and late evening as they move between shelter and feeding areas. These are the hours when mule deer hunters most often score. During the middle of the day you can vary the plan with still hunting and try to walk up on a deer. But the wise ones bed down in places where they command a view of the countryside and catch a whiff of the odors from anything that might approach from the upwind side.

Buck Tracks

I know hunters who insist that they can look at deer tracks and tell whether a doe or buck made them. But no one can identify the sex of a deer, either mule or whitetail, by the tracks 100 percent of the time.

Some years ago Wisconsin deer hunter Bill Bates had all the proof he needed that it's difficult, if not impossible, to tell buck and doe tracks apart. In his hunting party of six men, half the hunters said it couldn't be done and half said they could pick out the buck tracks anytime. One of the buck-track boys offered to put Bill on a buck trail the next morning.

Eight hours and ten miles later the set of big tracks Bill had been started on circled and came out in the open, where he had a good look at the deer he had pushed all day. "There stood my deer," says Bill, "about four hundred feet from me and not a thing in the way. It was as big a doe as I had ever seen."

Between 1946 and 1949, deer specialists of Wisconsin's Conservation Department were conducting feeding experiments on several hundred wild deer, all tagged and their sex known. They tried every way they could to find some basic difference between the doe and the buck tracks, all without success.

One Arkansas deer expert says, "I don't believe anybody can look at a whitetail deer track and say for sure whether the animal that made it is a doe or a buck."

The problem comes when you try to separate the big doe from a buck. There are some indications of the sex of the animal that left the track. Old bucks are usually heavier than old does of the same area. For this reason a buck's tracks may be deeper and the spread between the sections of the hooves greater than a doe's. But there is no dependable difference in shape between the two. The terrain and soil, the diet, and the animal's age all affect the shape of the foot. If you come on a big track, follow it. Unless you're out for a trophy buck or hunting in a state with a buck-only law, it seldom matters. And at any rate you should be right 50 percent of the time.

Tracks left by large deer hold special interest for hunters everywhere. Tracks with water moving into them, or with edges sharp and not yet eroded, are signs of recent movement. Big tracks, widely spread, may or may not be buck tracks.

Guides

The less you understand the country and the haunts and habits of the game, the more you need a guide. A few states require nonresident deer hunters to hire guides. There are wilderness regions where a guide and outfitter are almost essential. The guide packs, handles horses, establishes camp, cooks, skins game, and helps his hunter select the best heads.

The skilled guide is proud of his work; he is a walking handbook on camping, hunting, woods lore, natural history, and human relations. He also has more than average energy. Most states in which guides are important require guides to have licenses.

To obtain the names of guides in an area, ask for a list from state game and fish department, check the advertisements of outfitters in outdoor magazines, or write to the chambers of commerce in the towns you plan to hunt near.

A good guide wants his client to go home satisfied. And he always hopes for clients who are easy to get along with in the hunting camp. A hunter should not insist on personal favors, and he should be willing to help with chores around camp, especially when the guide is busy with pack animals and trophy skins.

No guide is fond of the client who insists on giving him instruction in deer hunting. I know one hunter who admits that his guide told him the second day out, "Maybe I should have hired you." The client took it well, however, and he and the guide became good friends.

The best guides I've known seem to have similar characteristics. They are relatively quiet people and they seem at home in the woods. They impart confidence to those who travel with them. They enjoy the outdoors and never seem in a hurry to return to town. They know what to do at every turn, whether cooking a pie in a reflector oven or portaging a canoe around a waterfall.

Most of these men, if they weren't guides, would find some other reason for spending time in the backcountry. They're happy in their work, not overly critical of their client's lack of experience, and eager to see that he gets more than his money's worth.

FOUR
THE DEER RIFLE

One of my friends, who has hardly missed a deer season in the last forty years, is fascinated by guns of all kinds. With the glint of adventure in his eyes he can expound for hours on the individual merits and demerits of his guns and the history that figured in their design. He took a gun census at his house a few years ago and found that he had acquired fifty-eight. Thirteen of them could be called deer rifles, because deer hunting is one of his cherished sports.

"Even I was a little bit shocked to find I had that many guns," he said. He began thinning the collec-tion down. It now stands at fourteen, which seems to be rock bottom. Why, one might ask, doesn't he just pick out the best deer rifle and let the rest go to somebody who needs them? The reason, of course, is that there is no such thing as a "best" deer rifle.

The rifle is the traditional gun of the deer hunter. The shotgun holds forth in the thick-growing brush country of the Southeast and parts of the East as well. On the West Coast, where the blacktail is hunted in the dense underbrush, the shotgun again comes through as a major deer gun. In Missouri, where hunters are permitted to use either shotguns

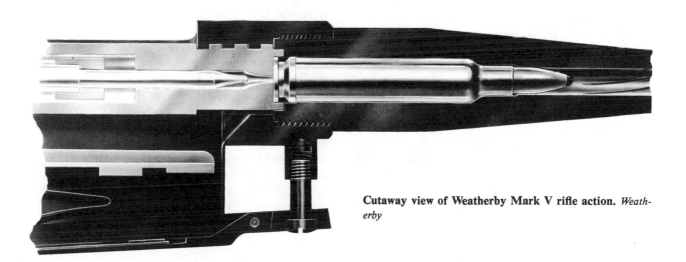

Cutaway view of Weatherby Mark V rifle action. *Weatherby*

or rifles, 80 percent of the deer hunters carry rifles. The calibers come in wide variety, but the most popular are the .30-06, .30-30, 8mm., .300 Savage, .270 Winchester, and .35 Remington. Success among rifle carriers may run a little higher than it does for the shotgun hunters.

Choosing a Deer Rifle

The average hunter setting forth to select his first deer rifle has probably waded through enough of the confusing information on calibers, bullet weights, types of actions, and barrel length to have some idea of the rifle he can best use. He need not, before choosing a deer rifle, become an expert on guns. Most deer hunters are not. It is not essential to make a long, detailed study of firearms and their history.

Some rifles will serve better for a given task than others. And this is the challenge: to select from the long list of excellent firearms available the deer rifle fitted to your needs.

To accomplish this, you must take into consideration these major points. Consider the type of country in which you will hunt, whether or not you will also use the gun to hunt other kinds of game, the laws of the states where you plan to hunt. And probably you must also consider the price of the gun.

Whitetails and blacktails are hunted mostly in brushy, thick-growing cover. Mule deer are more likely to be hunted in open mountain country.

These considerations are important. They determine which kind of ammunition you are most likely to need. For shooting in brushy country, the need is for a heavier bullet. Lightweight, high-velocity bullets are more likely to veer off course or disintegrate when they strike brush.

On the other hand, for open mountain country you want a lighter-weight bullet that whips along at a good pace and follows a fairly flat trajectory for longer shots, then disintegrates or expands well when it penetrates.

What you're after, of course, is the proper combination for quick, certain kills at any reasonable range in the territory in which you're likely to be hunting.

"Well," you say, "there should be a single deer rifle that will do this for me." And so there should. If you're going to restrict your hunting to deer in one type of territory, you can eliminate the confusion by settling on a gun that pleases you. If you're hunting brush country, you will do well to settle for a gun in that medium-caliber group represented by such weapons as the .30-06, or the old favorite .30-30, and 150- to 170-grain loads.

For long-range shooting you'll have trouble beating the .270, .280, or the .25-06 Remington. But if you're going to hunt both in the brushy cover of the eastern states and the open mountains of the West, a .30-06 or a .270 would be a good compromise.

What we're referring to in these figures is not the rifle itself so much as the cartridges it will handle. The bullet and the powder that pushes it does the work, and this is where you have to begin. You choose the load you want to use, then select a gun to handle that ammunition.

The caliber of a bullet is its diameter, measured generally in hundredths or thousandths of an inch. The cartridge is composed of four major parts: bullet, powder, primer, and casing.

Even within a caliber, cartridges come loaded with different weights of bullets. The weight of a bullet is designated in grains. The lighter bullet will go farther and get there faster than a heavier bullet when everything else is equal. You can, for example, buy .30-06 shells with 180-grain bullets or with 150-grain ones. The lighter-weight bullet is better suited to open country, because energy delivered at greater distances might be more important.

There is an almost endless variety of ammunition from which to choose for deer hunting. You will, of course, check the game laws and see that the rifle you're considering will be legal in the state where you plan to hunt. Some states prohibit the hunting of deer with rifles. Most of those that permit rifles place minimum limitations on the caliber. Check the legal angle very carefully before buying any rifle that calls for ammunition of under .25 caliber. Most of these are too light to take care of deer reliably time after time, even if they are legal. Regardless of the fact that you often hear of somebody who killed his deer with a .22, this is not a deer rifle and neither are the special hot loads, such as the .22 Hornet. The .25-20 is another gun too light for good work on deer.

Unfortunately, once you begin to dig into this topic of calibers, you soon realize that there has

m/700 ADL, bolt action, centerfire.

Remington Deer Rifles

m/7, bolt action, centerfire.

Sportsman 78, bolt action, centerfire.

Sportsman 76, pump action, centerfire.

Sportsman 74, autoloading, centerfire.

m/Six, centerfire, pump action.

m/7600, centerfire, pump action.

m/Four, centerfire, autoloading.

Remington Arms

never been any standard naming practice followed by the manufacturers of cartridges.

About the only thing you can be fairly sure of is that the first figure in a cartridge name refers to its caliber, the diameter of the bullet. Even this is expressed in several different fashions. Usually it is stated in thousandths of an inch or abbreviated and stated in hundredths of an inch. Europeans, however, state the caliber in millimeters.

The caliber designation gets a variety of information tacked on to it. Perhaps the best way to understand this is to take a few examples of ammunition and explain the background of their names.

Take a look at the .45-70 Government version of the old .45-70-500. The old .45-70-500 gave the caliber in the first figure. The 70 told the number of grains of black powder it contained. The 500 gave the weight of the bullet. The .45-70 refers to caliber plus weight of black powder used in the cartridge. Black powder, of course, is no longer used. The idea of having caliber and bullet weight in the same breath seems like a sensible one. Modern loads that still retain the meaningless black-powder information include the .38-40, .32-20, and .44-40.

Then there are those that give the caliber plus the name of the developer or manufacturer. Examples are the .35 Remington and the .257 Roberts. In the latter case the cartridge was designed by Roberts.

What of the .30-06? The .30 refers to the caliber and the 06 refers to 1906, the year it was adopted by the armed forces.

In the .300 H & H Magnum the initials are for the manufacturer, Holland and Holland, and the Magnum refers to an especially high-powered load in that caliber.

The 7 × 57 mm illustrates the European method of giving the caliber followed by the length of the cartridge casing, both stated in millimeters. One millimeter is roughly .039 inches. The 7 × 57 is therefore a .276 caliber.

The most important thing to bear in mind about cartridge names is that the first part gives you the caliber in practically any rifle you're likely to come across.

The general rule followed today for selecting deer-hunting ammunition is to choose a cartridge and bullet-weight combination that will deliver a minimum 1,300 foot-pounds of energy at the maximum distance you might expect to shoot. The following choices are suitable depending on the kind of terrain you hunt.

Open-Country Shooting

.270 Win. 130-gr.

.30-06 Springfield 150-gr.

6mm Rem. 100-gr.

.25-06 Rem. 120-gr.

7mm-08 Rem. 140-gr.

.308 Win. 150-gr.

300 H & H Mag. 150-gr.

.243 Win. 100-gr.

.280 Rem. 150-gr.

7mm Rem. Mag. 150-gr.

Brush-Country Shooting

.250 Savage 100-gr.

.270 Win. 150-gr.

.30-03 Win. 170-gr.

.30-06 Springfield 180-gr.

.303 Savage 190-gr.

7mm-08 Rem. 140-gr.

.444 Marlin 240-gr.

.257 Roberts 117-gr.

7 mm Mauser (7 × 57) 140-gr.

.300 Savage 180-gr.

.308 Win. 180-gr.

.280 Rem. 165-gr.

.30-06 165-gr.

Once you've selected a caliber of ammunition to fit your need, the next problem is to choose the rifle to handle it. Here, too, a number of factors must be considered. Various manufacturers make rifles in several models for many of the more commonly used cartridges. Points you may want to consider in narrowing the choice down include type of action, weight of rifle, length of barrel, and the way the gun "handles," or feels.

Type of Action

The action of a rifle is that part of it that does the loading and unloading. There are four types of breech actions used in deer rifles. These are bolt action, lever action, slide or trombone or pump, and semiautomatic. For example, if you want to use .300 Savage ammunition, you can have a choice of

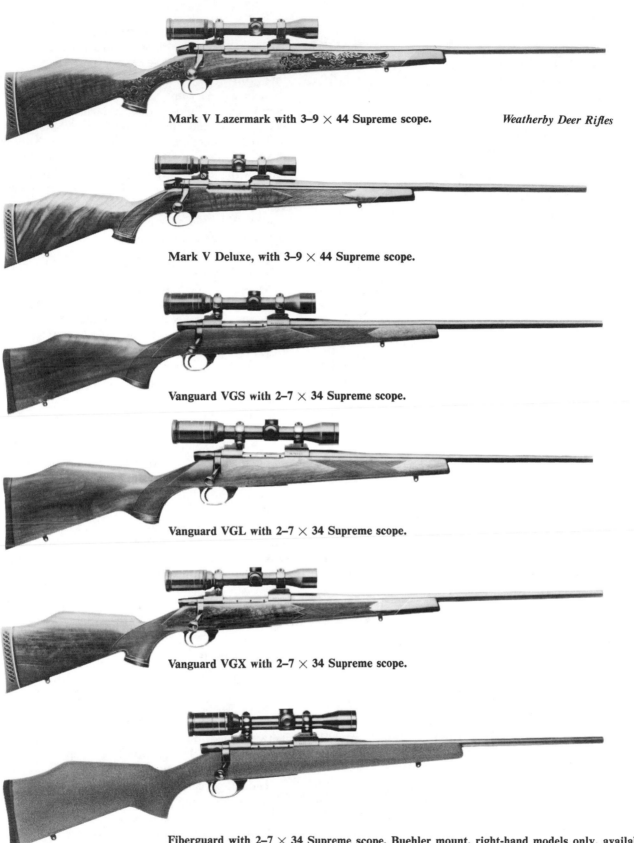

Mark V Lazermark with 3–9 × 44 Supreme scope.

Weatherby Deer Rifles

Mark V Deluxe, with 3–9 × 44 Supreme scope.

Vanguard VGS with 2–7 × 34 Supreme scope.

Vanguard VGL with 2–7 × 34 Supreme scope.

Vanguard VGX with 2–7 × 34 Supreme scope.

Fiberguard with 2–7 × 34 Supreme scope, Buehler mount, right-hand models only, available .223 Rem., .243 Win., .270 Win., 7mm Rem. Mag., .30-06 and .308 Win. *Weatherby* bolt-, lever-, or slide-action rifle. There are both slide- and bolt-action guns to accommodate .270 and .30-06 loads.

1. A bolt-action rifle ejects the cartridge case when you pull the bolt upward and backward; as the bolt is closed, another cartridge goes from the magazine into the chamber.

2. The lever action has a handle beneath the breech that is pulled down with the fingers of the shooting hand to eject the cartridge case. Another cartridge is pushed into the chamber when the lever is pushed back into position.

3. The slide or pump action ejects the cartridge case when the mechanism beneath the barrel is pulled back and reloads when it is slid forward.

4. Shell ejection and reloading in the semiautomatic loader is accomplished by recoil or gas from the cartridge activating the breech mechanism.

The best of the lot as far as accuracy is concerned is the bolt action. This becomes especially important in long-range shooting. Consequently the bolt action is highly popular through parts of the West. But there are other considerations. It takes more than once-a-year shooting to maintain efficiency with any rifle. You can get a bolt-action rifle for left-handed use. The user of a bolt-action rifle usually has to move the gun away from his shoulder, or at least his cheek away from the gun stock, to work the action. There are a lot of shooters, of course, who grew up with bolt-action rifles and don't feel at ease shooting any other style. It's a rugged and dependable type of action that merits its popularity.

The lever-action rifles have had more advocates among deer hunters than any other style of gun. Most famous of the lot is doubtless the Model 94 Winchester, first developed in 1894 and used since then on more deer, probably, than any other rifle. This old-timer, in either .30-30 caliber or .32 special, is still a highly popular choice in such places as the woods of Michigan and Maine and in Minnesota, Wisconsin, and Pennsylvania. It has long been a general-utility scabbard gun, carried by western range riders.

The lever action permits the shooter to handle his gun fast because he can keep the gun at his shoulder while sliding a second cartridge into the chamber. And its short barrel length and light weight make it especially good for those fast shots

in brushy territory. They are not, however, as accurate or as strong as bolt-action rifles.

If, in upland game shooting, you've relied on a pump gun, the slide-action deer rifle may well be what you should choose. Remington's Model Six and 7600 come in several calibers and are faster to handle than either the bolt- or lever-action jobs. And, while some may argue the point, there are those who can shoot a trombone-type rifle practically as fast as most people can shoot an autoloader. With the slide-action rifle you can reload without taking the gun from your shoulder or your finger off the trigger. Therein lies its major advantage over either of the other manually operated rifles. It falls short of the bolt or lever action in accuracy and strength, however, and this may have something to do with the fact that it has never threatened the popularity of those two styles.

The semiautomatic rifle is in a class by itself, because it does its own work in ejecting the old cartridge case, loading a new one into the chamber, and cocking. All the shooter does is pull the trigger. The shell fires and the gun is ready for the next shot. The ideal situation, of course, calls for taking a deer with a single shot. But there are times when the best of deer hunters need that second shot. If they happen to be using an autoloader, no time is wasted getting that important second shot off. This can be especially helpful in brushy country, where the deer may get out of sight so fast he leaves you blinking. But, on the other hand, the autoloader is less accurate than the bolt action, and accuracy may well be more important than fast shooting when you're out for deer.

Inside a Rifle

The inside of a rifle barrel is cut with a series of grooves, usually four or six. These grooves, usually .004 inch deep, follow a spiral pattern. The areas between the riflings are called lands. The true caliber or bore of the barrel is the inside diameter of the barrel before rifling is cut into it.

The rifling causes bullets to spiral or rotate as they travel through the barrel; they retain the spin after they leave the gun.

Here is what happens when you fire a rifle. You

pull the trigger of a cocked rifle and the firing pin is released to strike the primer in the back of the cartridge. The primer is highly explosive and it ignites the powder charge. Expanding gas released by the burning powder forces the bullet from the cartridge casing and along the barrel. The bullet has an extremely tight fit, to prevent the escape of gas. The escape of the bullet and the gas creates a partial vacuum. Air rushes in to fill the vacuum and probably causes the muzzle blast.

Barrel Length

The length of the barrel is related to the velocity of the bullet fired through it. In black-powder days the explosive needed a long barrel to develop full force in sending the bullet on its way. But as faster-burning powders came into use, the pressures could be built to maximum levels in shorter lengths of barrel—producing, incidentally, a muzzle blast that can be uncomfortably loud. The length of the barrel also has a relationship to the weight of the gun, an important factor on a full day's hunt.

Rifles in recent times have followed a trend toward shorter barrels. A few newer models have barrels only eighteen and a half inches long. With today's fast-burning powders, there is no great difference in the velocity of bullets from the same barrel before and after an inch or two has been cut off it. Arms manufacturers have made detailed tests of this factor. Some years ago the research department of Remington Arms fired a series of rounds from several guns with barrels of different lengths. In one .30-06, for example, 180-grain bullets from the standard twenty-four-inch rifle barrel traveled at 2,700 feet per second. With the barrel cut to twenty inches, the same load traveled at 2,640 feet per second. In the same series of tests, a .270 Winchester firing 150-grain bullets produced a muzzle speed of 2,800 feet per second with a twenty-four-inch barrel and 2,675 with a twenty-inch barrel.

A shorter gun makes it easier to get around through the brush; you can carry it comfortably in a saddle scabbard or tote it on your back in mountain or wilderness hunting. The ease of handling and accuracy will be more important than the differences in velocity. An exceptionally lightweight barrel, however, is usually harder to hold steady than a heavier one.

The Kick

As one of the more hilarious tricks where I grew up, the "big boys" would induce some ten-year-old to shoot a 10- or 12-gauge shotgun to see whether or not the youngster stood up under the impact. Well, recoil is just not that funny.

Every time a gun is shot there is recoil. The pressure pushing the gun backward is equal to the pressure exerted to send the bullet forward. The push must be absorbed by the gun and the shooter's shoulder. Some shooters seem to take it better than others.

A lot of shooters who can't hit a mark regularly either don't know or don't want to admit that they're flinching as they pull the trigger. It's a psychological reaction—fear of the noise and the jolt delivered—every time the trigger is pulled. There have even been attempts to explain away misses as the result of the recoil throwing the gun barrel off when the bullet was fired. But high-speed photos in ballistics laboratories took away this excuse. The pictures showed that the gun muzzle doesn't jump until after the bullet has left it. What was blamed on recoil had to be marked down as flinch.

The significance of recoil in choosing a rifle is considerable. A heavier gun generally absorbs the recoil better than a light gun. Some shooters afflicted with flinching have had to turn to firing .22 rifles and .410 shotguns until they conquered the trouble.

One thing is certain: the bigger the caliber, the more likely you are to develop trouble from flinch. But most of the medium-caliber deer guns, those in the .30-caliber class, pack no more wallop than the average person can absorb without worrying about it.

If you are bothered by recoil, you would not choose a gun such as the .375 H & H Magnum or the .300 Weatherby Magnum for deer. These are more gun than you need for deer anyhow.

If a hunter using one of the smaller calibers and lightweight bullets hits a vital area, the deer is more than likely to stay right where he is. If, on the other hand, the bullet hits the game a little bit off the mark, it may not cause enough trouble to bring him down until hours or days later in some hidden glen.

Deer rifles in the .30-caliber class are a wiser choice for the average hunter. Heavier bullets from these medium-caliber rifles pack the wallop needed to do the job and still don't carry an unbearable recoil. The .270 and the newer .280 caliber, for which you can get a variety of choices in bullet weights, also belong in this group.

Foreign Guns

There seems to be no end these days of "bargain" priced military rifles, especially foreign makes, available to the outdoorsman. The prices look tempting. But unless you know your way around the gun counter, you had better proceed with caution before buying one of these guns in the hope of "sporterizing" it. It's true that some of them can be excellent hunting rifles. "A major consideration," says Charlie Grossman, a highly competent gunsmith of Milford, Ohio, "is how easily available the ammunition will be for the gun you choose. I usually rechamber them."

One friend of mine who made regular runs for the United States Navy into Salerno back in the 1940s acquired a Model 98 8mm Mauser. When he was back home, the gun's new owner went into the hills on a beautiful fall day carrying a few shells that he had bought from the same place he obtained the gun. He spotted his mule deer, a fine buck, and touched off two fast shots that might as well have been blanks. The third turned out to be a tracer bullet which showed him he was missing his deer by three feet. "I sat down and had a good laugh," he says.

This gun has since become his favorite deer rifle. It has been restocked, had a four-power scope added, and been rechambered to accommodate 8mm-06 cartridges for more powder. He usually chooses 150-grain bullets, which have a muzzle velocity of about three thousand feet per second. He realized from the beginning what the military gun would need if it was to measure up in the field.

Federal Premium brand cartridge for .30-06 Springfield, 150-grain bullet. *Federal Cartridge Corp.*

Bullets

The bullet that does the job has been the subject of long years of highly scientific research. There are many kinds, each designed for a specific purpose and each expected to work in a special fashion when it strikes the target.

An important consideration is how much and how fast the bullet will expand when it hits a target. High-speed varmint bullets, for example, as a safety measure and also to give immediate kill of small game, are made to disintegrate if they hit the ground. What you're asking of a deer load is that it penetrate the skin, explode or expand for great shocking power, and kill the animal cleanly. It must expand inside the deer and not pass on out the other side to leave a small wound and probably a crippled animal.

A jacketed bullet is one in which the lead, or part of it, is covered with a thin coat of tough alloyed metal to make it hold together on impact. Jackets also help to give bullets better accuracy and performance. But full-jacketed bullets are a poor choice for deer because the jackets hold the bullets together and won't let them expand. The lead nose of the bullets should be left exposed and not covered by other metal. When one of these soft-nosed bullets strikes a deer, the bullet mushrooms, makes a

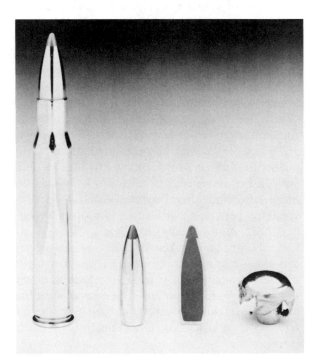

large path, and carries great ability to render shock.

Hollow-point bullets should not be used on deer. They're intended for heavier game.

Slings

A sling on your rifle may seem to be a small item; it is just a leather strap, but it can be highly important to you at the moment you want to take a carefully aimed long shot. There are two jobs you ask of a sling: to serve as support for carrying the gun over your shoulder and to steady your gun while you aim.

As an aid in aiming, it has its greatest utility in western locations where you may have time for a long shot taken carefully. There is seldom time to use a sling in close brush shooting. But you will need the sling for carrying your rifle when you start dragging a deer out of the woods. Some hunters equip the gun with removable swivels and carry the sling as a belt until it's needed.

Care and Cleaning of Rifles

Equipment you should have to keep your hunting rifle in good shape includes a bottle of lubricant, which probably also contains some anticorrosive agent and solvent, a brass brush of the right caliber, a steel cleaning rod, flannel patches, and an old toothbrush.

Some guns are cleaned too much. "I've seen gun owners sit in a deer camp and in a single evening of cleaning their gun shorten the life of the barrel as much as five hundred rounds of ammunition would," says gunsmith Charlie Grossman, for fourteen years a deer guide in the Adirondacks. It's possible to damage the lands in a barrel with a cleaning rod. This is especially true if the rod is dirty. Damage is also easily done with those supple aluminum rods that buckle and rub the inside of the barrel. Use a steel cleaning rod of the right caliber, one that won't bend as you run it through the barrel.

You may also want to include a rod guide in your gun-cleaning kit. This fits into the action of the rifle and guides the cleaning rod so that it won't nick the barrel on the way in.

Here is the procedure for cleaning your deer rifle. If you have been out in the rain and there is a chance that the barrel is wet, run a dry patch through it. Follow with one of the newer products containing a desiccant to remove moisture and protect the barrel. A dry patch alone is not enough to remove moisture from metal pores, while plain oil tends to trap moisture. Typical desiccant-containing products include Rem Oil or Break Free.

If you haven't been out in the rain or snow, there is no need for daily cleaning of your hunting rifle even if you have shot it during the day. One pass of a dry patch is a good idea if you can't look through the barrel to be certain it is free of foreign matter.

When you do clean the rifle—and you should before you store it for the winter—start by making a pass through the barrel with a patch carrying a solvent. The rod should be run from the action end of the barrel toward the muzzle if your rifle has the bolt-type action that will permit this. If you don't use a rod guide, grip the cleaning rod between thumb and finger and guide it to keep it centered in the barrel. And if you must clean from the muzzle toward the action, take special care to see that the rod doesn't scrape the muzzle.

Next, pass a bronze or brass brush of the right caliber in the same direction all the way through in one movement, then bring it back. If you've fired the gun only a few times, this step probably won't be necessary. But two or three passes with the metal brush should loosen any lead or other foreign materials that need to come out.

Now, with the dirt loosened, pass through the barrel a few more patches soaked with solvent. Don't feel that you have to run enough dry patches through the barrel to get them coming out snowy white. If you're going to store the gun in the rack, run one more oiled patch through it. If you intend to do some more shooting with it shortly, finish with a dry patch.

Between cleanings, keep the gun brushes in a sealed container so they won't collect dust and grease.

If you want to give the gunstock a little extra care, go over it with a fine grade of furniture wax, then polish it.

The biggest mistake made in taking care of the action of a rifle is in overoiling it. That is no place for pouring or splashing oil. If you want to lubricate the action, strip the gun down partway. Use a thin petroleum-based solvent to remove the dirt. Then re-oil the parts lightly with a good gun lubricant and work the parts to spread it around. Take it easy. All you need is a thin coat of lubricant to protect the action. Too much lubricant can, in freezing weather, make the action so stiff it won't work.

In storing your hunting rifles, you want to protect the guns and the members of your family—not necessarily in that order. Keep the guns in a locked rack or cabinet and the ammunition in another locked compartment if there is any possibility at all that curious citizens of any age will have access to them.

Guns look nice in a glass-fronted cabinet, but they are usually safer from rusting when they are kept in an open wall rack. If you do use a cabinet, most good gun stores can supply you with a compound for keeping down moisture and rust.

Wall racks can be either purchased or made with bars that enable you to padlock the guns in place.

Sights on the Deer Rifle

As a boy on the home place I don't recall driving nails with my little .22, or lighting matches the way the spellbinders did in the traveling shows of those days. But that little gun brought walnuts from the tops of the big trees behind the house. And I recall one day when I took careful aim and hit a length of baling wire sticking out from a fence post at about fifty feet. With open iron sights that wasn't doing too badly.

In those times practically the only sights available to the average farm boy with limited resources were open sights. He could knock off squirrels with them and collect sitting rabbits. But those open iron sights are not easy to use, in spite of the fact that they're still standard equipment on most rifles.

Rifle sights are classified in three groups. There are the open sights, the peep receiver sights, and the scopes. Their purpose is to improve your chances of hitting the target. Deer hunters who restrict their shooting to the deer season may not realize what a variety of sights are available to them.

Rifles normally come from the factory equipped with open iron sights. There is a front bead which you line up in a notched rear sight. This type of sighting aid forces your eye to focus on three planes at once, the rear sight, front bead, and target. This isn't always easy, especially for eyes past thirty-five years old.

The best arrangement is the front bead seen through a receiver peep sight. It gives you only two planes to worry about, because the front bead seems to the eye to become part of the peep sight aperture. Also the sight doesn't mask out as much target as does the V-shaped or buckhorn-type rear sight. You can ordinarily see the entire deer in the circular field of your peep sight. The front bead is simply centered in the aperture and placed on the point of aim. This centering is taken care of by the eye automatically.

One rifle I acquired had both a peep sight and, mounted in front of it, an open notched sight. The peep sight could be swung aside if the shooter wanted to rely on the open sight. But strangely enough, as I looked through the peep sight, the open sight in front of the peep was easily ignored, at least on this rifle. The natural tendency, in spite of the extra sight, is to center the bead in the peep sight. The size of the aperture in a peep sight isn't highly important for accuracy, especially when sighting on a target as large as a deer, although a large aperture does give added light.

The Front Sight

If you use iron sights on your rifle, you should be able to find the front bead in a hurry, even in dim light. For this, the shape, color, and size are important. My preference is for one with a flat surface on the back. The sharper edges are more easily defined by the eye.

Target shooters blacken the bead, if it is not already black, but the best color for deer hunting is determined by the color of the background against which you're shooting. White is a good color under many circumstances but the worst possible against a snowfield. The bead on the .280 Remington I use for western deer hunting is gold, a good and popular choice in colors. Red is also a good choice. I carry a hood cover over the front bead to protect the bead from hard knocks which can damage it.

If you're not happy with the iron sights you're using, it's possible to change them or various parts of them.

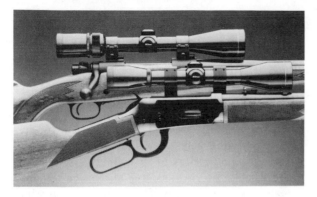

Nikon Riflescopes, 4× and 3–9× *Nikon*

Scopes

Civil War sharpshooters utilized scope sights. So did snipers in both World Wars, and American soldiers returned with accounts of amazing performances for the scopes. In some cases they returned with the scopes as well.

Before long, scope sights were becoming increasingly common on the target ranges, and they next began showing up in hunting camps. American manufacturers started turning out scopes that were increasingly sturdy and dependable.

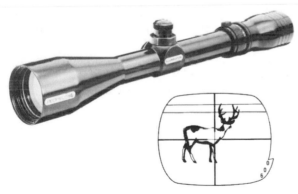

The ILLUMINATOR: 3X-9X Widefield® Accu-Trac® Variable

Redfield Illuminator: 3×–9× Widefield, Accu-Trac Variable. *Redfield*

With a scope, big-game hunters get single-plane precision sighting, and deer hunters are turning to scope sights in constantly growing numbers. There are, of course, hunters who wouldn't consider switching from open sights to a scope. The reason usually given and often debated is that iron sights are faster to use.

I have seen men bring down an elk at 275 yards with open sights. I have also seen hunters kill whitetails in thick cover with the use of a four-power scope. It depends on what you're accustomed to handling.

Actually, there is little advantage to the iron sight except lower cost. Most shooters who have both iron sights and scopes on their deer rifles, with scopes mounted so they can swing them aside for a fast close-up shot, soon make little use of the iron sights. One generalization can be made: the greater the distance from gun to target, the poorer the hunter's chance of making a clean kill with iron sights.

Inside a Scope

The tube of a scope has various lenses, known as elements, mounted rigidly within it. In most scopes there are four such elements. Out in front is the objective lens. Behind it is the reticle, which is a marker to line up on the target. Farther back is the erector lens, which turns the inverted image right side up and puts it in its proper left-to-right position. Finally, nearest the eye, is the ocular or eyepiece.

Choosing a Scope

The hunter shopping for his first scope sight often places too much emphasis on magnification. The tendency is to choose a scope too powerful for the task.

Most experienced deer hunters are content with a 2.5-power scope, which, in effect, brings the target two and a half times closer to your eye. This is enough magnification for practically any deer-hunting situation. Probably the scope most often chosen, however, is the four-power. This is a good choice if you're going to combine deer and antelope hunting in open mountain country where you're likely to have some long-range shots. Anything larger than a four-power scope provides too much magnification for the deer woods.

You can't have both great magnification and wide field of view in a scope. The more powerful the telescope, the narrower the section of landscape you can see through it. When you look through a scope, you need to see as much territory as possible to pick out the target rapidly. This is especially important when sighting on a running target. Remember too that the more powerful a scope, the more it magnifies the motion of your gun and makes aiming difficult.

At one hundred yards a four-power scope has a field of view about thirty feet wide. This automatically means a sixty-foot field at twice that range and only fifteen feet at fifty yards. And you're much more likely to have a shot at a deer at fifty yards than at two hundred. A good 2.5-power scope will have a field of view of about forty-three feet at one hundred yards, or 21.5 feet at fifty yards. Highly popular choices today are low-power variable scopes of 1.5 to 5× or 2–7×.

Reticles

The reticle can be obtained in a variety of designs. Most popular are the cross hair, the post, and the dot. Western shooters favor the cross hair. A large fraternity of eastern whitetail hunters want nothing but post-style reticles, either flat-topped or pointed.

Advocates of the cross-hair reticle argue that the post type obscures too much of the target on those shots where you must "hold over."

The dot-type reticle also has its fans. They point out that it hides but little of the target and that, given practice, the shooter can learn to judge ranges by how much of the deer's body the dot covers.

The reticle is usually made of fine wire mounted in a metal frame, or of lines engraved on glass. Cross-hair reticles can be purchased in various thicknesses: fine, medium-fine, medium, and coarse. Thickness of the wire has little to do with accuracy as long as the wires permit a good view of the target. The best choice for deer hunting is the medium.

Parallax

Parallax is simply what appears to be movement of the reticle on the target. The sighted object and reticle seem to be on different planes. A good gunsmith usually checks and corrects for parallax when he mounts a scope.

As far as hunting scopes are concerned, the subject of parallax gets more play than it deserves. There is some parallax in all scope sights. They are factory-set to be parallax free at a given distance, usually 100 or 150 yards. The short ranges at which deer are usually shot make parallax an insignificant cause of error in marksmanship.

Mounting a Scope

Today's high-powered rifles, with the accompanying recoil, make it imperative that scopes be mounted rigidly. Just as there is a wide variety of scopes, so are there a number of mounts from which to choose.

You can select a fixed mount which holds the scope in one position, or you can get a hinged mount that lets you move it aside if you want to use iron sights.

Some rifles eject shells from the top of the breech, and consequently the scope cannot be mounted directly on top. For this type of rifle there is a side mount. Some shooters like this because it permits instant availability of both scope and iron sights.

Scopes should be mounted by a good gunsmith. It is not a costly procedure and it's worth the price in added peace of mind and confidence in your weapon. If your rifle is already tapped and drilled for mounts, however, you can easily install them with a screwdriver.

Focus Your Scope

One of the better features of the modern hunting scope is that you can focus the eyepiece or ocular to match the needs of your eye. On most scopes it is accomplished by turning the entire eyepiece, which is threaded in the housing. Bring it into sharp focus at one hundred yards by sighting on some object with sharply defined lines. Once it is in focus, leave it alone.

Scope Troubles

Before you go hunting, get lens caps to protect your scope. They're inexpensive and may spell the difference between getting a deer and not getting a deer.

A friend of mine a few years ago had an opportunity to hunt in Wyoming. He borrowed a .30-06 equipped with a four-power scope. He packed into a wilderness camp and after two days of hunting had his first shot. It was late in the day and a wet snow had fallen through most of the afternoon. He brought the gun to his shoulder but everything was blurred through the scope. For all his efforts to protect it, the lens had still caught enough snow to make sighting through the scope impossible. He flipped the scope mount aside and squeezed off a shot with the help of the iron sights. But the distance was more than two hundred yards and he missed the deer completely. It should have been an easy shot with the scope, and probably would have been if he had equipped it with lens caps before leaving.

Lens covers come in several designs. Some are hinged. My preference is for the type in which the front and back lens caps are attached with elastic bands. These can be fastened to the gun and flipped off quickly when you get a chance at a shot.

Sighting In

Before you set forth for the hunting fields you should sight your weapon in. The first problem may be finding a place to sight-in a hunting gun. City hunters must often travel considerable distances to sight-in their guns.

Some gun clubs permit nonmembers to use their ranges. But not all ranges are equipped for shooting high-powered rifles. Some police and city recreation departments make their ranges available. Your sporting-goods dealer, local outdoor columnist, or conservation officer should know how to contact local gun clubs.

In most cities and in many smaller communities there is a gunsmith equipped to mount scopes. You can usually find him through a sporting-goods store. Allow two weeks for the job, especially if you wait until late in the summer, when deer hunters are swamping him with work on hunting guns. He will probably bore-sight the rifle after mounting the scope. Some gunsmiths, with this simple method, bring the point of impact amazingly close to the mark.

You can bore-sight a bolt-action rifle yourself by removing the bolt and fixing the rifle in a rigid stand. Sight through the barrel at a target fifty, then, one hundred yards distant so that the bull's-eye is centered in the barrel. Then, with the gun in the same position, adjust the scope so it too is centered on the bull's-eye. Now you are ready to shoot a few rounds and see how close you have come.

You can bore-sight a rifle that does not have a bolt-type action by opening the breech and inserting a small bore-sighting prism manufactured for the purpose.

Adjustments to the right or left are made with the windage-adjusting screw. To make the rifle shoot lower or higher, adjust the elevation screw. These adjustments are generally graduated in click stops, with each click measuring an angle of .25 minute. At one hundred yards, a minute is one inch. Consequently, if you're sighting in at one hundred yards and want to move the point of impact one inch in any direction, you correct the adjustment by four clicks. Packed with most scopes are directions for making these adjustments.

On the range, the first difficulty may be in getting the shots "on paper." You can sometimes shoot a couple of boxes of ammunition before getting close to the bull's-eye.

The thing to do if you have trouble getting on target is to move in to a distance of twenty-five yards. Try a few carefully released shots with your gun rested on a rolled blanket. Sight-in with the same ammunition you will use for deer hunting.

High-powered rifles are usually sighted in at two hundred yards and medium-powered ones at one hundred yards. If you're making a long trip to the hunting area it's a good plan, when possible, to shoot a few rounds after you arrive to be certain that the sights weren't bumped out of line during the trip.

Recoil makes your rifle jump back when you shoot. The scope must be mounted far enough forward to keep it from hitting you in the eye. The distance from your eye to the ocular is known as "eye relief." Eye relief for a scope on a high-powered rifle should be at least two and a half inches. Some of the better scopes have an eye relief of three to five inches. I know of at least one deer hunter who took a healthy blow in the eye from a scope set too far back in the mount.

Don't assume that your rifle stays sighted-in from year to year. Check it out before every hunt.

Gun Terms

BALLISTICS. The study of projectiles in motion. In the case of firearms the term includes ballistics both inside the barrel and after the bullet leaves the barrel.

BORE. Diameter of a gun barrel interior before rifling.

BULLET ENERGY. Term used to express bullet's ability to do work at a given range expressed in foot-pounds. A foot-pound is the energy required to lift one pound of weight one foot.

CALIBER. Diameter of a bullet or bore of a rifle barrel, usually in hundredths or thousandths of an inch.

CARTRIDGE. Container that fits into the chamber of a gun and holds powder, primer, and bullet, shot, or slug.

CHAMBER. That part of the gun into which cartridge is fitted for firing.

FIRING PIN. The part of the action released by the trigger to strike the primer and fire the powder.

LANDS. Those high areas separating the grooves cut into the barrel of a rifle.

RIFLING. A system of spiraling grooves cut into the inside of the rifle or handgun barrel to make the bullets spin as they are pushed through and out of the barrel by the exploding powder.

TRAJECTORY. The path of flight of a bullet from the time it leaves the gun until it hits an object. The bullet in flight is subject to two forces which, considered together, make it follow a curved path. The forces are gravity and air resistance. Gravity causes the bullet to drop toward the earth, and air resistance causes it to lose speed. Knowledge of trajectory data for the loads he uses will help a shooter set his sights properly for various ranges and correct his aim to compensate for shots at various distances.

TRAJECTORY, MIDRANGE. That point at which the bullet, traveling from gun to target, reaches the greatest height in its path.

VELOCITY. Speed of a bullet at a given point after leaving rifle muzzle. Measured in feet per second.

FIVE

SHOTGUNS FOR DEER HUNTING

The shotgun has stacked up quite a record in the deer woods of the eastern half of the country. Some states permit hunters to use either rifles or shotguns for deer. Others, fearful for human safety in highly populated regions, prohibit the taking of deer with the traditional deer rifle. In these states the deer hunter has little choice in firearms. He hunts with a shotgun.

It's difficult to argue with the legislators and game commissions that have restricted deer weapons to shotguns. In Ohio, with its 235 people per square mile, fear of the long-range rifle is easy enough to understand. And Ohio is only the seventh most heavily populated state. Just how dangerous deer rifles would actually be in such places, no one knows for certain.

But there is no reason for weeping at the gun counter. Some hunters, in fact, are better off with a shotgun than with a deer rifle.

This is often true of hunters, especially through much of the Southeast, who have wide experience swinging a shotgun but who seldom use a rifle. The shotgun feels right to them. Quail hunters, over the years, become highly proficient at swinging on the covey rise and picking out a couple of small high-speed targets. This practice comes in nicely when they shift to deer hunting with the same gun.

Thick-growing underbrush makes the shotgun especially well suited to deer hunting. Even the old rifleman Teddy Roosevelt said of the whitetail in heavy brush, "The shotgun is really the best weapon wherewith to attempt its death." Through

Some highly populated states prohibit hunting deer with rifles. These two Ohio hunters prove that shotguns are excellent for deer hunting. *Ottie M. Snyder, Jr.*

swamps and river-bottom thickets you may get only a fleeting glimpse of your buck as he slides past an opening twenty yards away from your stand. Usually he's in high gear, because the hounds, which are legal deer-hunting aids through part of the South, are pushing him. A hunter unfamiliar with his rifle hardly has time to find the game in his sights. But give him the old familiar shotgun and it's a different story.

The modern shotgun had its origin in the old smoothbore, muzzle-loading musket. Then followed the double-barreled muzzle-loaders, and

Well ahead of opening morning, the shotgun-carrying hunter will have fired practice rounds of identical loads to know how the rifled slug will perform.

eventually the breech-loading shotguns from which today's models developed.

Most of the gun people, hoping to improve the shotgun as a deer-hunting weapon, have concentrated on the ammunition. Only in recent years has there been a conscious effort to build a better shotgun for handling rifled slugs.

Two manufacturers, Ithaca and Remington, have shotguns directed at the deer-hunting market. Ithaca led the pack with development of its Deerslayer which, logically enough, had its birth in the frustrations of a hunter who failed to bag his deer with slugs from an old standard shotgun.

Ed Thompson, head of Ithaca's service department, told of the neighbor who dropped by one evening with a sad tale of how he thought he had missed the biggest buck he had ever seen. He had a shot at the buck at one hundred yards right out in the open. He knew, as any shotgun hunter of experience knows, that this was too far for a shot with a

slug. But the temptation was great and he lined up on the buck. The buck bounded off and the hunter figured he had scored a clean miss. But he hadn't.

The following morning he went up the ridge with his hunting companions to search for the deer. In a fine old stand of pine, they found the eleven-point buck down on a bed of needles. He had settled there and never lifted himself. The hunter stood over the magnificent animal and said sadly, "I wish I had missed him clean." His slug had hit the buck far back and low in the paunch, the kind of shot that often kills a deer but only after sending him so far away that the hunter may never find him.

The fact that this is fairly common among shotgun hunters set Ed Thompson to thinking. He and his neighbor took turns shooting the unhappy hunter's gun. It consistently shot far to the right of the mark.

Ed couldn't get the episode off his mind, and the next morning, when he was back in his shop, the company began a project of building the best gun they could design for commercial rifled slugs. After several years of trials and detailed scientific laboratory checking, they came up with their Deerslayer.

In test firings by an independent testing laboratory, the Deerslayer, shooting at one hundred meters (109.4 yards), grouped five slugs in a pattern with a vertical spread of 7 inches and a horizontal spread of 4¾ inches.

The new shotgun performed equally well in numerous other tests and has been making a reputation for itself in the field. In Hobart, Oklahoma, the family of radio sports editor Wayne Robison used this gun to bag three deer the first year they had it. They killed the first one at seventy-five yards and the other two at slightly more than one hundred yards each.

Development of such guns as this and Remington's special versions of the Model 1100 and the Model 870 pump for slugs gave deer hunters more confidence in the old smoothbore as a big-game weapon. One reason for their greater accuracy is the special boring that makes the entire length of the barrel fit the slug, with none of the usual choke near the muzzle.

Few shotguns are bought for deer only. Its use during the deer season may be a minor part of its annual duties.

There are several styles of shotgun, all of which are used for deer hunting. They can be classified as single and double barrel. Double barrels come in two styles, the old side-by-side and the over-and-under. Among the single barrels are the autoloaders, pump guns, bolt actions, and break-open singles.

The autoloading shotgun utilizes gases from the explosion to eject the empty shell and slide a fresh one into the chamber, all with a single pull of the trigger. The autoloaders commonly offered on the market are made for three or five shells. Some states require plugging them to hold a maximum of three shells for deer hunting.

The pump gun, most popular of all scatterguns, ejects the empty shell when the shooter slides back a lever beneath the breech. The forward motion runs another shell into the chamber. An experienced shooter accomplishes this with lightning speed.

Bolt-action shotguns are less expensive than other repeating-type shotguns and somewhat slower to use. The old break-open single shot is the least complicated, one of the safest, and the least expensive. It's a good gun for a boy to start with.

If you're setting forth to purchase a new shotgun especially for deer hunting, choose a single barrel. You can sight more accurately with it than you can with a double barrel when using slugs. Double-barreled, side-by-side shotguns have a tendency to cross over in their shooting. The load from the right barrel tends to cross over to the left and the one from the left barrel wanders to the right. If you use a double barrel without some special sighting device, you shoot by guess and instinct. If your guess and instinct are good, you may score.

If you're going to use a shotgun for deer, the problem of gauge is important. Shotguns commonly come in 12, 16, 20, 28, and .410 gauge. You can get rifled-slug ammunition in any of these sizes. But not all are suitable deer guns. The only two that should really be used on deer are the 12- and 16-gauge. The 20-gauge is in the doubtful range as far as power and energy are concerned, and if you're headed for the deer woods the .410 is a peashooter and should be left at home. True, you can kill a deer with a .410. You can also kill one with a croquet mallet if you get in close enough and smack him in just the right spot often enough.

For comparative purposes take a look at the ballistics figures on various shotgun ammunitions. A 16-gauge, shooting 2¾-inch shells, throws a slug having more foot-pounds of energy at one hundred yards than a .410, shooting a 2½-inch shell, develops at the muzzle. The .410 develops only 650 foot-pounds of energy at the muzzle with its .20-ounce slugs. The 20-gauge, developing 1,550 foot-pounds of energy at the muzzle, does take a fair number of deer every year. But the slug's energy dissipates rapidly along its trajectory. Any shot over thirty-five yards is a long one for a 20-gauge with rifled slugs.

The 12-gauge, with a muzzle velocity of 1,600 feet per second, develops a walloping 2,485 foot-pounds of energy at the muzzle, and at seventy-five yards the slug still rips along with 1,040 foot-pounds of energy. The 16-gauge, only slightly under the 12-, has the same muzzle velocity, using slugs from shells of the same length, and it packs 2,175 foot-pounds of energy at the muzzle. The slug in a 16-gauge shell weighs only an eighth of an ounce less than the one-ounce slug from a 12-gauge.

Rifled slugs expand but little when they hit an animal, but from the larger-gauge guns they hit with a smashing impact that, properly placed, will bring down far bigger animals than deer.

Barrel length doesn't have a lot to do with how successfully your shotgun will perform for you in the deer woods. In these days of smokeless powder a shotgun packs about the same power whether its barrel is twenty-six, twenty-eight, or thirty inches long. The longer barrel develops somewhat less muzzle blast. The shorter barrel, logically enough, is easier to manipulate in heavy brush, where a lot of the shotgun deer hunting is done.

Don't worry about rifled slugs damaging the choke in your shotgun. Like a load of shot, slugs constrict as they pass through the narrower part of the barrel, whether the choke is built into the barrel or added in a choke device.

The gunstock should be comfortable to you. Your gun dealer can help you pick one that is. It should swing into place smoothly yet have a stock long enough to keep the recoil from bringing your thumb back against your nose.

What about gun weight? A light gun with heavy loads lets your shoulder absorb too much of the recoil. But because you won't shoot very often while deer hunting, recoil isn't highly important. You don't want a shotgun so heavy you can't carry it all day with ease. Strike a happy medium between weight and recoil.

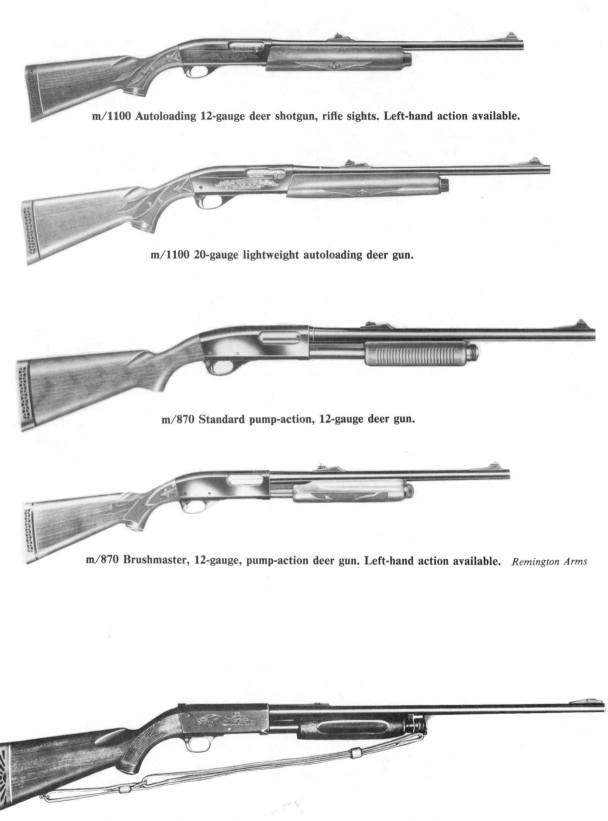

m/1100 Autoloading 12-gauge deer shotgun, rifle sights. Left-hand action available.

m/1100 20-gauge lightweight autoloading deer gun.

m/870 Standard pump-action, 12-gauge deer gun.

m/870 Brushmaster, 12-gauge, pump-action deer gun. Left-hand action available. *Remington Arms*

Ithaca Model 37 Super Deluxe Deerslayer shotgun. *Ithaca Gun Company, Inc.*

Shotgun Sights

Some kind of sighting aid is almost essential for deer hunting with a shotgun. Nothing that ordinarily comes on a shotgun is of much help with slugs. Without some type of receiver sight, you are mixing a lot of guesswork with your aiming. Shotguns vary from one gun to the next in their accuracy with slugs. A good set of sights helps you center the slugs and shoot a tighter group.

Open sights are not as good for the job as are peep sights. Flat or notched sights hide part of the target. The Williams Gun Sight Company of Davison, Michigan, makes an excellent low-priced peep sight for shotguns. Some shotgunners have even taped the guide from a fishing rod to the barrel of their shotgun to help them line up the target. This can be of some help, but a good commercially made sight is well worth the money. Such sights can be removed when you want to switch from deer hunting to bird shooting.

Deer Loads for Shotguns

The two kinds of ammunition used for deer hunting with shotguns are rifled slugs and buckshot. The buckshot, generally 00 or single 0, are traditional loads in parts of the South. These loads are at their best on close shots at fast-running deer in thick cover.

Hollow-point rifled slugs for shotguns ranging from 10-gauge, 3½-inch Magnum to .410. *Federal Cartridge*

Any load from a shotgun can kill a deer. Even bird shot has done it. But either double or single 0 buck carries only nine to fifteen pellets in a 2¾-inch, 12-gauge shell. Each of these pellets carries a muzzle energy of around two hundred foot-pounds. They spread into an ever-widening pattern once they leave the muzzle. Their sometimes imperfect shape, plus imperfections they gather if they hit obstructions such as brush, spread the pattern still more. The farther the deer from the muzzle, the fewer pellets are likely to hit him in vital spots. The hunter who strikes a deer a killing blow with a single buckshot pellet has been leading a clean life. A neck shot is your best bet.

The rifled slug is descended from the old solid-ball loads or "pumpkin balls." The minié balls of the Civil War days were of the same family. Later, in an effort to add the spin of a rifle-propelled bullet to the solid balls, munitions makers began working on shotgun loads. They came up with a rifled slug, a ball of soft lead, heavy in front and hollow in back, and carrying along its outer surfaces spiraled lands and grooves which are said to give it the spin that keeps it from tumbling. And it does spin. But, more than the lands and grooves, it's the shape of the slug that keeps it from tumbling. One manufacturer says, "The hollow base simply can't get ahead of the weighty nose until it's slowed down to walking speed." The effective range of shotgun slugs is generally considered to be seventy-five yards or less for deer.

Slugs vary in weight from one ounce for a 12-gauge to one-fifth ounce for a .410.

Practice Can Bring Venison

By all means take your shotgun out ahead of the deer season and get in some practice. Knowing what it will do on "birds" won't tell you where it throws a rifled slug. Practice shells are not costly when you figure that they may mean the difference between venison on the table and no venison on the table. Use the same loads throughout your practice and for hunting.

South Dakota game warden Cletus Kachel once said that hunters need more preseason shooting practice. He interviewed nine successful deer hunters who shot their deer with shotguns. The nine hunters blasted off 172 rounds to get their nine deer, for an average of nineteen shots per deer. One hunter shot forty-three slugs to get his deer.

Most experienced deer hunters will tell you that

you have about a twelve-inch circle into which to get a good killing shot on your deer if you aim at the vital "boiler room." When, by shooting without a rest, you can put a group in a pie-plate-sized target, you're ready for opening morning.

You need to sight-in your shotgun and practice shooting it enough to know how far it throws slugs to the right or left at various distances.

This subject of distances is highly important. The shotgun deer hunter needs to be a good judge of distance. Measure off twenty-five yards, fifty yards, seventy-five yards, and one hundred yards and familiarize yourself with those distances by shooting from each of them.

Know how far a rifled slug, or a load of buckshot of given size, will drop at any measured distance from the muzzle of your gun. At seventy-five yards a one-ounce slug from a 2¾-inch, 12-gauge shell falls off 5.3 inches below the point of aim. At one hundred yards it drops 10.4 inches. Practice will tell you where to hold to deliver a slug at the point of aim at various ranges.

Because different brands may act differently in your gun, do all your practice shooting with the kind of shells you will carry when actually hunting.

Bringing a deer down with a shotgun can call for as much skill as the same feat accomplished with a rifle. And one thing is certain: when you take the old scattergun out for venison next fall, you've joined a big fraternity.

TRAJECTORY DATA — BUCK SHOT

				Velocity in f.p.s. at							*Energy in ft-lb per pellet at*						
Gauge	Shell Length	Size	No. of Pellets	Muzzle	10 Yds.	20 Yds.	30 Yds.	40 Yds.	50 Yds.	60 Yds.	Muzzle	10 Yds.	20 Yds.	30 Yds.	40 Yds.	50 Yds.	60 Yds.
12	2¾	00	9	1325	1220	1135	1070	1015	970	930	210	180	155	135	125	110	105
12	2¾	00	12	1325	1220	1135	1070	1015	970	930	210	180	155	135	125	110	105
12	3	00	15	1250	1160	1085	1030	985	940	900	185	160	140	125	115	105	95
12	2¾	0	12	1300	1200	1120	1055	1005	960	915	185	160	135	120	110	100	90
12	2¾	1	16	1250	1135	1050	990	935	885	835	140	115	100	90	80	70	65
12	2¾	4	27	1325	1195	1095	1020	960	905	860	80	65	55	50	45	40	35
16	$2\frac{9}{16}$	1	12	1225	1115	1040	975	925	875	830	135	110	95	85	75	70	60
or	2¾																
20	2½	3	20	1200	1100	1025	970	915	870	825	75	65	55	50	45	40	35
or	2¾																

				Drop in Inches at							
Gauge	Shell Length	Size	No. of Pellets	10 Yds.	20 Yds.	30 Yds.	40 Yds.	50 Yds.	60 Yds.	Barrel Length In.	Choke
12	2¾	00	9	.1	.4	1.0	2.0	3.2	4.8	30	Full
12	2¾	00	12	.1	.4	1.0	2.0	3.2	4.8	30	Full
12	3	00	15	.1	.5	1.2	2.2	3.5	5.2	30	Full
12	2¾	0	12	.1	.5	1.1	2.0	3.3	4.9	30	Full
12	2¾	1	16	.2	.7	1.7	3.2	5.2	7.8	30	Full
12	2¾	4	27	.1	.5	1.1	2.1	3.4	5.1	30	Full
16	$2\frac{9}{16}$	1	12	.2	.7	1.8	3.3	5.4	8.0	28	Full
or	2¾										
20	2½	3	20	.1	.5	1.3	2.4	3.9	5.9	26	Full
or	2¾										

TRAJECTORY DATA — RIFLED SLUGS

Gauge	Shell Length	Slug Wt. Oz.	*Velocity in f.p.s. at* Muzzle	25 Yds.	50 Yds.	75 Yds.	100 Yds.	*Energy in ft-lb at* Muzzle	25 Yds.	50 Yds.	75 Yds.	100 Yds.
12	2¾	1	1600	1365	1175	1040	950	2485	1810	1350	1040	875
16	2⁹⁄₁₆	⅞	1600	1365	1175	1040	950	2175	1585	1175	920	765
or	2¾											
20	2½	⅝	1600	1365	1175	1040	950	1555	1130	840	655	550
or	2¾											

Gauge	Shell Length	Wt. Oz.	*Drop in Inches at* 25 Yds.	50 Yds.	75 Yds.	100 Yds.	*Midrange Trajectory in In. for a Range of* 25 Yds.	50 Yds.	75 Yds.	100 Yds.	Barrel Length In.	Choke
12	2¾	1	.5	2.1	5.3	10.4	.1	.6	1.5	3.1	30	Full
16	2⁹⁄₁₆	⅞	.5	2.1	5.3	10.4	.1	.6	1.5	3.1	28	Full
or	2¾											
20	2½	⅝	.5	2.1	5.3	10.4	.1	.6	1.5	3.1	26	Full
or	2¾											

SIX

HUNTING WITH MUZZLE-LOADERS

When pioneering gunmakers first began building their revolutionary breech-loading rifles in the 1800s, there must have been predictions that the muzzle-loaders were headed for museums and scrap heaps. The military found during the Civil War that breechloaders were more reliable than the front-end-loaded guns and, furthermore, that riflemen equipped with breechloaders could shoot far faster than they had with muzzle-loaders. All signs pointed toward the retirement of the muzzle-loading rifles.

But after a hundred years or so the muzzle-loader entered a remarkable revival beginning in the 1950s. Increasing numbers of outdoorsmen found that there was special appeal in handling and shooting the kinds of long guns once carried by the rugged independent mountain men and others who opened this country's wilderness.

The revival gained momentum rapidly until the muzzle-loader shooters had their own books, periodicals, and organization—The National Muzzle Loading Rifle Association. Today, many manufacturers supply the guns, kits, and other equipment needed for this growing fraternity of shooters.

Those who speculate on what lies behind this revival of black-powder guns manage to come up with various reasons. It has to be more than the fact that numerous states now allow special primitive-weapons seasons during which hunters carrying muzzle-loaders might take an extra deer. The muzzle-loader is a piece of American history. Besides, there is satisfaction in knowing that you are accomplished enough as an outdoorsman to take a deer with one of these old-time guns. Carrying a muzzle-

When the smoke clears, the shooter learns how well he aimed his muzzle-loader. The growing popularity of these antique firearms is rooted in tradition. *Jerry Pickrell*

Ohio rifleman, Virgil Longacre, reloads his muzzle-loader during a preseason practice session with friends.

loader, you have time for one shot and, if you do everything right, one is enough.

Most important of all may be the fact that the muzzle-loader links today's hunter with a breed of outdoorsman who lived as close to being absolutely free and independent as any people in historic times. Hold a muzzle-loader in your hands and you begin to recall the deeds and the way of life of the mountain man, the ultimate woodsman. Some historians believe the mountain men who pursued the beaver trapper's trade in the Rockies early in the 1800s were better outdoorsmen than the Indians whose land they invaded. Jedediah Smith, Jim Bridger, Thomas Fitzpatrick, Kit Carson, Joe Meek, and the rest of the free trappers could survive in the wilderness by their knowledge, wits, and handling of their muzzle-loading guns. To hunt deer with black powder today is to walk in the footprints of those old-timers and sample the outdoors as they knew it.

Whatever the reason, new recruits are joining the muzzle-loader clan every year. Once you understand your gun, there is no reason to look upon the muzzle-loader as a handicap. Many of those carrying muzzle-loaders shoot as accurately with them as they do with breech-loading guns. Effective shooting with muzzle-loaders, however, is limited to moderate range. A hundred yards is close to the maximum range that most seasoned muzzle-loader carriers would try for a deer. Half that distance is a far better shot to take. Besides, the shooter must remember that the trajectory is not very flat. A deer hunter's muzzle-loader shooting, for example, a .50-caliber ball, and sighted in at fifty yards might shoot four inches below the mark at one hundred yards, depending on the powder load, rifling, and type of projectile. Preseason practice will tell you what your gun can be expected to do at various ranges.

Some deer hunters carry flintlock rifles, but more carry rifles with cap- or percussion-type firing mechanisms.

The shooter with a percussion-type firing mechanism loads the gun through the muzzle then places a little copper cap on the nipple beneath the hammer while the hammer is at half cock. The cap contains a priming compound. Before shooting, the hammer is brought to full cock. When the trigger is pulled the hammer strikes the cap sending a spark through the flash hole in the nipple. This fire touches off the main charge.

The flintlock, which is an earlier design, strikes a spark using flint against steel. After the gun is loaded with powder and ball, a small amount of primer, a very finely granulated powder, is placed in the pan. The piece of flint is secured in a vise or cock. When the cock is pulled all the way back and the trigger is then pulled, sparks ignite the powder beneath the frizzen, or pan cover, and this sends sparks through a touchhole to the main charge.

There are all manner of black-powder rifles available today. Some come in kit form, others are factory built. Some are such faithful copies of antique rifles that they are difficult to tell from the originals, others are of modern design. One of the more popular designs is the Hawken, a heavy-duty, half-stock rifle first made by the Hawken brothers in St. Louis and carried on the Western frontier.

Which rifle you eventually choose for deer hunt-

Mark I Hawken

Left-hand Hawken

Country Boy rifle

Morse rifle
Navy Arms Company

ing, and perhaps use on other game or the shooting range, will probably depend on personal preference, your feeling about history, your studies of guns owned and shot by friends, and your reading. Some purists insist on carrying flintlocks, but the caplock has taken over much of the territory.

In the projectile you have a choice between the round lead ball or the conical bullet. Which you choose bears a relationship to the rifling inside the barrel. The two common riflings are the slow twist, which is one twist per sixty-six inches, and the fast twist, which commonly means one twist in forty-eight inches. The slow twist is better for round projectiles, but one in forty-eight is considered a fair compromise for both ball and bullet.

Deer hunters widely believe that .50-caliber is the best choice for black-powder shooting.

Hunters who carry muzzle-loaders use one of two kinds of powder, either black powder or Pyrodex. Black powder intended specifically for muzzle-loaders comes in clearly labeled containers. If in doubt about the suitability of a powder for your gun, don't use it. Pyrodex is a modern product compounded to have similar characteristics to black powder but safer to use. It works satisfactorily in caplocks.

You will see black powder labeled Fg, FFg, FFFg and FFFFg. Think of the g as standing for granulation or fineness of the powder, and the more F's there are in front of the g, the finer the powder. The very finest powders are used as primers in shooting flintlocks. The medium granulations are the ones most commonly selected for charging the rifle. Special care is always in order when handling or storing powder.

The muzzle-loader is loaded by pouring a weighed or measured portion of black powder or Pyrodex down the barrel. The best plan is to carry premeasured charges of powder in small containers available commercially. Next the ball is forced down the barrel to rest against the powder. A patch of cloth is normally wrapped around the ball to give it a tight fit and prevent loss of gasses around it. Standard patches are available commercially. The lead is started down the barrel with a short starter which has a ball on one end, making it easy to apply pressure. Then the ramrod completes the loading as the patch and ball or bullet are forced firmly down on the powder.

Finally, the cap is put in place after crimping the open end of the brass cup slightly to make it stay in position over the nipple or, in the case of the flintlock, the primer is placed in the pan. Be sure that the nipple is open. You can check this either by running a thin wire through it or firing a cap or two through it before loading the gun.

Much of the fun of working with muzzle-loaders comes from practice firing on the range. This is also essential if you want to assure yourself a fair chance of collecting a deer during the season. Practice will tell you what to expect of your gun and your level of skill at various distances.

Black-powder guns require special care and cleaning after shooting and one reason is that potassium nitrate, or saltpeter, which is a major ingredient of black powder, is corrosive. It is hygroscopic which means that it attracts moisture. If you fire the gun even once, the film of residue must be cleaned out or the inside of the barrel may be damaged.

There are numerous recently developed black-powder solvents and moisture-fighting lubricants to help the shooter protect his muzzle-loader.

This "possibles" box built by Virgil Longacre keeps lead, patches, and other essentials easily available during practice.

Deer hunter equipped with muzzle-loader, and wearing orange cap for safety, knows from extensive practice exactly where the lead ball should go when he gets a shot at an approaching whitetail.

HOW TO SHOOT A MUZZLE LOADER

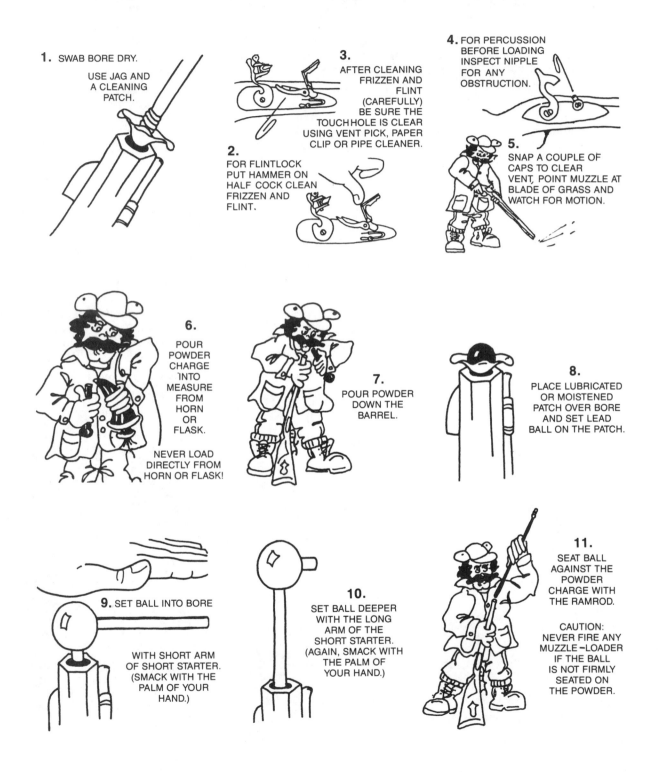

1. SWAB BORE DRY.

USE JAG AND A CLEANING PATCH.

3. AFTER CLEANING FRIZZEN AND FLINT (CAREFULLY) BE SURE THE TOUCH HOLE IS CLEAR USING VENT PICK, PAPER CLIP OR PIPE CLEANER.

4. FOR PERCUSSION BEFORE LOADING INSPECT NIPPLE FOR ANY OBSTRUCTION.

2. FOR FLINTLOCK PUT HAMMER ON HALF COCK CLEAN FRIZZEN AND FLINT.

5. SNAP A COUPLE OF CAPS TO CLEAR VENT, POINT MUZZLE AT BLADE OF GRASS AND WATCH FOR MOTION.

6. POUR POWDER CHARGE INTO MEASURE FROM HORN OR FLASK.

NEVER LOAD DIRECTLY FROM HORN OR FLASK!

7. POUR POWDER DOWN THE BARREL.

8. PLACE LUBRICATED OR MOISTENED PATCH OVER BORE AND SET LEAD BALL ON THE PATCH.

9. SET BALL INTO BORE

WITH SHORT ARM OF SHORT STARTER. (SMACK WITH THE PALM OF YOUR HAND.)

10. SET BALL DEEPER WITH THE LONG ARM OF THE SHORT STARTER. (AGAIN, SMACK WITH THE PALM OF YOUR HAND.)

11. SEAT BALL AGAINST THE POWDER CHARGE WITH THE RAMROD.

CAUTION: NEVER FIRE ANY MUZZLE–LOADER IF THE BALL IS NOT FIRMLY SEATED ON THE POWDER.

12. MARK YOUR RAMROD WHEN BALL IS IN PLACE.

13. **REMOVE** RAMROD AND STORE UNDER THE BARREL.

14. FOR FLINTLOCK, PRIME PAN ¼ to ⅓ FULL.

15. CLOSE FIZZEN AND BRING HAMMER TO FULL COCK

16. FOR PERCUSSION PLACE CAP FIRMLY ON NIPPLE AND BRING HAMMER TO FULL COCK

17. BE CERTAIN OF YOUR TARGET AND WHAT IS BEHIND IT! AIM AND FIRE.

18. RUN A DAMP SWAB DOWN THE BARREL AND START ALL OVER!

National Muzzle Loading Rifle Association

The standard procedure with removable barrels, however, is to cleanse the inside of the barrel thoroughly with hot, soapy water. Removable barrels make this fairly simple. The solution can be drawn up into the barrel by holding the end of the barrel in a pail and forcing a cleaning patch attached to the ramrod jag up and down from the muzzle end. After washing the barrel, rinse it with clear hot water, then finally treat the inside of the barrel with a thin coating of oil made especially for this use.

Take special precautions to protect the stock when cleaning the muzzle-loader, especially if the barrel cannot be removed.

If you buy a new muzzle-loader, it should be thoroughly cleaned to remove excess oil and lubricant before it is loaded and shot.

The following companies are a few of those making and selling kits, assembled guns, and other equipment for the hunter who chooses to take up a muzzle-loader.

Hearing protection is an excellent idea for those who do extensive shooting in preparation for the deer season. Preseason practice familiarizes the shooter with his gun and its capabilities.

Browning
Rt. 1
Morgan, Ut. 84050

Connecticut Valley Arms
Saybrook Road
Haddam, Conn. 06438

Dixie Gun Works
Gunpowder Lane
Union City, Tenn. 38261

Lyman Products Corp.
Rt. 147
Middlefield, Conn. 06455

Navy Arms Co.
689 Bergen Blvd.
Ridgefield, N.J. 07657

The address for The National Muzzle Loading Rifle Association, and its monthly periodical *Muzzle Blasts,* is P.O. Box 67, Friendship, Ind. 47021.

As with any gun, be especially careful to observe all safety precautions. Handle and store powder carefully. Talk with experienced shooters. You will learn that they take pride in understanding their equipment and materials, and learning the skills required for success with the muzzle-loader.

Using stapler, targets are quickly replaced. Gun rack mounted on tractor makes it easy to reach backcountry shooting range in all weather.

Friends with space enough can easily build an inexpensive shooting range for muzzle-loader practice. The spotting scope gives each shooter an instant reading on his score.

SEVEN

HUNTING WITH BOW AND ARROW

On the way back to our northern Michigan hunting camp from an unsuccessful morning hunt, Frank chose the path that would take us past a sagging, old abandoned lodge that he had not seen for a long time. He was less interested in the old building than he was in scouting for fresh deer sign.

We walked around the weather-beaten structure and came out thirty yards away on the edge of a rarely used lane lined with a few old apple trees. What interested us at once was the fact that the falling apples were not being left to rot on the ground. They had been cleaned up almost as fast as they dropped. And the abundance of fresh deer tracks beneath the trees left little doubt about the identity of the apple lovers.

For several days we had tried every way we could devise to get close enough to a deer for a telling shot. Our party had staged drives, stalked, and spent long hours on stands. There were plenty of deer in that section of Schoolcraft County in the Upper Peninsula. We had seen them frequently. Gun hunting, we would long since have had a deer hanging, but our trouble had been getting close enough for telling shots with bow and arrow. The few arrows we had released had failed to find their way through the thick brush.

Finding the apple trees was one of the more promising developments in the week-long bow hunt. At the right time of day, we agreed, this abandoned orchard should be an excellent place to get a shot.

The right time of day, in this case, would be just ahead of dark when the deer first came out to start

Does as well as bucks are legal game in many bow-hunting seasons, and the archer has only to wait until the cautious deer moves into a position allowing a clear shot.

Skilled bow hunter, completely camouflaged and knowledgeable about habits of the whitetail, has an excellent chance of collecting trophy antlers as well as a supply of venison. *Ottie M. Snyder, Jr.*

feeding. Apples are a delicacy to deer and the first place they would probably head for when they got out of bed would be these apple trees.

It was almost dark when the deer came, a doe and two half-grown fawns. They had slipped from the woods on Frank's side of the abandoned building and spent twenty minutes working slowly toward the apple trees. Just as they should have come in range for Frank, they made a little detour up around the hill and never came closer than seventy yards from his stand.

They were, however, working steadily closer to me and, although Frank could no longer see them, he did not move. I waited until the unsuspecting doe lowered her head to pick up an apple, picked a spot, and released an arrow from the fifty-five-pound recurved bow I carried in those precompound-bow days. I can still see the white shaft of that arrow on its way, and it still seems to me that it pierced her neck. She vaulted forward and all three deer were out of sight in seconds.

We searched the ground beneath the tree carefully. I found the arrow but there was not a hint of blood on point, shaft, or fletching. Perhaps the arrow had grazed her as she lifted her head because Frank was sure her tail was down as she dashed into the woods. A thorough search for a blood trail revealed no signs and we finally concluded that the shot was a clean miss.

But even a near miss is a memorable event for the hunter who carries a bow. The success of the hunt may be measured in the number of good shots the archer has because the odds favor the deer. Whether you fill your tag or not, the hunt is rich in promise and excitement because in no other kind of deer hunting is the taking of game a bigger accomplishment than it is for the bow hunter. The hunter who carries bow and arrows may accumulate many stories such as my apple-orchard episode before he brings home that first venison. One of the good reasons for hunting deer with the more primitive weapon is that bow hunting calls out the woodsman in you.

Many bow hunters also hunt with rifle or shot-gun in season. In the bow, they have simply found a way to extend their deer-hunting season by taking advantage of the additional seasons for bow hunting in many states.

Many bow hunters are former gun hunters who have taken so many deer in earlier years that they turn to the bow and arrow for the added challenge. Some years ago, while on a hunt for whitetails and fallow deer in Kentucky's Land Between The Lakes, I was talking about this with Douglas McKellar of Nashville. "Gun hunting lost its kick for me," he said. "I began to feel that, with a gun, I was taking advantage of the game, so I turned to the bow and arrow." A few archers go a step further and limit themselves to homemade equipment and even use flint arrow points of their own making. This is a step further than I need to go to give the deer an even break.

There are some other reasons behind the remarkable growth of bow hunting in recent times. As hunting pressures increase, the use of the bow stretches hunting opportunities. Besides, archery is an inexpensive year-round form of target practice. You may even have room in the backyard to set up a practice range where the entire family can participate.

Hunters who stick to guns sometimes complain that early bow seasons spook the deer for the gun hunters, but this is not what my experience tells me. In bow season I have seen the same deer moved around their territories every day, and sometimes several times a day, without being run out of the area. In spite of the human movement through

From his stand along the edge of a woodlot, the bow hunter may have a variety of shots early and late in the day when deer are moving.

their home country, they are probably still going to be there, scarcely disturbed, at the end of the bow season.

Besides, the bow season can give the hunter who also hunts with a gun the opportunity to learn about the movements of deer before he goes forth on the opening morning of gun season. If he fails to bag his deer with the bow, he at least knows where to look for them. Gunfire, however, can cause the deer to shift around and perhaps move some distance into a different kind of cover. A small-game season, falling between gun and bow seasons, can also disturb the deer's daily routine. Severe weather changes can also make them move.

There is another plus for archery—the fundamentals are easy to learn.

The story of the long bow reaches so far back into man's history that there is no way of telling just how old this weapon is. For hundreds of thousands of years early people fought a touch and go battle to survive. Then, some ancient tied the ends of a bent stick together with a piece of vine and found that the device helped propel his spear faster. The longbow had come into the world, and this early invention helped our ancestors make the grade. This was the first instrument invented to use stored energy. The earlier spear, or even the throw-

ing stick or atlatl, had utilized only the energy transferred directly to it from the human arm. Creation of the bow stored energy and added speed to the cast of the spear, which was the ancestor of the arrow. Among primitive people, the bow and arrow came into use on every continent except Australia.

In addition to giving early people an edge over the nontool-using creatures around them, the bow became an instrument of warfare and great armies ruled the known world with arrows. In the famous battle of Agincourt in 1415 some eight to nine thousand English and French soldiers fell to arrows over a two-day period. But with the development of gunpowder the arrow was no longer the latest thing in weapons. Progress.

Archery continued to slide toward oblivion until it appeared that this age-old weapon that had served man so well was relegated to the past forever.

Then two brothers, Maurice and Will Thompson, breathed new life into archery as a sport. Maurice was born in 1844, in a little town in eastern Indiana where his father, Matt, preached the gospel in the Baptist church. After returning from the Civil War the Thompsons soon became widely known for their uncanny marksmanship with home-fashioned arrows cast from homemade bows.

Fred Bear (light shirt) bagged this fine fallow buck with bow and arrow in Land Between The Lakes, in Western Kentucky. *Bear Archery*

But Maurice Thompson was more interested in hunting with the bow than he was in the genteel sport of lawn shooting. Hunting drew him to the woods and fields. His practice was at short distances, because he knew what archers still know, that most game taken with bow and arrow is shot at reasonable distances. Thompson could, and did, hit woodpeckers on the wing, which is illegal today. He hit a lead pencil at ten yards five times in succession. On another day, his arrows broke thirty-seven out of fifty small glass balls tossed into the air at distances of twelve yards.

But it was not until Thompson began writing articles about the pleasures of taking game with the long bow that people paid much attention to him. Times were right for a new sport, and within a few years archery clubs sprang up around the country. While Will earned his place as a five-time national champion, Maurice continued to write about the fun of shooting the bow and arrow, and there is no doubt that his teachings played a major role in the revival of archery as a shooting sport. Archery clubs continued to flourish after Maurice Thompson died in 1901.

But credit for the present-day popularity of archery as a hunting sport goes to Dr. Saxton Pope and his hunting companion Art Young. Dr. Pope wrote his book *Hunting with Bow and Arrow* in 1923, and the sport has been growing ever since. By the mid-thirties, bow hunters were beginning to invade the deer woods in numbers, and in 1934, Wisconsin established the first bow-and-arrow season for deer, to see if the idea held appeal. A year later

Oregon followed, then Pennsylvania, and in 1937, Michigan's first archery deer season attracted 186 hunters. Michigan bowmen killed four deer that year. Now the number of archery licenses sold by Michigan each year, as well as the deer taken there with arrows, number in the thousands.

The Bow Hunter's Outfit

The archer needs a fairly simple list of equipment. His or her bow and arrows, quiver, arm guard, glove, and some kind of target at which to shoot are enough for a start.

The bows carried by modern hunters are the best the world has ever seen. Modern materials and remarkable new designs have moved the ancient weapon away from its prehistoric form and into the world of advanced technology.

For thousands of years bows were made of wood and some still are, at least in part. The most popular hunting bows today are either solid fiberglass or bows made of fiberglass and wood laminate. Fiberglass, in addition to its strength, develops less fatigue than other materials that have been tried.

Laminated bows are not really new. Ancient Turkish warriors, who were among the finest archers the world ever saw, made laminated bows. They backed their bows with sinews of animal tendons and faced them with the horn of water buffalo.

The longbow consists of logically named parts. It has two limbs and, because of the handle, the lower

Before settling on a new recurved bow for hunting, you may want to check out those designed to break down for easy carrying during travel. If you are fortunate enough to find a dealer who maintains a shooting range, you may be able to try different bows before settling on your choice. Friends may also permit you to shoot their bows, and there is no shortage of advice from competent archers if you locate a local bow-hunters group.

The Compound

As the archery industry began to flourish following World War II, most of its leaders believed that the bow had reached the ultimate design and never again would anyone create a new and better bow. For thousands of years there had really been very little that was radically new in the design of the bow and arrow. Then came the compound bow, an entirely new design. The inventor of this bow reasoned that by attaching a system of wheels, or pulleys, to the limbs of the bow, he could increase the energy it stored—therefore the cast of the arrow—without increasing the strength needed to draw the instrument. He built the first such bow in 1942.

The problem he soon met was that the old wooden bows would not stand up under the added pressure. But the idea for the compound bow was born. Most people first learned of this in 1967 when noted archer, manufacturer, and writer Tom Jennings described the new bow in *TAM,* the archery magazine. A patent for this bow was issued to H. W. Allen, of Kansas City, Missouri, in 1969.

In due time, compound bows were on the market, and once available they swept the country. Instead of four eccentric wheels, the compound bow was largely standardized as a two-wheeler with one wheel on the end of each limb. The two-wheelers shot more consistently than bows with four wheels, and also did not require the constant "tuning" that the four-wheel models demanded.

The big advantage of the compound bow is that,

limb is shorter than the upper limb, and the whole piece is balanced so it will pull in an even arc.

As you hold the bow in shooting position, the side away from you is the back, and the side facing you is the face or belly. On the end of each limb is a groove to hold the bowstring and these are known as nocks.

The Turks of old came up with a variation on the simple bow by recurving the end of each limb, and the recurved design replaced the original straight bow. Many archers still shoot the recurved bow. The recurved design provides greater leverage, and this enabled the bow to send an arrow faster than the old straight bow could. The archer's word for arrow speed is "cast." The bow stores energy when drawn, and its return to its original position when released casts the arrow. How fast the bow returns determines the arrow's velocity. The recurved bow, for all its rugged strength and force, may not shoot as accurately as the straight bow did.

For the hunter, one advantage of the recurved bow is its shorter length. Deer hunters, pursuing game through brush and timber, have always searched for a way to shorten the bow while retaining smooth shooting ability and good cast. The recurved bow offered an advance in this direction.

These rugged bows come in a wide variety of shapes, lengths, handle designs, and draw weights.

during the draw, it has a "let-off" point beyond which the archer can complete the draw then hold the arrow on target using only a fraction of the full draw strength for which the bow is rated. The percentage of let-off varies with the bow but is often in the vicinity of one third of the peak draw weight.

An outgrowth of popularity of the compound was the eventual commercial rise of the popular "cam" bow, in which the wheels are replaced by elliptically shaped cams. Although there is a widespread belief among archers that the cam was a later development, the original patent granted on the revolutionary bow shows not a wheel, but an elliptical cam. Early manufacturers found the eccentric wheel easier to produce than the cam, and the wheel provided ample stored energy anyhow. Years would pass before the pressures of commercial competition would send bow makers back to the drawing boards for another look at the cam. The result is the modern cam bow. The archer has to pull harder to draw the cam bow than the two-wheel compound but the cam bow performs better, giving the arrow greater cast, therefore a flatter trajectory, than even an equivalent two-wheeled compound bow.

The strength of the bow is known as the pull and is measured in pounds. The pull of a straight or recurved bow is the number of pounds needed to bring a twenty-eight-inch arrow to full draw. If you use a compound bow, draw weight is the peak weight the shooter must draw bringing the bow to the let-off point.

The biggest mistake made by many beginners is to purchase a bow that is too heavy for them. Avoid choosing a bow heavier than you can handle comfortably. The average deer hunter's bow requires a pull of fifty to fifty-five pounds. Some states place minimum legal limits on the bow strength needed for hunting deer—usually around forty-five pounds.

Sometimes you are better off starting with a lighter bow, practicing with it, and learning to shoot until your muscles are conditioned and you have gained strength and confidence. Then, well ahead of opening day, begin using the heavier bow you will carry into the woods.

Ahead of opening morning, the bow hunter should practice with arrows that match broadheads in weight, and shoot from a wide variety of positions. *Jerry Pickrell*

This compound bow by Bear Archery permits owner to set draw weight at 50, 55, or 60 pounds to match his strength.

In recent times, bow-sighting devices have appeared on the market in growing numbers. Many bow hunters go afield without them, relying strictly on instinctive shooting. But the modern sighting device can probably improve your chances of hitting what you aim at, once you have it adjusted and have gained proficiency in judging unmeasured distances to targets.

The bowstring also deserves careful attention. In addition to the one on your bow, carry a spare when you go into the woods. Be sure the extra is the same length and strength as the one on your bow. Your dealer should be able to help you select a bowstring if you need help over and above the details printed on your bow. It is good planning to use the new bowstring a few times before setting off on your hunting trip so it is conditioned and you have confidence in the fit.

There is a specific spot on the string where the arrow should be fitted or "nocked" if it is to rest at an angle of exactly ninety degrees to the string. You should mark this "nocking point" in a way that enables you to avoid fumbling and looking at the string when you should be concentrating on an approaching deer. This will help give you consistency in shooting. My preference has always been to mark the nocking point by wrapping the bowstring with enough turns of fine thread to catch the nock of the arrow. A spot of shellac will keep the thread in place. Equally good are a number of commercially offered nocking points.

In addition, equip yourself with a bowstringer which, not only simplifies stringing the bow, but also helps protect the bow from damage during the operation.

Finally, outfit the string with a pair of silencers, one near each end, to quiet the string as you shoot and help keep from alerting the deer. A deer that hears the string returning to its normal position may have time to "jump the string." There are several commercially made silencers that are popular and your dealer can probably offer you a choice.

The Arrow

Even more important than your bow are the arrows you shoot. Some years ago I met a Kentucky bow hunter eighty years old who was carrying a bow he had made from Osage orange wood grown on his home place and cured in the kitchen. The pull, he said, was sixty pounds. His aim was still good and his marksmanship admirable in spite of the unfinished-looking home-whittled bow. His secret was to purchase good factory-made arrows matched to his bow weight.

You might think that because the arrow rests on the left side of the bow as you shoot, it should fly off toward the left. But that is not the case. The force of the bow buckles the arrow to the right around the bow. The arrow must recover to fly in a straight direction. The quality of the arrow responsible for this correcting factor is known as spine.

The arrow with too much spine for its bow will correct itself back to the left too far and hit to the left of the mark. If it has insufficient spine it will not come back far enough and this will make it hit to the right of the mark. If you consistently shoot to the right or left of your mark you can be fairly certain your arrows are not matched to your bow.

Hunting arrows are made of wood, fiberglass, or aluminum. Most of them are aluminum.

One of the most important points to consider in buying or making arrows is to get them the right length. The average adult male will require a twenty-eight-inch arrow, but the length may vary from twenty-six to thirty inches, depending on your arm length. If you choose too short an arrow you may draw it past the bow and endanger your bow hand.

Here is how to measure the exact length of the arrow you should use. Lay your outstretched arm along a yardstick. Right-handed shooters should measure on the right arm, left-handed on the left. Lift your arm until it points straight out from your shoulder and is level with the floor. Mark the spot where the second joint of your index finger comes on the yardstick. This gives you the arrow length if you draw the string back to a spot beneath your chin. If, as many archers do, you prefer an anchor point farther back beside your cheek, add two inches to this measured length.

Another method for measuring correct arrow length is to hold your hands palm to palm with arms outstretched in front of you. The arrow should reach from the base of your neck to the tips of your fingers.

One quality you need if you're to score in the field is consistency. If you're using the same equipment in the same manner each time, the arrows should go reasonably close to the same point. If

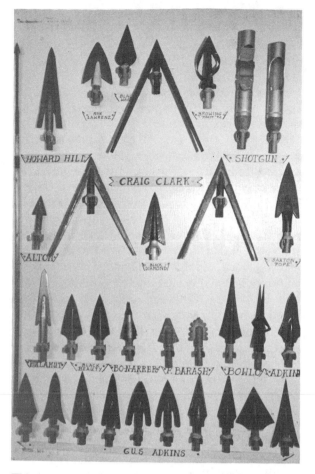

This is a small part of the collection of hundreds of historic broadheads owned by Floyd Eccleston, a Michigan hunter and collector. Broadhead collectors have their own association.

rows. Each has its advocate and almost any of them is capable of making a kill for the archer who sends it to the right place at the right moment. Perhaps the most widely used steel broadhead has three rigid blades. I also like the one Fred Bear invented some years ago which utilizes a razor blade steel insert to create a broadhead with four cutting edges. Broadheads with a center post and blade inserts are very effective and thus highly popular with hunters.

The projectile from a gun kills largely by shock. The broadhead arrow, on the other hand, cuts blood vessels and kills by hemorrhage.

Some modern arrows are made to accept different points so the archer can switch from field points for practice, blunts for small game, or broadheads such as this one with replaceable blades for big game.

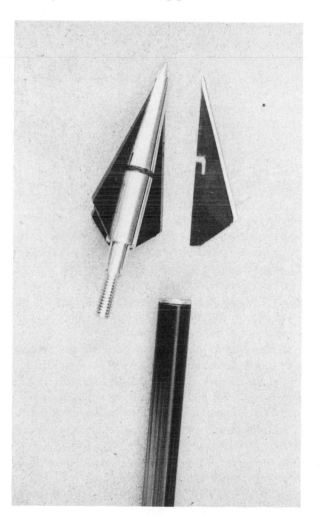

they don't, your arrows may not be matched. When you begin to practice for a deer hunt buy matched arrows. This means arrows matched for weight, spine, and straightness so that you can come to predict accurately the course of the properly released arrow.

Some archers like arrows painted in dull colors on the theory that they're less noticeable to deer. I have never been able to associate the spooking of a deer with the color of the arrow.

One way, incidentally, that you can often find a practice arrow lost beneath the grass of the yard is to walk over the area in your sock feet. You can often feel the arrow and stop, thus avoiding snapping the shaft. One should obviously not try this with a lost broadhead and risk cutting one's feet.

There are several suitable styles of broadhead ar-

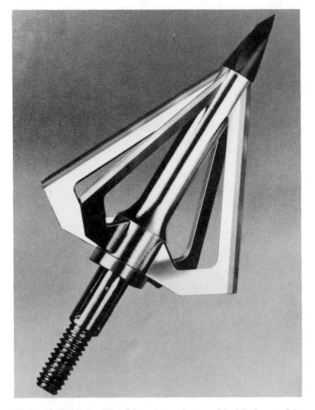

**This quality broadhead has interchangeable blades and is
critically machined for perfect balance.** *Anderson Designs,
Inc.*

The Indians knew that a sharp broadhead was
important, so they traveled long distances to collect
flint which they could chip into sharp edges with a
section of deer antler. The flint points had ragged
edges, which added to the cutting surface. Some
modern bow hunters even file notches into the cutting edges of their steel broadheads.

Arrows tipped with broadheads are too dangerous to use for backyard practice. For practice, use
field points. They are available in weights to match
the broadheads. Sometime ahead of deer season,
use a few of your matched broadheads for practice.
Try them in a bale of straw, from which you can
extract them easily. Make it a habit to shoot every
hunting arrow at least once before packing it for a
hunting trip, to see that it flies properly. Then inspect each one and, where necessary, touch up the
points with a file.

Field archers are always beset with the problem
of how best to carry extra arrows. The standard
quiver is a deep leather pouch carried across the
back with a shoulder strap. It keeps the tops of the
arrows where you can reach them across your
shoulder as you need them.

Such a quiver will serve all right for field practice
and target shooting, but when you're trying to stalk
a deer through close-growing brush the quiver becomes a genuine threat to the success of your efforts. It catches on every limb it comes close to. For
this reason many bow hunters fit their bows with
bow quivers. These are brackets which carry extra
arrows alongside the bow. The bow quiver is excellent equipment for the deer hunter, but, as with all
your hunting equipment, you have to get used to it
well ahead of your hunting trip. Attach it early and
practice shooting with it on the bow.

Some hunters prefer hip quivers. The advantages
are that they are lightweight and arrows are protected and easily available. The disadvantage is that
arrows carried in a hip quiver can get caught on
heavy brush.

Whatever quiver you choose, remember that it
has multiple jobs to do. It should protect both the
arrow and the archer from injury. If possible, it
should keep broadheads separated and not allow
arrows to rattle together, making noise that could
alert the deer you are stalking. It is important that
arrows be easily available with minimum movement.

Before you go into the field to hunt, remove from
your quiver all arrows except those you have carefully chosen as suitable for deer. Few things can be
more frustrating than hitting a big buck in the side
with a blunt-tipped arrow intended for squirrels.

You need two other pieces of equipment, a finger
glove and protective sleeve. The leather sleeve fas-
tens around your bow arm with elastic bands to
protect your forearm from the bowstring and to
keep loose clothing from catching on the bowstring.
With a tight-sleeved hunting jacket you may not
need a sleeve. The shooting glove is either a tab or a
finger glove to protect the three fingers with which
you draw the bowstring.

If your backyard provides space for an archery
practice range, a couple of straw bales will provide
ample backstop for your targets. Sporting-goods
stores carry animal targets which you can pin to the
straw with spikes or short pieces of wire cut from
clothes hangers.

Archer files notches in broadhead to increase cutting surfaces for deer hunting. The bow hunter's equipment should include a small file.

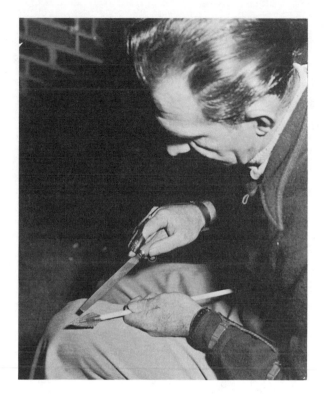

Don't worry about taking long practice shots. Start out practicing at twenty yards and later at thirty yards. The chances are that your shots at deer will be at similar distances.

As you gain proficiency in shooting, you will want to get in some special practice to sharpen your aim for the coming deer season. There are a lot of tricks you can try that will accomplish this and also prove to be fun. If there is a nearby archery club, a field range might be available to you in which animal targets are set up at varying distances through a variety of cover. Ranges such as this are usually shot by a few archers together who keep score and check their scores against each other or against their previous score on the same range.

There are other preseason practice ideas that can help too. A deer will seldom give you a clean shot free of underbrush and other obstructions. Every shot will carry its own set of obstacles. Consequently it's good to practice under as wide a variety of conditions as possible. Practice shooting at targets through a woven wire fence. Or practice on a cardboard target rolled downhill in an old automobile tire for experience in shooting at moving animals.

Shooting the Bow

My friend the late Jim Blackburn, who in addition to being a champion target archer, had at least fourteen deer to his credit, always said, "A lot of people can shoot better than they think they can once they learn to do the same thing the same way every time."

Jim knew what he was talking about. As manager of a large archery center for the city of Cincinnati, he taught hundreds of people the basics of handling the bow and arrow. Some of his students went on to become champion shooters.

If you've never shot a bow, begin by first learning the proper shooting form. Accuracy will come later.

If you're right-handed, you will hold the bow with your left hand and pull the bowstring with your right. Stand with your left side toward the target and your feet pointed ninety degrees away from the target.

Your feet should be a foot or so apart so that your weight is comfortably distributed on both of them.

Your head is turned sideways now so that you are looking along your left arm at the target.

Lay an arrow on the arrow rest on the left side of the bow above your hand. The odd-colored feather should point away from the bow. Some bows provide an offset shelf to hold the arrow.

Place the bowstring on the notch in the end of the arrow; this is known as nocking the arrow. Pull the string with the first three fingers of your right hand, the arrow lying between the forefinger and middle finger.

Next, with your left arm fully extended, draw the string back until the knuckles touch the corner of your mouth. The point to which you draw your hand is known as your anchor point. It's important to draw to the same anchor point every time.

The bow is pulling now against the base of your hand. Do not hold the bow tightly: tenseness can throw your aim off.

This picture illustrates good shooting techniques. Instructor Jim Blackburn taught the rudiments of archery to hundreds of people, including some who went on to become champions. Weight should be distributed comfortably on both feet, left side toward target, left arm straight out when drawing bow, right arm held high—about parallel to ground—arrow on rest above hand, nock held lightly between first and second fingers, arrow brought to full draw at anchor point at corner of mouth. Shooter aims over point of arrow, holds, releases arrow by relaxing fingers, and follows through by holding fingers at anchor point until arrow strikes target.

The manner in which you release the arrow is highly important. Relax the three fingers and let the string slip off their ends without moving your thumb from your anchor point. Once the arrow is

away, hold this position until the arrow strikes. This follow-through will prevent you from moving your hand forward before you release the arrow.

If you're left-handed, reverse the procedure.

These are the essentials you need to know about shooting. Practicing them can help you develop shooting skill faster than you expected. The *best* way to learn to shoot a bow, however, is from an instructor. He can save you time and help prevent the development of incorrect habits.

It's better to practice shooting at a small mark than at a big target. Mark a spot the size of a milk bottle cap on your animal target and shoot at that. It's not enough to hit a deer; you have to hit him reasonably close to the spot you choose.

Instead of shooting at a paper plate at thirty yards, mark a small black circle in its center and shoot at that. Or stand a matchbook on a stick in the ground and shoot at close range. You'll hit these small targets surprisingly well after a little practice. Begin by practicing at ten and fifteen yards on the small targets, then move back and shoot from a wide variety of distances.

Preparing for the Hunt

The challenge to the bow hunter, far more than to the gun hunter, is to fit himself into the landscape. The deer knows the trails and the trees and the skylines, and if any of it looks strange to him he is immediately suspicious. His sense of smell and his sharp ears aid him in his constant efforts to size up the landscape around him. He is nervous by nature, and once his suspicions are aroused he usually won't wait around to double-check. Your task is to get close enough to him for a shot before he gets suspicious.

The clothing you wear can be important to a bow-hunting expedition. Most bow hunters wear camouflage suits that make them melt into the background. They often go a step further and paint their faces and cover their bows with camouflage tape.

Footgear is even more important here than it is for the gun carrier. Foot comfort is important at any time, but the bow hunter in the deer woods will often rank silent walking ahead of foot comfort. In many places the bow season comes ahead of the bitter winter weather. If the ground is dry enough to make them practical, moccasins or tennis shoes are good. Wearing true moccasins, not those with sewed-on composition soles, you can often feel a stick beneath your foot in time to avoid breaking it and alerting every deer for a quarter mile around you. But such moccasins are for toughened feet. For wet country in moderate temperatures it's hard to beat combination rubber and leather boots such as those sold by L. L. Bean, Freeport, Maine.

Some clothing is noisy in the brush. It is almost impossible to work your way through thickly growing cover quietly if you're dressed in clothes with a hard surface. One of my primary objections to most of the camouflage clothing on the market is that it scratches noisily in the brush. If you're going to hunt on stand, stage drives, or stalk your deer in fairly open woodlands, these work well. But if you're planning to slip up on your deer in thickly growing cover, I'd suggest going into the clothes closet for an old outfit. Depending on the weather, a good outfit may be a pair of woolen trousers, a sweater, tennis shoes, and an old felt hat. Some bow hunters prefer a tight-fitting woolen knit cap. But the felt hat is far better protection if it rains or snows. And you may, of course, need rain gear.

How Bow Hunters Get Deer

Hundreds of bow hunters would agree with Bob McDuffy that the most productive plan for bagging a deer is to seek out a first-rate stand and stay there until a deer comes within reach of your arrows. And probably a few have made mistakes as basic as the one Bob made in his early days of hunting deer with the longbow.

"I came upon this beautiful glade in the woods," says Bob. "The sun was filtering down through the leaves and I could see all along this slope ahead of me. There was deer sign there, too."

The next morning, when the season opened, Bob was on hand early. He installed himself in the hollow stump of a big tree that offered nearly perfect concealment. "I stuck some arrows beside me," he says. "It was a fine place to wait."

A half hour later Bob saw a fine buck come picking his way into the setting. For fifteen minutes the buck worked toward Bob's blind, unaware that he was observed. The buck stopped occasionally and lifted his head to sniff the air and look around, and

each time he did this he seemed satisfied and moved steadily closer to where Bob waited.

When the buck was thirty yards away, Bob, his hands slightly shaky by now, nocked an arrow and began to draw his bow. That was when he realized that he had overlooked one important fact in his choice of a blind. "My stump was too small for me to get more than about a twelve-inch draw on the bow," he admits. "But I managed to stand up and get off two shots at that buck before he got excited and left." Bob was so disconcerted by this time that his arrows never touched the buck.

The time to choose a stand is before the season opens. Go into the deer-hunting region and scout the terrain quietly and thoroughly. If you can find two trails where deer travel in both directions you have an excellent place for a stand. Sometimes even the most promising of crossings doesn't work out for a bow hunter. In southern Ohio some years ago, I followed a heavily used deer trail into a creek bottom thicket for a quarter of a mile and came to a place where another trail came out of a nearby hollow and crossed the first trail. The cover was so thick that getting an arrow through it to an unsuspecting deer was an impossibility and I had to give up the busiest deer crossing I was to find for years, for even a twig can send an arrow veering off at an angle.

I found another crossing some years earlier in Kentucky. Deer had crossed a small creek time after time. I took up my stand behind a small bush twenty yards downwind before daylight on opening morning. This was exactly what I should have done. What I didn't know until daylight was that another bow hunter had taken up a stand forty yards upwind. No deer with a normal olfactory sense would come between us, so I abandoned the crossing.

It is seldom necessary to build a blind, but if it is, make it simple, use materials that are natural in the locality, make it as far ahead of the season as possible, and be sure you clear all sticks off its floor. A low blind is preferable to a tall one. Plan to shoot over the top of it instead of through it.

A deer hunter doesn't have to be perfectly camouflaged or completely hidden from sight. The closest a deer ever came to my stand was during a northern Ohio hunt several years ago when I was fully visible from the belt up. All that broke up my outline was the remains of a rotting stump behind which I stood. Drivers were moving deer through

Ohio bow hunter gets shot at whitetail at twenty yards. Timing is important. Try to choose moment when deer is relaxed, or looking in other direction.

the woods toward this stand, and the woods in that spot were filled with deer. I saw a fine buck come up opposite me. He stopped inside the protective cover directly across from me and two does joined him. Three other deer followed shortly.

I could hear the drivers coming up now behind the deer, and the animals were getting increasingly nervous. So was I. Finally one of the does bolted out into the open, then the entire herd broke. Those deer came directly toward the stump that only half-hid me, and at the final moment they split into two small bands and passed on either side of me.

Before I chose that stump for a stand, however, I had checked to make certain that I was not outlined against the sky. Trees behind me broke up my outline, and I was downwind from the drivers. Movement and noise were the only things left to scare the deer away from my stand. They never knew I was there until I lifted my bow.

Bow hunters make good use of tree blinds. Deer will sometimes walk directly under a hunter waiting in a tree for them.

In selecting or using a tree blind take care to check it out in advance of the season to see if it

permits you to draw a bow and shoot from a variety of positions in various directions from which deer might approach. Know where you will hang or rest your bow and quiver of arrows during those long periods of waiting so the bow can be brought into play with minimum movement or loss of time. The tree blind that worked perfectly during gun season may place limitations on you when you carry a bow. Know in advance.

It is also an excellent idea to practice shooting from a tree blind or a similar elevation so that once given the opportunity to shoot at a deer you will not be astounded by where your arrow goes.

Wherever he hunts, the bowman must move quietly and unperceived and must be able to blend into the landscape.

Bowmen Get Close to Deer

Whatever the Indians didn't know about marksmanship with bow and arrow, they made up for in hunting ability. They could stalk game silently for hours or wait patiently beside the trail as long as necessary. They had to get close to the game, and they knew it. Today's archers, even with better equipment, still have to get close to the deer.

In 1911, Dr. Saxton Pope had as good an opportunity as any white man ever had to see how primitive Americans hunted deer. Dr. Pope had made friends with Ishi, last of the Yana Indians. Ishi was captured, half starved, in the wilds of California and was brought, the last of his tribe, to the University of California at Berkeley, where scientists studied him as a living exhibit out of the past.

Ishi, when captured, knew no word for iron, horse, or road. But he was a superb hunter. Dr. Pope hunted often with Ishi, whose bow was made of mountain juniper and backed with sinew. When he hunted deer, Ishi sometimes wore a stuffed buck's head, which he would bob up and down behind the brush until some curious deer came to investigate.

But it was caution and preparation more than trickery that helped him make his kills. He would study his hunting ground. He would learn where the old bucks bedded down in daytime, and figure out how he could best get to them undiscovered.

The day before the hunt Ishi smoked no tobacco, and when he arose on the morning of the hunt he would bathe in the creek then rub his dark skin with aromatic leaves until the man smell was masked. He would wash out his mouth, and on the day of the hunt he would drink water but eat no food.

In final preparation Ishi would change his clothes for a loincloth, which would help in two ways. It would make less noise in the brush than standard clothing and would prompt the hunter to move more cautiously in thorny thickets.

When to Shoot

The deer is a bundle of steel springs. His mind is alert and his reactions fast, and you must get your arrow away at precisely the right moment. It is in timing the shot that many an archer makes his mistake. Often he shoots at distances too great for accuracy; the deer might come closer if he waits. If he won't come close, it is wise to wait for a better shot than to take a chance on injuring and losing him. There is seldom a good chance of scoring on deer at more than fifty yards, and the twenty-five-yard shot is a far better choice.

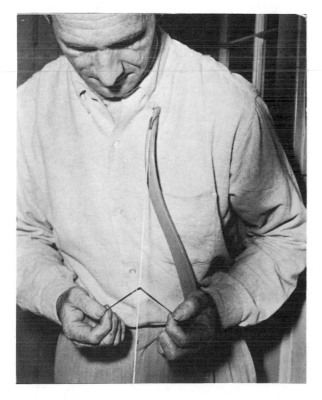

Even if your deer is close enough for a shot, some moments are better than others for shooting. If the deer is feeding, he will probably lower his head and eat, then lift his head and look. He is most vulnerable when his head is down, because he won't leap until he lifts his head. Wait for him to lower his head, then choose your spot and release your arrow.

You can sometimes accomplish the same thing by waiting until his head is behind a tree. Never try to shift your position while he is looking at you. If you have no choice but to draw your bow while the animal is alert, you have to be capable of getting off a fast and accurate shot.

A nervous deer is difficult to shoot for still another reason. If he senses trouble and is uneasy, he may hear the string released in time to jump out of the arrow's path. Some deer do "jump the string"— although their numbers are probably far fewer than claimed by archers who miss.

You can quiet your bowstring by threading a pair of rubber beads, known as "brush nocks," over the ends of the bowstring so that they hit the limb of the bow when the string is released. One bow-hunting friend of mine ties a three-inch length of ordinary yarn around the string near each end to absorb the sound. Whether or not the yarn is responsible, this archer has killed a dozen deer.

Shooting at a running deer with bow and arrow is, in most cases, a bad thing to do, especially if the deer is frightened badly and moving fast. Already alarmed, if he is wounded, he will probably find that added burst of strength which enables a wounded deer to travel amazing distances. And you may have a long trailing job at hand.

But the running shot is a temptation difficult to resist, and I'm certain that Ohio deer hunters Paul Jordan and Dick Compton would not agree that it's always best to pass up a shot at a running deer. They can offer as proof one of field archery's strangest episodes, which occurred on the second day of Ohio's bow season some years ago. Jordan and Compton, hunting side by side, were moving slowly up a logging road which promised to bring

Short lengths of yarn tied to the bowstring near the ends will help to muffle the twang when the bow is shot. Brush nocks, which are rubber beads made to fit over the string, accomplish the same purpose.

Mini-Magnum. For beginning archers. Draw weights 15 to 25 pounds at 22-inch draw length.

Jennings T-Star Hunting Bow. Various draw weights for target shooting or hunting. Let-off: 40 to 50 percent.

Whitetail Hunter. Draw weights 35 to 70 pounds, depending on draw length and adjustment.

Jennings Lightning. Adjustable. Sound choice for beginner.

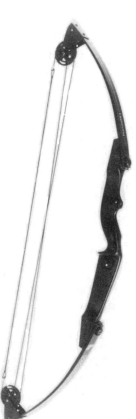

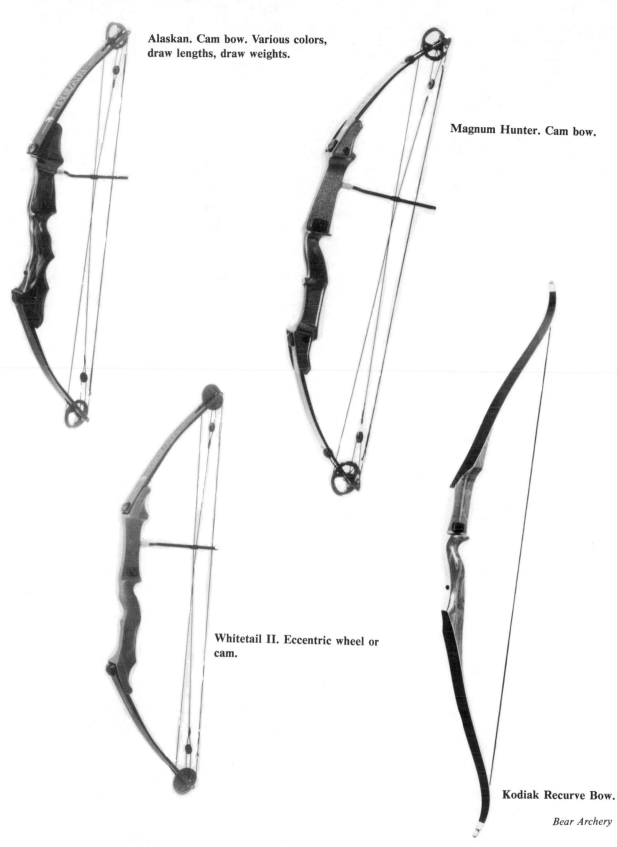

Alaskan. Cam bow. Various colors,
draw lengths, draw weights.

Magnum Hunter. Cam bow.

Whitetail II. Eccentric wheel or
cam.

Kodiak Recurve Bow.

Bear Archery

them out to the head of a long, deep hollow. Both of them saw the buck at the same moment.

As Jordan recalls it, "We both raised our bows and froze in place." They watched the antlers, then the whole deer, come into view through the brush. It was a big buck, coming directly down the road toward them. He closed the distance rapidly and Jordan slowly drew his bow until his fingers touched the anchor point on his cheek. Not until the buck reduced the distance between himself and the hunters to fifteen yards did he spot them and angle sharply to the left. This was what Jordan was waiting for. He saw his arrow sink into the buck's side.

What he didn't yet know was that Compton had also shot. The buck dropped dead only twenty-five yards from where the archers stood. Both archers had shot at the same spot and both had scored. Their arrows had actually rubbed against each other where they entered the buck. One tipped the heart. The other barely missed it. They divided the meat and while one settled for the hide the other took the head. Both archers received the Art Young Big Game gold pin for killing the same deer.

If you do try a shot at a running deer, your lead must be much greater with an arrow than with a rifle. While a 170-grain bullet from a .30-30 will rip along at about 2,000 feet per second, an arrow covers only about 150 feet per second.

If a deer isn't thoroughly spooked, you can sometimes appeal to his curiosity and get him to stop long enough to give you time for a shot. Whistle or make a slight clucking noise. Often this will stop him.

The best point at which to aim is where Jordan and Compton both hit their buck, just behind the front leg and low in the chest cavity.

An archer who has just shot a deer should wait, not run after the deer. Often a deer hit by an arrow doesn't even know where his trouble came from. He feels like lying down. If he lies down and nothing disturbs him, he will lie there and stiffen. Jim Blackburn told of three deer he saw shot in the rear quarters. This is not ordinarily considered a very effective place to shoot a deer, but every one of those deer lay down within thirty yards and stayed there.

If you set off to run a deer down, you are certain to spur him to frantic action. Even a mortally wounded deer can muster amazing strength and

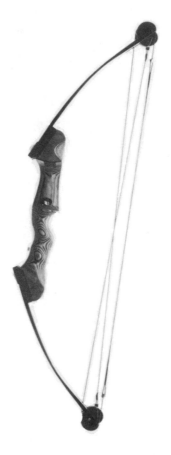

Cam Master. Adjustable, 50 to 60 pounds.

stamina. He may run a mile or more, depending on how badly wounded he is. And he may find his way into cover where you'll never find him. If he's moving slowly, however, you can usually pick up his blood trail later and track him down.

After you've scored a hit with an arrow, or even if you're not certain you've scored, sit down and wait. Wait half an hour. Then get up and move in slowly in search of him.

When you do come upon that deer you've taken with one of the world's oldest weapons, you have a feeling you've earned your venison.

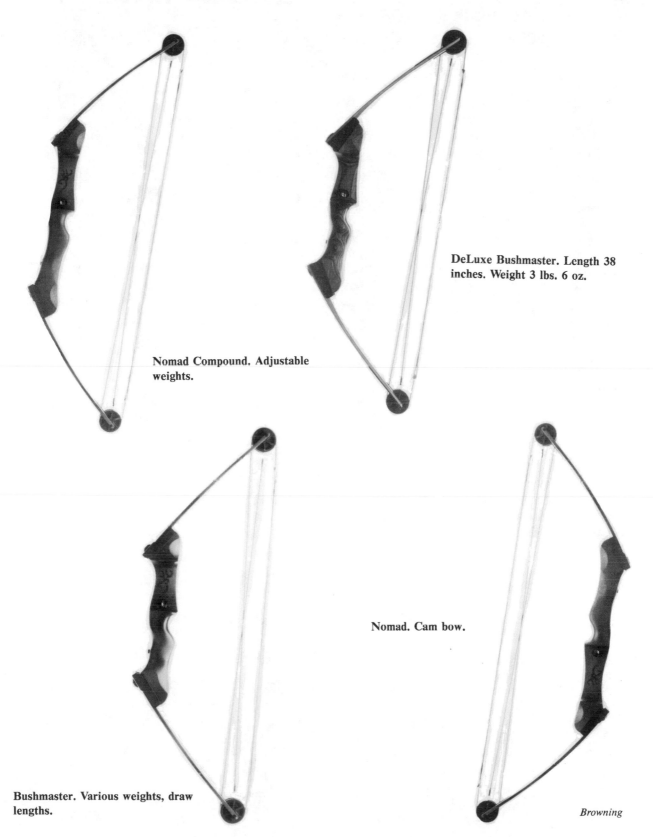

DeLuxe Bushmaster. Length 38
inches. Weight 3 lbs. 6 oz.

Nomad Compound. Adjustable
weights.

Nomad. Cam bow.

Bushmaster. Various weights, draw
lengths.

Browning

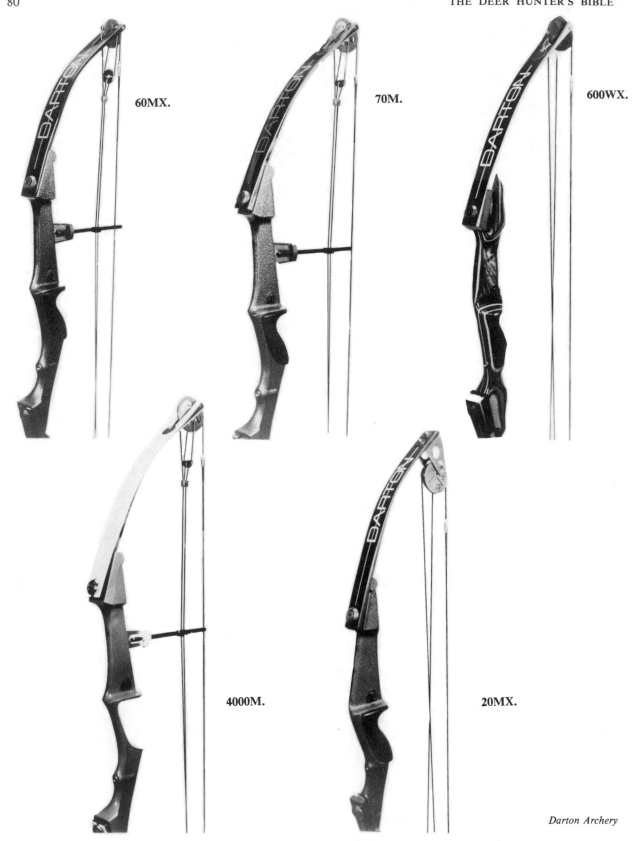

60MX.

70M.

600WX.

4000M.

20MX.

Darton Archery

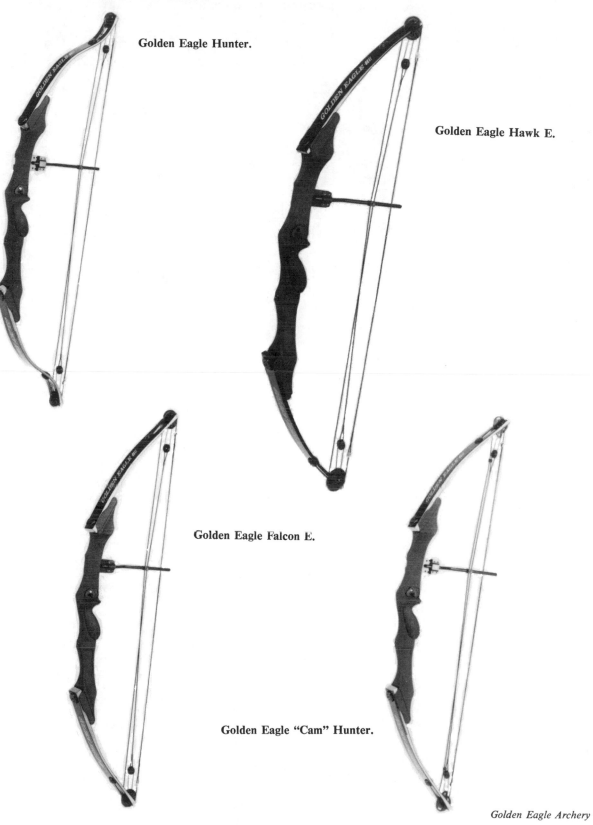

Golden Eagle Hunter.

Golden Eagle Hawk E.

Golden Eagle Falcon E.

Golden Eagle "Cam" Hunter.

Golden Eagle Archery

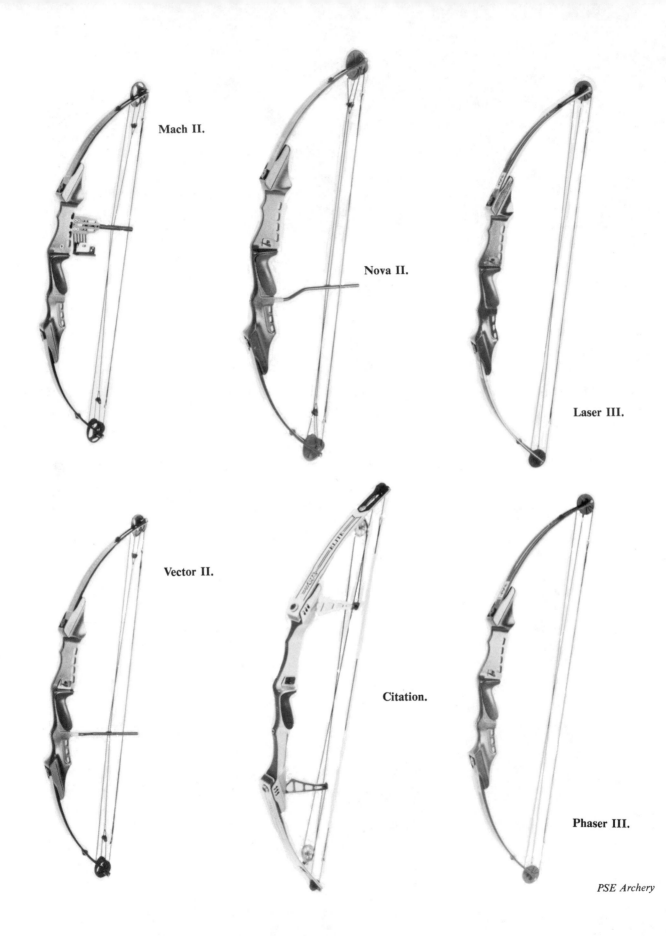

Mach II.

Nova II.

Laser III.

Vector II.

Citation.

Phaser III.

PSE Archery

"Ole" Norm's Bow Sight features red sighting light.

Vibra-Lock Sight. *Browning*

Mongoose. *PSE*

Range-Indicating Sight. *Mason*

The archer seeking to protect his bow and arrows in transit can purchase a foam-lined, hardcover case. *Penguin Industries*

Camo Stalking Quiver. *PSE*

Shoulder Quiver. *PSE*

Dual-Mount Quiver. *Browning*

Take Care of Your Tackle

Archery equipment deserves good care whether in use or in storage.

Your bow should be stored hanging up and not stacked in a corner where the tips might warp or get damaged. Unstring the bow before putting it away, regardless of what kind of bow it is. Put it in a bow sock to protect it from being scratched.

If a bowstring is worn, replace it. Sometimes the bow also breaks when a string breaks.

It's a poor practice to draw a bow without an arrow in it. You may overdraw and break it or put too much stress on one limb or the other. And never dry-fire a bow. Without the arrow to help absorb shock, this puts too much strain on the limbs of the bow and can break it.

Be certain the arrows you shoot aren't too long for the bow. If they are, you may overdraw and break the bow.

Store your archery tackle where humidity and temperatures are not severe. Both dry heat and dampness can harm bow and arrows. A little furniture wax will help protect the wood surface of your bow.

Arrows are best stored in a vertical position. Wooden arrows stored in a leaning position may warp after a while. They should not be left bunched together in the quiver, for this can damage the fletching.

Many arrows are ruined while being removed from targets. They should be grasped ahead of the fletching and pulled straight back, with no side pressure on the arrow. If the arrow goes deeply enough into a target to imbed part of the fletching, draw the arrow on through from the back of the target. This will do it less harm than backing the fletching up to get the arrow free of the target.

Shooting arrows at rocks, bottles, and tin cans can, obviously, ruin the arrows.

For Safety's Sake

Discard weakened and cracked arrows; don't shoot them. Never shoot metal arrows that are bent or any arrow that has a damaged nock. And never shoot an arrow too short for your draw length. Use arrows with spine matched to the strength of the bow.

Keep an eye on everyone on the firing line and the sidelines. Have one person in charge of target shoots to give the word when to retrieve arrows.

In rough country do not carry an arrow nocked on the string. If you slip or slide, you could fall on the arrow and puncture yourself.

There is always the temptation, especially with beginning archers, to shoot an arrow straight up into the air to see if it will go out of sight. It will, if shot by a hunting bow. And it will come down in an unpredictable location at a speed that could render a serious blow.

Take special care in stringing and unstringing your bow, especially a recurved bow, to see that the strings are centered in the grooves at the tips of the bow.

The Crossbow

In recent times the crossbow has found a new life in the hands of deer hunters and its popularity is growing remarkably. This ancient instrument dates back to the Middle Ages, when it became a feared weapon of war because its projectile was capable of piercing a suit of armor.

The crossbow is a short, powerful bow mounted on a wood stock similar to a rifle stock. The bolt or arrow lies along the top of the stock and the string that propels it is released by a trigger.

Bringing a crossbow to full draw requires the use of both hands and feet. A stirrup on the front of the

Trophy whitetail that fell to a well-placed arrow.

Crossbows have grown in popularity in recent times and are now available with a wide variety of sights. *Jerry Pickrell*

bow is held down by the shooter's feet while the string is drawn into the cocked position, where it is locked in place until released by the trigger. Some crossbows are cocked with a mechanical device. Crossbows commonly have a 125- to 175-pound draw weight.

Modern hunting crossbows can be equipped with a variety of aids for the shooter, including various sighting devices and rifle scopes.

What the deer hunter should understand is that the crossbow has definite limitations. It is in no way a substitute for a gun. The deer taken by a crossbow dies of hemorrhage, the same as one shot by an arrow from any other bow, and is unlikely to drop in its tracks as if taken by a gun. Furthermore, the crossbow limits the hunter to close shots, preferably forty yards or less.

EIGHT

THE DEER HUNTER'S EQUIPMENT

There are many aids manufactured for the deer hunter, some of them essential, some frivolous. There are devices to help him walk, talk, shoot, rest, carry deer, enjoy warm drinks, mask his human odor, and make it seem like fun to get lost.

The problem for the hunter, all fired up and enthusiastic as opening day approaches, is to figure out what he really can use to advantage in addition to gun and ammunition, or bow and arrow.

The final choice of equipment depends on several factors including where you will hunt, how long you will stay, how you will get there, how you will live during the hunt, who your companions will be, and how much you are willing to burden yourself as you take to the woods and fields. The following information should help guide you in making equipment choices and also serve as a partial checklist to help you round out your pack.

Compass

Whether you travel in the wilderness regions of the West or the woodlands of the East, a good compass can be a valuable part of your outdoor equipment. The compass that helps you avoid being lost for several hours, or spending a night in the woods, is worth many times its price. The best plan is to invest in a quality instrument. Buying one with luminous points for easier use at night is a good idea. You may also want one equipped with map scales.

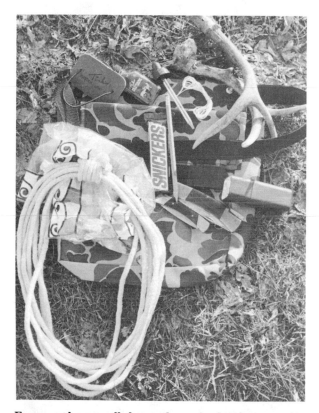

Fanny pack or small day pack carries lunch, rope, rattling antlers, pad and pencil, camera and film, meat bags, rope, scents, extra knife, dry socks, first-aid items, and more, all kept handy but out of way, allowing freedom of movement. *Jerry Pickrell*

The more remote the country hunted, the more important the hunter's compass. Good quality is a sound investment, and some hunters carry a spare compass in pocket or pouch. *Silva*

Often, reliable compasses made for outdoorsmen are advertised in outdoor magazines.

There are compasses to carry in your pocket, hang on a string, suspend from the zipper pull on your jacket, fasten on your wrist, or pin to your lapel. The pin-on style is handy and you do not have to remove gloves and dig into a pocket for it. The pin that holds it, however, may spring if caught on brush and the result is a lost compass. A string attaching the compass to a buttonhole can serve as a backup safety measure.

A second, perhaps less expensive, compass as a backup is good insurance if you hunt in remote areas or regions where there are large blocks of woods or uninhabited country.

Maps and Cases

For more than a century the U.S. government has been creating and publishing fine topographic maps which are highly detailed records of features of the landscape. These maps are helpful for the hunter to carry in the woods. They are also fun to study at home before opening day arrives. With some study, the outdoorsman can translate the map's colored symbols into features seen on the land. The topo maps show contour lines that reveal the nature and steepness of slopes and locations of cliffs, as well as water, marshes, woodlands, shorelines, and man-made features. They are excellent aids for planning deer drives to take advantage of natural features of the landscape. The U.S. Geological Survey distributes more than seven million copies of these maps annually.

The topo maps are published in various scales. Small-scale maps show less detail while large-scale maps show more. One popular choice with hunters, and the most common topo map, is the 1:24,000-scale quadrangle map. One inch on this map represents 2,000 feet (24,000 inches) on the ground.

To order topographic maps, first obtain an index for the state in which you will hunt. This index, which is free, tells you the name, number, scale of the maps you need, as well as price and how to order.

Depending on your location in the country, order index and maps from the following addresses.

If you hunt east of the Mississippi River, write to:
Eastern Distribution Branch
U.S. Geological Survey
1200 Eads Street
Arlington, Va. 22202

If you hunt west of the Mississippi River write to:
Western Distribution Branch
U.S. Geological Survey
Box 25286, Federal Center
Denver, Colo. 80225

Alaska residents may order from:
Alaska Distribution Center
U.S. Geological Survey
New Federal Building
Box 12
101 Twelfth Avenue
Fairbanks, Ak. 99701

If you want to give your maps longer life and make them easier to handle in the field, you can mount them on cloth. Here is the procedure suggested by one publication from the Geological Survey. Stretch a single piece of starch-free bleached muslin the size of the map over a board. Hold it in place with tacks.

Next mark lines on the back of the map showing where you want to make folds in it. Using a sharp knife or razor blade, cut the map into sections along these lines.

Float the sections of your map in a pan of water for a minute or so, then apply a layer of paste to the back of the pieces, one at a time. Place the pieces on the cloth, leaving about one-eighth inch between them. Use a damp sponge or cloth and gentle pressure to smooth them out. Leave the map to dry on the board for at least twenty-four hours. After trimming the newly mounted map with a straightedge and razor blade, it is ready to use.

If you choose to avoid the mess, you can obtain backing cloth from a photographic supply or art supply store and use a hot iron to bond it to the back of the map.

Some counties issue maps that are helpful, especially if you are hunting in farm country. If the county has such maps, they can be obtained from the county engineer or clerk. A number of state game and fish agencies also issue maps. Western states are usually divided into numerous big-game-management areas. State wildlife agencies publish boundary maps to show where it is legal to hunt at various times, and these maps often carry considerable detail on numerous natural and man-made features of interest to deer hunters. For hunting in Canada, you can obtain excellent maps from the Canadian Department of Mines and Technical Surveys, Ottawa.

For weather protection, carry your map in a waterproof plastic case or large Ziploc-type bag.

Camping Equipment

In some sections of the country the best plan is for the deer hunter to pack along everything he needs for easy living and camp out. Modern deer camps often feature the latest in fancy recreational vehicles complete with television. There are still those hunters, however, who get away from all the frills when they go after deer, living in a cabin or under canvas and cooking over open fires.

Modern deer hunters often use a recreational vehicle as hunting headquarters, and enjoy the comforts of home in the field.

Tents

In recent times, there has been a revolution in tent designs. They come in modern shapes that would astound old-time hunters. More important than color or shape is the quality of construction, weight, ease of erecting, and stability. Some hunters still prefer the longtime favorite Baker tent, which leaves the whole front open to a fire that reflects warmth into it. For hunting-camp use you will have trouble beating a well-made wall tent that is roomy enough to permit your group to stand up, eat at a table, and move around.

Sleeping Bags

Anyone who goes afield, even infrequently, on hunting or fishing trips should own a good sleeping bag. The modern sleeping bag with air or foam mattress is the answer to getting a good night's sleep in the field. They come in wide variety and varying quality.

This item of equipment is important enough to justify paying for quality materials and workmanship. It is one thing to buy a sleeping bag for the kids to use camping out in the backyard in summer and another to select one suitable for a week or so in a deer camp when weather may be bitterly cold.

However, if you already have a sleeping bag that you use on summer vacations, you may be able to fit it out for deer hunting by inserting a blanket or two.

The best material for sleeping-bag insulation is still goose down. Down is also the most costly. It is generally considered worth the price, however, if you might be sleeping out in temperature lower than about ten degrees above zero. Most of the millions of sleeping bags sold these days, however, are filled with synthetic fibers, or with odds and ends of cheaper materials, even clippings and materials derived from clothing manufacture. Some modern synthetics are highly effective insulation said to rival goose down.

The bedding tag on the sleeping bag can reveal quite a bit about its materials. Some sleeping bags contain virgin synthetic fibers while others contain fibers that are reprocessed. In general, reprocessed fibers offer less protection against cold than virgin fibers. The fabric covering the bag should be strong.

Better sleeping bags all have good-quality zippers that go around the bottom so the bag can be opened flat, if desired. Inside the full length of the zipper there should be a wind-barrier flap to cut out breezes that might otherwise find their way through.

Air Mattress

The old pine-bough bed may be fine for the first few hours. Smells nice too. But a good camp mattress is less trouble, and, for most of us, provides greater comfort. Besides, less of the world is wilderness than it once was and the cutting of pine branches for bedding may be frowned upon.

Rubberized cloth is more reliable than a plastic air mattress, which may suffer a puncture from a sharp stick or stone—sometimes in the middle of the night. The plastic is more difficult to repair. An air-mattress repair kit is good insurance.

You might think about selecting one of the foam mattresses on the market, depending on space available as you pack your equipment and how far you may have to pack your load into camp.

Tarpaulins

A good tarp has many uses around camp, from covering a table or gun rack to giving you a smoother surface on which to make your bed. It may also be needed to form a wind barrier for the campfire, or cover the rest of the equipment as you pack it for the trip. Some hunters lay their deer on a tarp to protect the hide and meat as they drag it out of the woods.

Select a tarp that is equipped with grommets so you can tie ropes to it, increasing its versatility.

The space blanket is a smaller relative of the old tarpaulin. I carry one because it is lightweight, protects guns, optical equipment, cameras, food, and other items from the weather, serves as an emergency blanket for anyone who gets wet, and can offer a degree of weather protection for the hunter caught out in rain or snow.

A large sheet of heavy plastic is also frequently useful whether you camp or not.

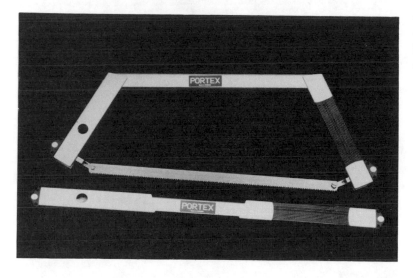

The Portex is one of several light-weight, folding saws. Interchangeable blades equip saw to butcher deer or cut wood. *Peco Sales, Inc.*

Axes

Few tools are more important in a wilderness or semiwilderness camp than a good ax, well sharpened. There is a natural tendency for the casual ax user to select a short-handled belt ax. This choice has a place for the hunter who is backpacking into his camp, or where it might be used only to help dress a deer. But if you plan to camp in, or near, a vehicle, pack in by horse or mule, or travel in a canoe, take a sharp, single-bladed ax with a thirty-inch handle. For safety, include some kind of sheath.

Saws

If you are packing into backcountry and weight is a problem, you may want to pack a small folding bucksaw instead of the ax. If traveling by horseback or vehicle, take both tools. For its weight, a small saw can be an extremely valuable tool for cutting firewood or sawing poles for a shelter.

Furthermore, the saw is going to come in handy when you dress out your deer. Some saws, made especially for deer hunters, are compact, lightweight items equipped with both wood-cutting and bone-cutting blades. An extra blade is good insurance for the folding saw.

Portable folding seat, which adds comfort to deer stand, swivels to permit shooting from any direction.

Hunting Knife

The trend among outdoorsmen in recent years has been toward folding, lock-blade knives carried on the belt. I favor these compact knives over the heavier standard belt knives. In addition, I carry a small pocketknife for two reasons. First, a knife is so important in the field that I like to have a spare in case it is lost. Besides, there are many jobs the small knife handles perfectly well. The truth is that many of us carry knives bigger than we will ever need. The bigger the knife, the more weight there is to carry, and you will seldom need a blade longer than four inches, whether spreading butter or quartering a buck.

Many hunters carry folding, lock-blade, sheath knives which are heavy-duty enough to handle all jobs on a hunting trip. *Buck Knives*

Which hunting knife to carry must be a personal choice, but remember that the knife on a deer-hunting trip has a variety of jobs. Good quality is important in both knife and sheath. *Buck Knives*

If you do carry a standard belt knife with a fixed blade, give special attention to the sheath. It should be made of heavy leather, both stitched and riveted. The rivets help keep the point from working through worn leather. Better yet, use a sheath that is lined with metal.

A stainless-steel blade is good protection against rust. The handle may be bone, plastic, metal, or wood. Wood may not be the most rugged handle but it may be easier to grip, especially when wet, and also will be warmer to the touch in sub-zero weather. Overall, plastic is probably the most widely used handle material. It is rugged, long-lasting, and inexpensive.

When choosing a knife, select one that fits your hand comfortably. The size and shape of the handle should protect your hand from accidental contact with the sharpened blade. The edge should curve up to form a point.

Good knives deserve good care. The knife is never improved by using it as a hammer, throwing it at targets, or sticking the blade into the ground.

A small sharpening stone is a good addition to the hunter's equipment, and using it properly, and often, is insurance that the knife will serve you well whenever needed. The longer you will be away from home base, the more likely you will need the sharpening stone.

This 9½-ounce folding Game Hook is an easily carried gambrel capable of handling all large game. *Black Timber*

Packs and Bags

A prime rule for packing is to store everything in as few packs as you can. Shaving kits, repair kits, and other small items scattered about increase the chance of forgetting essentials, and complicate loading and unloading your vehicle. Although a written checklist is the best insurance against forgetting the necessities, a packing plan can also help. Try to have a place for everything needed for the trip, and to keep some order in the packing.

Soft bags are better than standard suitcases, especially if you travel by small aircraft, on foot, or by horseback. The exception may be a hard case to protect your gun and scope. Outdoors stores and department stores offer canvas bags in wide variety and it is fairly simple to select one to match the length of your trip and the time you will be in the field.

Include a fanny pack in your outfit. These small belt pouches hold a remarkable assortment of items useful during the day's hunt. They have room for lunch, an extra candy bar, coil of rope for dragging and hanging a deer, dry socks, insect repellent, fire starter, small first-aid kit, and more.

Some equipment, including scopes, binoculars, lanterns, and glass bottles, should not be allowed to shift or bounce around in transit. Any fragile, uncased equipment can be wrapped in blankets or paper, and braced with duffle bags, sleeping bags, or blankets. Vibration can damage cameras and other fragile equipment. Padding under these items protects them.

The Hunter's Clothes

Manufacturers of outdoor clothing have, in recent times, produced the finest lightweight, energy-conserving clothing the world has ever known. The days are long past when discomfort comes with the territory.

Pocket fire-starting pack, such as this Fast Fire kit, by Mountain Products, Inc., is insurance in case of emergencies.

That deer slipping up from behind can be spotted without turning if a hunter has a folding mirror from Deer View Corp.

Outdoorsmen are always searching for the perfect boot, one combining comfort with protection against wet and cold. This Gore-Tex-lined leather boot, made by American, is both lightweight and waterproof.

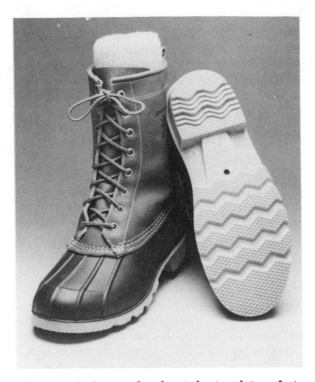

Where terrain is rugged and wet, boot-pack-type footwear is highly serviceable. Insulated boots are usually a good choice. *Browning*

Beginning with the inside layers, those old red flannels, once prominent around deer camps, have been replaced by more modern underwear for outdoor people. For hunting in moderately warm weather, the waffle-design thermal wear is excellent. It provides warmth but permits enough air circulation to keep you comfortable even if the day warms up.

If you are going to hunt where the thermometer may hit basement levels, the best plan is to invest in insulated underwear. These are tops and bottoms filled with layers of synthetic fiber and quilted to keep the insulation in proper shape and distribution. One secret to warmth and comfort in the field is to wear layers of loose-fitting clothes.

Wool pants and shirts are excellent garments for deer hunting in cold climates. They are warm, quiet in the brush, and help retain body heat even when wet. In moderate climates a good combination is a wool shirt and field trousers made of cotton, synthetics, or a combination of them.

Depending on where you hunt, rain gear can be important. The heavy outfit you wear on fishing trips may serve but, before leaving home, try it on over your hunting outfit to be sure it is not too tight.

The poncho has been both praised and cursed. I find that it has much to recommend it. If there is

For bitterly cold weather, this hunter's mitt-type glove, made to hang from the belt, provides spaces for keeping both hands warm. *Berlin Glove Company*

even a slight possibility of rain during the day, I carry a lightweight, olive-drab poncho made of rubberized nylon. I arrange it in a square and fold it over my belt behind me. This way it can hang down far enough to provide a waterproof seat in the woods.

I would recommend that lightweight, flimsy plastic raincoats never be taken into the deer woods. They are seldom rugged enough to withstand the hard use they get on a hunting trip.

Color of the outer garments is highly important. In many states, the color of the deer hunter's outer garments is regulated by laws enforced by conservation officers, and with good reason. The deer hunter needs to be seen by other hunters. Exhaustive testing has shown that the most visible color is blaze orange. Check your state regulations. But regardless of the safety regulations, a blaze-orange hunting hat and jacket or vest is a sound idea.

Select your hunting boots to meet the needs of the country where you plan to hunt. For hunting in wet lowlands or slushy snow at above-freezing temperatures, it is hard to beat shoe packs with rubber lowers and leather uppers. They should fit loosely enough to accommodate an extra pair of heavy wool socks.

For most dry hunting situations, eight-inch leather boots are a popular choice. Good boots of this type, well broken in, are hard to beat for comfort. Manufacturers have tried for years to make leather boots waterproof. Silicone treatment has helped. Most are water resistant at best and there is a difference between water-resistant and waterproof. The best I've encountered are lined with Gore-Tex which is waterproof but also breaths so moisture can escape through it. For genuine waterproof leather boots of this kind, the Gore-Tex lining must be held in place without stitching. The result is a relatively expensive boot, but just probably the finest hunting boot one has ever worn.

If you plan to hunt out of a hunting camp, an added pair of light shoes is a good idea for around camp.

Select your gloves to match the weather. In cold country mittens may be the best protection against low temperatures, providing the one for your shooting hand permits the finger to fit the trigger.

You may want some added insurance against cold hands, such as fleece-lined pouches the hunter can wear on his belt as hand warmers.

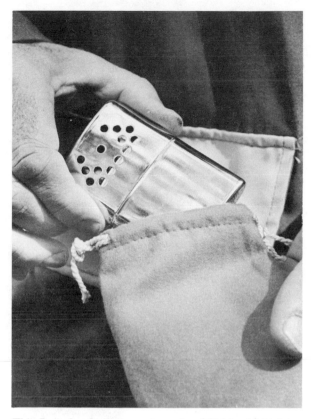

This Jon-e hand warmer, compact and lightweight, glows for twenty-four hours.

After several hours on a cold deer stand you can appreciate a pocket hand warmer. This little heat maker burns fuel without flame, and will glow for twenty hours or more with one filling. It is lightweight and easy to carry in pocket or pouch.

Meat Bags

If you skin and quarter your deer in the field, you can use cloth sacks to protect the meat from insects. You can purchase these bags ready-made, and large enough for an entire deer.

Also carry along a few plastic sacks for the liver and heart to keep this organ meat clean until you get it back to camp or kitchen. These plastic bags are handy for a variety of purposes, ranging from protecting cameras and film to waterproofing snacks.

Binoculars

A good pair of binoculars can help you avoid mistaking a branch for an antler, or the white patch on a hunter's clothes for the tail of a deer. Binoculars are especially important if you are trophy hunting and want to avoid limiting out on an inferior rack. They are most valuable while on stand or still hunting.

The four binoculars most commonly used by deer hunters are 6×30, 7×35, 7×50, and 8×30.

The first digit tells the magnification. A 6×30 lens makes your deer appear six times as close as it does without the binoculars. The second figure is the diameter of the objective lens in millimeters. This lens size is important because it indicates how much light the lens admits, and this in turn helps determine how well you see the image. The measurement should be at least 30 mm. The field of view is the width of the field you see through the binoculars at a designated distance—usually one thousand feet.

Which pair of binoculars should you buy for deer hunting? Given a choice, most deer hunters prefer the 7×35. This is my choice for general use. The best one for hunting in thick brushy country is probably the 6×30. The 8×30 would serve better for long distances in wide open country. The 7×35 is a satisfactory compromise for both conditions. The higher the magnification, the more difficult it is to find what you are looking for through the glasses and to hold them steady.

Good binoculars have coated lenses. This means the glass has been treated with a thin chemical coating to hold down reflections.

There are two types of focusing arrangements used on binoculars. Some have a single central adjustment so that one knob adjusts both lenses. Others have oculars that adjust individually. Those with individual adjustments are slower to use but more satisfactory if your eyes don't test the same. You can obtain binoculars with corrected lenses if you need them.

Old binoculars sometimes get out of alignment. This essentially ruins them until they are taken to the shop for realignment.

Your binoculars should have a neck strap for easy carrying, but shorten the strap so the binoculars hang only six inches or so below your chin. This way they can be brought to the eye faster, and will also bang against your body less than with long straps. It is possible to attach a leather flap to the binoculars and cut a buttonhole in it so they can be secured by buttoning it to your coat when you are moving.

Materials, design, and workmanship determine the price you pay for binoculars. For the better-known brands, price is closely related to quality.

A past president of the American Academy of Optometry, and a veteran deer hunter, once said, "A lightweight binocular is better because of the problem of packing it around. Coated lenses are an absolute necessity, particularly for early morning and late evening hunting.

"Binoculars," he added, "can cause headache and considerable eye strain when there is anything wrong with the alignment of the lenses. It pays to get the best pair one can afford. Binoculars are a real precision piece of machinery and the cost is in keeping with the material purchased."

Cameras for Hunters

Good pictures made during the deer hunt can bring back memories, and provide a record of trophies for years to come. Furthermore, with today's cameras anyone can make pictures that range from satisfactory to excellent. Modern cameras can take much of the guesswork out of picture making, some even adjusting automatically to the amount of light available, focusing automatically, and advancing the film for the next shot.

Most still cameras carried by amateurs today, as well as by many professionals, are the small, compact, single-lens-reflex 35mm models. Film for this size camera, either color or black and white, is widely available.

A 35mm camera is best if you want to make slides for projecting on a screen at home or at club meetings. The simplest of all, and perhaps the least expensive, are the compact 35mm models with one fixed lens. These lightweight miniatures fit neatly into a hunting-shirt pocket. They are also simple to use with flash if you want to make pictures in cabin, tent, or dark woods after the sun goes down. Ask your photo dealer to show you these neat little 35mm cameras. There are several manufacturers.

For those who want to get deeper into photography there are 35mm cameras that take interchangeable lenses. Again, there are several manufacturers,

This selection of spotting scopes shows models considered suitable for hunting big game. Prominent and respected names in manufacture of spotting scopes include Bushnell, Swift, Weatherby, Bausch and Lomb, and Celestron.

most of them Japanese. The 35mm camera most often used by professionals, as well as a host of amateurs, is the Nikon. Lenses for almost any reasonably well-known brand of 35mm camera on today's market are manufactured with computer-controlled precision and are generally reliable. If you want more than one lens for a 35mm camera, the best basic selection might be the standard 50mm or 55mm, a wide-angle lens, probably 28mm, and a medium-length telephoto lens in the neighborhood of a 200mm.

Polaroid cameras can be fun because you get almost immediate results. Shoot a picture, wait a minute, see the picture. Furthermore, these cameras are low-priced. The film, however, can be expensive. They are capable of turning out satisfactory color pictures, although seldom of the quality obtainable with the cameras and film used to make slides. One advantage of the Polaroid is that if you take a picture you do not like, you can immediately make another and correct your error while the hunt is still in progress.

Another route for the picture-taking deer hunter is to carry a movie camera or video outfit.

Buying used cameras of any kind is risky business. The safest procedure is to deal with an established photo dealer.

Spotting Scopes

Western deer hunters pursuing mule deer in the wide open spaces often need a spotting scope. The spotting scope is especially helpful for the trophy hunter. In other seasons the scope can double for use on the target range and for studying migratory waterfowl.

The working optics in a spotting scope include the ocular, or eyepiece, which provides the magnifi-

Bushnell 10–30× Zoom Stalker with tripod. *Bushnell*

cation, the objective, or light-gathering lens, on the front of the scope, and mounted between them, various combinations of lenses, prisms, or mirrors. The most widely used magnification is probably 20×. Some come with more than one eyepiece to give a choice of magnifications. The zoom lens gives a variety of magnifications with a single eyepiece.

The good spotting scope should last a lifetime. Buy a recognized brand and pick the best one you can afford. Factors to consider before making a choice include the field of view, magnification, exit pupil, relative brightness, relative light efficiency, weight, length, price, and quality of construction.

The field of view is usually expressed as the diameter of the field viewed at one thousand yards. The wider the field, the easier it is to find and follow moving animals with the scope.

Too much magnification can work against you. The greater the magnification, the less landscape you can see through the scope. The high magnification amplifies motion as well as image size and this means more problems with wind and tripod stability. Increased power also cuts down brightness by reducing the amount of light reaching the eye. Consequently, if your scope offers a single magnification, 20× may be far better than a 40×.

Relative brightness is a term sometimes used as an index for comparing binoculars or telescopes. Relative brightness is the square of the exit pupil, which is the point within the scope where light rays are concentrated to be sent to the eye. Size of exit pupil decreases as magnification increases. The relative brightness of a scope with an exit pupil measuring 3mm would be nine. Sometimes you may hear the term RLE, or "relative light efficiency." This refers to relative brightness, plus a factor gained by coating the lens with a chemical that can increase relative light efficiency by decreasing reflection. Coating can increase relative light efficiency by 50 percent, and good-quality lenses offered nowadays are coated.

Judging quality of construction is difficult, but anyone can check to see that moving parts work smoothly and appear to be machined to close tolerances. A well-made scope promises to hold up better under field conditions than a cheaply manufactured one.

NINE
ADVANCED DEER HUNTING

In recent times deer hunting has become increasingly sophisticated. The basic hunting techniques still apply, as they did for the Indian and the pioneer, because the nature of deer remains much as it always was. But biologists, tracking herds of radio-collared deer to see what they do as hunters pursue them, have given us a better understanding of the ways of deer during those autumn weeks when hunters tramp the fields.

Body Language

The hunter can now know what the various actions and movements of deer mean. Deer do communicate. They get their messages across to each other in ways they have evolved over the centuries. Most of their messages are sent by sign language. For example, deer can relay messages with their tails and ears, and the experienced hunter knows this. It is probable that Indian hunters knew how to read this deer sign language, and that we are now relearning it.

On an old Midwestern hill farm I know well there is an open meadow sandwiched between two woods and the deer often come out into this open area, especially in the evenings. This has frequently given me the opportunity to watch as the alert deer alternately eat a few bites then lift their heads to study the world around them.

The best-known signal by the whitetail is the

Intensive study of deer reveals secrets of body language and behavior that help hunters understand how big bucks act under various circumstances. *Erwin A. Bauer*

flashing of the white underside of its tail as the escaping animal, sensing danger, bounds away. Day or night, this is an alarm signal to other deer, especially the doe's fawns. Bucks are less apt to lift their white flags than are does, perhaps because they are less concerned about notifying other deer of danger. Furthermore, keeping the tail down helps the buck escape attention and may prolong his life.

Watch the way a doe holds her tail when not alarmed. If she holds it straight out, and angling off to one side, she is an estrus doe at peak readiness for breeding.

Hunters in tree stands often see a doe mincing along the trail with her tail at this angle. Commonly, she stops occasionally and inspects her backtrail, walks on, then stops again. Where does are legal game, the hunter can either take the doe, or hold off. By waiting, he stands a fair chance that a buck has picked up the doe's clues, is trailing her, and, unless alarmed, may soon afford the hunter a shot.

Often the whitetails coming to the edge of the meadow—which I frequently watch from the house, with binoculars—keep their tails swinging from side to side, as if scaring flies away. This is a sign that the deer are not alarmed. But if the tail stops swinging and is held straight out, I know that the deer has picked up warning signals and could take flight at any moment.

Ears are also excellent indicators of what the deer is doing or about to do. Deer can swivel their ears independently as they gather clues about possible hazards in their world. If you are watching an approaching deer displaying this kind of behavior, you can be relatively sure that it is not alarmed—at least, not at the moment. But if the deer suddenly stops and turns both ears in the same direction, it has picked up some alarming sound, perhaps from people or dogs that you have not yet heard. Then, if the deer lays its ears back, expect its instant departure.

The more you learn about these subtleties of deer body language, the better your chances.

Scrapes and Rubs

Deer use their sensitive noses for more than detecting danger. The odors they pick up, especially during the rut, tell them when other deer are in the vicinity. Furthermore, scientists now know that deer can identify other individual deer by odor. In this autumn season, when the breeding occurs, the deer are particularly sensitive to the odors left by the other sex. There are special odors that warn bucks away from the dominant buck's home areas, that lead bucks to estrus does, and that tells does when they have come into the range of a rutting buck.

Between the deer's hooves are the interdigital glands that lay a trail wherever the deer puts its feet. On the inner surface of the deer's hind legs are

In fall, with the approach of the rutting season, bucks polish their antlers on saplings, establishing territory and leaving sign for does to read. *U.S. Forest Service*

the tarsal glands that produce odors unique to the individual deer. Tarsal glands, which appear as tufts of hair, are used in conjunction with urine when deer urinate on their hind legs.

Metatarsal glands are on the outer surface of the hind legs. Scent from these glands is believed to signal alarm, and biologists believe this is especially true for black-tailed and mule deer.

In the corner of the deer's eyes are the preorbital glands which, in addition to being tear glands, yield secretions the deer uses to leave its mark on bushes and low-hanging limbs.

Does in estrus discharge sex attractants with their urine and, in this manner, leave trails that lead bucks to them. As a warning to other bucks, as well as a notice to does, bucks mark their ranges, especially their scrapes and the surrounding bushes and ground, with the odors they discharge with their urine. Bucks also mark bushes by rubbing them with their foreheads. Because these marked areas are so highly advertised, they become important in the plans of deer hunters.

Small trees rubbed clean of bark tell hunters where the big bucks are active.

When the dominant buck is nowhere around, other deer may investigate the scrape, giving the hunter on stand a choice of shots. According to highly respected whitetail hunter Bob McGuire, who has developed several aids for deer hunters, you can tell whether or not the buck seen at the scrape is the dominant male in the area or one of the lesser bucks. The top-ranking buck comes to the scrape with a sense of confidence and sniffs around the scrape before checking the overhanging branches for information. Other bucks are more likely to first check the branches.

Another interesting discovery is that whitetail scrapes may be used year after year, sometimes by successive generations of dominant bucks.

McGuire, who makes a profession of studying deer behavior, went one step further when he decided to create and test artificial scrapes to see if bucks would come to them. Using a stick as a substitute deer paw, and taking care not to contaminate the area with human scent, he created a scrape then treated it, as well as overhanging branches, with the appropriate deer urine and other scents. The plan works, and McGuire and his hunting companions have taken numerous trophy bucks to prove it.

When he sets off to make a mock scrape, Mc-

Those who best understand the behavior of deer are the full-time professionals, the trained biologists. In recent years they have pinned down facts of deer behavior that add new interest to deer hunting. Instead of simply heading for the favorite hunting area, the modern hunter profits by searching for scrapes and rubs, especially if he or she hunts with a bow.

The dominant buck scrapes aside leaves and litter, using his front feet alternately, and when the scrape is complete, he showers it with his urine. In addition, he will generally mark the low overhanging branches by biting them and rubbing them with sex-attractant odors from his forehead and preorbital glands. Unless the branches above a scrape have been chewed on by a deer, the scrape is seldom that of a dominant buck.

The buck may have made other, less developed scrapes in his range simply to mark a part of his territory, and these may be unproductive places to take up a stand.

Deer scents applied to pads on bottom of boot leave a trail wherever hunter walks.

Guire carries a plastic sheet on which to lay his supplies when he works: a pair of rubber gloves, a short forked stick for scraping and knocking branches, and a collection of buck scents, as well as materials he has collected from estrus does. McGuire explains in his book *Advanced Whitetail Hunting Techniques* that five of his biggest bucks taken with bow and arrow were taken at mock scrapes. Bob, who has also produced a cassette tape on deer-calling and -rattling techniques, as well as a "mock scrape paste," can be reached at P.O. Box 3213.CRS, Johnson City, Tenn. 37602.

How Hunters Use Scents

With the knowledge that scents play such a highly important role in the day-to-day life of deer, especially during the rut, it was not surprising that hunters would begin mixing and bottling scents to attract deer into range. A wide variety of scents has come to the shelves of sporting-goods stores. There are scents to mask human odors, scents that smell like various deer foods, and scents to imitate the natural sex attractants to bring in the bucks during the rut. Properly used, these scents are important aids in deer hunting, especially for bow hunters

One of several methods of laying a scent trail is using this penlike container strapped to boot to leave even trail of drops as hunter walks. *Buck Stix*

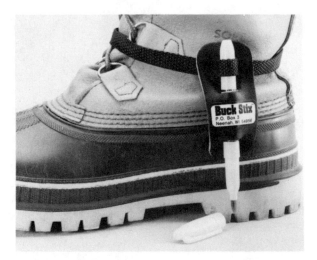

who must get close to their game for a good shot.

The most important scents that the hunter has to worry about are his own body odors. The downwind deer picks up your human scent and recognizes you for what you are. Then he probably slips away over the ridge before you even know he is close by. Indian deer hunters understood the importance of minimizing human odors.

Today's hunter can obtain scents that help mask the human odor. Perhaps the best known of these is skunk odor. Some bow hunters skunk up their camouflage outfit so thoroughly that they must leave their hunting clothes hanging in the barn or shed between hunts. There are two schools of thought, however, about skunk scent. Some outdoorsmen refrain from using it on the grounds that the skunk only discharges its protective odor when alarmed, therefore the deer smelling skunk might suspect a foreign intruder.

Smokers, on the other hand, or those who associate with them and pick up smoke odors on their clothes, might make good use of a skunk scent to mask the tobacco odors. If you use other kinds of masking scents, for example a scent carrying the odor of evergreens, use it only in areas where these are natural odors, in this case evergreen trees with similar odors.

It makes sense to have the body as clean and odor free as possible before going into the field. The deer's sensitive nose can probably pick up the strange foreign odors of highly seasoned foods, smoke clinging to clothing, human perspiration on the body or clothing, and the fumes from alcohol. Antiperspirants that are unscented will help inhibit sweating and thereby diminish some body odors.

Using scented soaps, for either the body or clothing, can announce your presence to deer. Rinsing all the soap from freshly washed clothing is important. Hanging your hunting clothes out in the fresh air to dry instead of stuffing them into the clothes drier will help free them of telltale odors.

Baking soda is a commonly used substitute for soap powder among deer hunters. Clothes can be washed in it then hung out to dry. Hunting boots, soles and all, should be scrubbed with baking soda.

In general, what the hunter needs to remember is that the odors of his body and clothing, including his boots, will tell deer that there is danger nearby. Anything done to reduce these odors, especially if bow hunting, gives you some added advantage.

Scents that Attract

Among the most frequently used scents on deer hunts is a buck lure. There are many on the market. They are made to convince the buck in rut that he is approaching a doe in estrus. The doe ready to breed leaves her trail of sex-attractant odors behind her as she moves through the woods.

The hunter's challenge is to make an effective trail of this kind to lead the aroused buck right to his stand. One method of dispensing the scent is to apply it to pads that are worn on the bottom of the boots. It is best not to apply the scent directly to your clothes because the buck may approach you directly, look you in the eye when you are on stand, and leave you no opportunity to move without spooking him. For this reason too, it is good policy to remove the scented pads from your boots a short distance to one side of your stand or where you ascend to your tree stand.

Some manufacturers offer scent dispensers designed to mark the trail, a drop at a time, for equal strength all the way to the stand. This gets around the possibility that a trail made with boot pads

This is one of numerous easily used deer stands available to hunters. Complete with pillow, this one was designed by Bob Hice for all-day comfort. *Advanced Hunting Equipment, Inc.*

might grow progressively weaker and tell a buck that he is trailing the doe in the wrong direction. Another popular system for dispensing buck lure is a plastic holder that attaches to a Jon-e hand

This homemade tree stand in northern woods gives white-tail hunter a special vantage point. *Erwin A. Bauer*

Although they do not normally look up into trees for danger, the adaptable deer are catching on. *Official U.S. Navy Photograph*

warmer. Heat activates the scent as the hunter walks into his stand. Once you reach your stand you may want to decorate the nearby bushes with a few drops of the doe scent.

If you decide to use scents, the best plan is to first do all you can to guard against human odors. Then study everything you can about the scents available on the market, and finally experiment until you find which scents, or combinations of them, work best for you in your area.

Late-Season Deer

Opening day offers most hunters their best chance to get a deer. This is especially true if you have done your scouting and have some idea of where the deer feed and bed and of the trails they use traveling between these areas. On opening morning the deer are surrounded by new sights, sounds, and odors. Human odors drift through the woods. Gunfire is everywhere. Some of the deer will have been through this experience before.

Responding to these disturbances in the woods, deer may become more difficult than ever to find. The wariest of them will often move into heavy cover, sometimes traveling to seldom-used areas. But a deer does not need a large area in which to hide. A briar patch or a few pine trees may give cover enough. Furthermore, a hard-pressed deer may stick tighter than ever to its bed, sometimes allowing a person to come within a few yards and still not bolt unless there is direct eye contact.

Tree Stands

Hunting from tree stands has probably been practiced for hundreds, maybe thousands, of years. The first time I ever hunted from a tree stand I simply climbed to the rather low forks of a giant oak tree on the edge of an open meadow, where I had reason to believe deer would come out in the evening. This was years before the introduction of the fancy tree stands on the market today. Humans must have been doing this for a long time.

That early tree stand of mine was occupied during a bow season. Archers were the first to seriously take advantage of tree stands, but as word spread

Where trees are unsuitable as deer stands, elevated shooting platforms solve the problem. This 55-pound tripod with telescoping legs, is a Texas favorite. *Texas Hunter*

that the added elevation gives the hunter some advantage, gun hunters too began climbing to vantage points above the deer trails and crossings.

Standing uncomfortably in the crotch of a tree, trying to remain quiet and motionless while waiting for a deer, led a few pioneering hunters to build little platforms in the trees. Some of these were equipped with soft chairs, carpeting, roof, and handy shelves for hot coffee and snacks. You can still build your own tree stand, and many deer hunters do, or you can purchase one of the numerous tree stands on the market today.

Because the home-built stand is usually more or less fixed to its tree, there are some rules that apply. The hunter building such a stand needs either to own the tree that supports it or make some arrangement with the rightful owner. Building a fixed platform in a tree can damage the tree. So can nailing steps on the tree. There is always the possibility

This Baker tree stand permits hunter to ascend tree without use of steps by alternately "walking" platform and seat section upward.

After shooting buck from tree stand, hunter remains ready for second shot if needed.

Once in position, use a rope attached to belt to draw gun or bow to tree stand, and later to lower it to ground again.

The Treesling is a lightweight, versatile system for securing a hunter comfortably in a wide variety of trees. *Anderson Designs, Inc.*

that these stands will weaken in time and become unsafe.

Those who manufacture tree stands have been highly successful in creating stands that do not damage trees because they do not have to be attached with spikes and do not even require the use of steps. If steps are needed, they can be obtained in designs that keep each step in place temporarily without attaching it to the tree.

Points to consider when purchasing a tree stand include whether the design of the tree stand permits shooting in any direction, total weight of stand, if it can be easily carried, ease of erecting the stand, speed with which it can be moved to another tree, comfort, and safety features—especially a safety belt.

There is no need for the hunter to climb to the very top of a towering tree to find a good hunting position. In most cases a stand fifteen feet above ground is more than high enough to avoid being seen by deer that might walk beneath it.

Using a safety belt deserves careful thought by any tree-stand hunter. I know one hunter who dozed off and fell a dozen feet onto frozen ground, costing him the permanent loss of hearing in one ear. Safety in using tree stands, like safety in most situations, is a matter of combining good equipment and the usual caution.

Tree stands work because in their evolutionary history deer never had to scan the tree for enemies. Most of the natural predators that have attacked them have been at ground level. Consequently, deer often ignore completely the possibility that there may be trouble in the trees above them.

In recent times, however, increasing numbers of hunters have reported that the deer are catching on. Deer are highly adaptable animals. It stands to reason that, sooner or later, they would discover hunters perched on little platforms above them. So don't be too surprised if you are spotted up there.

Use of a tree stand still requires cautious attention to being quiet and not moving, as well as to wind direction and where the cone of odors from your body might be in relation to approaching deer.

Deer Calls

There are times when a deer call will help get an animal's attention and bring it closer to investigate the source. Increasingly, hunters who understand this are making good use of calls. Research by biologists reveals that all deer, young and old, commonly make more sounds than most people are aware of.

The vocalization best known to hunters is the explosive snort of the startled deer. What many do not realize is that a buck may also snort as a challenge to another buck. This is a brief series of snorts, and such a series issued on a deer call sometimes brings a buck to a hunter's stand in a hurry.

Another deer call imitates the bleat of the fawn as it tries to attract its mother's attention. This bleat has also been known to attract other deer, including bucks carrying heavy racks.

Calling deer is a specialized challenge, a technique the advanced hunter may add to his list of tricks as he learns more and more about deer behavior under various circumstances. Issuing just the right call to bring a deer within range adds to the excitement, and having a deer call available when nothing else seems to work might be enough to bring a deer into range.

Properly used, a deer call may bring a buck into range.

An excellent way to learn deer calls and rattling techniques is with the aid of one of the expert tapes available. Use of electronic aids when actually hunting is widely illegal.

Rattling Antlers

When two bucks fight during the rutting season, the sounds of their clashing antlers fill the surrounding woods, often drawing other bucks to the scene. This was certain to be noticed by hunters looking for new techniques for bringing deer closer. Texas whitetail hunters reasoned that the contest could be staged by a person rattling a set of antlers together. As a result, thousands of hunters became enthusiastic rattlers, carrying their sets of "horns" with them whenever they went deer hunting.

Their method is simple enough. Obtain a set of antlers, right and left, from a recently killed deer, take up a stand, and rattle antlers together. Skilled rattlers add refinements to make it sound even more like a struggle between two large bucks. They scuff their feet through the leaves, whip the bushes around a little, hit the antlers on rocks and trees, and anything else to set the rutting bucks into action.

The idea spread to many parts of the country because experience has shown that it will attract deer during the rutting season wherever it is tried.

Old dry antlers tend to lose their natural resonance and should be replaced by new ones. A Texas biologist created and tested a set of antlers made of plastic, working with the material until it matched perfectly the pitch of the genuine item. He reported that his artificial antlers brought in the big bucks as surely as did antlers collected from the heads of deer.

TEN
TROPHY HUNTING

Deer hunters may settle for a legal doe or buck with small antlers, but they dream of a genuine trophy buck coming within range. This outstanding whitetail was taken in Ohio, which is nationally famous for its trophy-size bucks. *Ohio Division of Wildlife*

When the New York deer season arrived some years ago, an Allegany County farmer named Roosevelt Luckey had his deer-hunting plan all figured out. There was one special buck he wanted. Several times he had seen the animal slipping through a strip of woodland at the back of the place. This whitetail monarch labored beneath a set of antlers that looked like twin sassafras trees.

One day Luckey, with his old 12-gauge in hand, managed to stalk the buck and send a rifled slug through the underbrush and the deer dropped on the spot.

It was the first year the deer season had been open in Allegany County since deer began returning to that part of the state about 1920. This no doubt helped to account for the fact that the fine rack was still in the woods. The chance of finding another like it there is slim indeed—and, for that matter, slim anywhere.

Luckey knew he had a good one from the beginning, but he probably didn't know just how good. But he saved the entire head, including the important lower jaw, by which biologists figure out the age of deer. The buck was four and a half years old, right in his prime, when Luckey got to him. He hung the head in his garage and sent word to the game protector to stop by. The game protector was as excited as a kid at Coney Island. He acquired the antlers for the New York Conservation Department. When the Boone and Crockett Club representatives finished measuring the rack, they scored it 198 3/8 points. The buck was the world's record whitetail in its class for many years.

This trophy was later moved to the New York Conservation Department's Zoo and Exhibit shop at the Wildlife Center off Route 43, southwest of Albany.

There's a little of the trophy hunter in us all. No matter how much a person talks about "good eating deer," it's the rare meat hunter who would pass up a magnificent rack. (For that matter, there's a good chance that the big buck, if he's fat, also offers the finest venison.) Big racks monopolize bull-session time in deer-hunting camps. The rack of the buck is a thing of mystery, a status symbol to the deer that wears it as well as to the hunter who hangs it on his wall.

There was a time, and not too long ago, when trophy heads were scored on simple measurements. Length and spread determined their rank. But this left many factors unmeasured and formed the foundation for many an argument. There was a need for a more detailed system of scoring.

In 1949 the Boone and Crockett Club, organized in 1887 by Theodore Roosevelt, and a few other hunter-conservationists, took steps to set up a scoring system to recognize trophies on the basis of their overall excellence rather than on one or two measurements. For a start, this committee had the detailed scoring plans worked out by Dr. James L. Clark in 1935 and famed trophy hunter Grancel Fitz in 1939. These two men served on the new Boone and Crockett six-man committee. The committee submitted the final system to 250 noted big-game hunters, taxidermists, guides, scientists, and wildlife administrators. Recognized authorities were chosen to make the measurements of record heads. This system was first put to use in 1950.

One thing the committee recognized was the wide variation that can show up in deer antlers. A normal or typical set is a beautiful, symmetrical, curved, and matched creation. But antlers often come in freak shapes. Consequently both mule deer and whitetails are judged in two classes, typical and non-typical.

At three-year intervals the Boone and Crockett Club determines the finest trophies, and grants awards and certificates for all that qualify. The classes for deer include whitetails, typical and non-typical; Coues deer, typical and non-typical; mule deer, typical and non-typical; Sitka blacktail; and Columbia blacktail. The deadline is December 31 of the last year of the period. Owners must pay crating, shipping, and insurance costs. Correspondence on the subject should go to Boone and Crockett Club, 205 South Patrick Street, Alexandria, Va. 22314.

The scoring sheets (on the following pages) show the numerous measurements made on a head to determine its rank. Heads are measured at least sixty days after the animal is killed to allow for uniform shrinkage, and measuring is done with quarter-inch-wide flexible steel tapes.

In recent years the taxidermist's art has flowered to the point where you may never be entirely certain that the rack of antlers on the wall is real. Antlers are now being reproduced from casts, which are then used to make as many fiberglass reproductions as the market demands. The fiberglass versions are almost impossible for the average person to tell from the real thing.

Some taxidermists even know how to increase the size of a set of antlers by adding inches to the length of the points, then making casts of them. Antler casts are sometimes sold for use as gun racks, hat racks, or wall decorations.

For some reason western and eastern hunters have developed different systems for counting the points on a deer's rack. In the West, they count only the points on a single antler. Easterners count the whole set. The western deer bearing four points will probably rate as an eight-pointer back east.

OFFICIAL SCORING SYSTEM FOR NORTH AMERICAN BIG GAME TROPHIES

Records of North American
     Big Game

BOONE AND CROCKETT CLUB

205 South Patrick Street
Alexandria, Virginia 22314

Minimum Score:
  whitetail 170
  Coues'   110

TYPICAL
WHITETAIL AND COUES' DEER

Kind of Deer_____

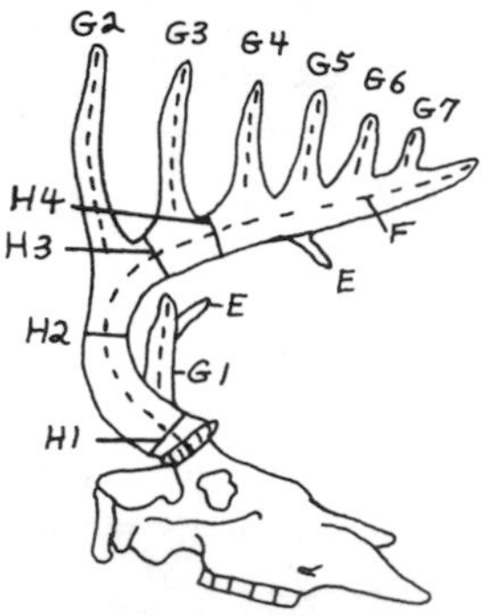

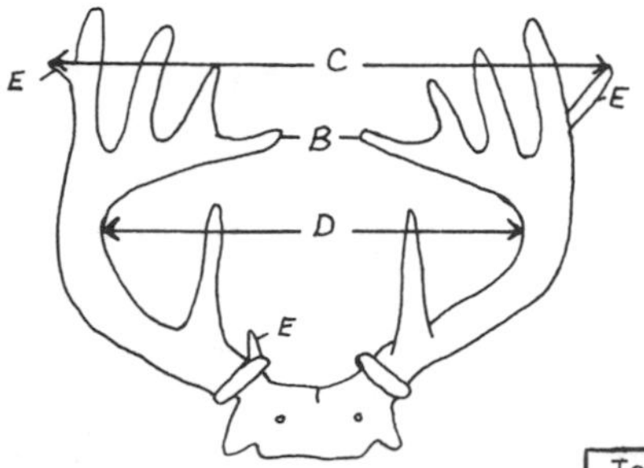

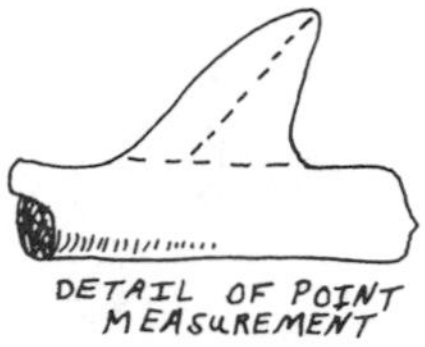

DETAIL OF POINT
MEASUREMENT

Abnormal Points	
Right	Left
Total to E	

SEE OTHER SIDE FOR INSTRUCTIONS			Column 1	Column 2	Column 3	Column 4
	R.	L.	Spread Credit	Right Antler	Left Antler	Difference
A. Number of Points on Each Antler						
B. Tip to Tip Spread						
C. Greatest Spread						
D. Inside Spread of Main Beams — Credit may equal but not exceed length of longer antler						
IF Spread exceeds longer antler, enter difference.						
E. Total of Lengths of all Abnormal Points						
F. Length of Main Beam						
G-1. Length of First Point, if present						
G-2. Length of Second Point						
G-3. Length of Third Point						
G-4. Length of Fourth Point, if present						
G-5. Length of Fifth Point, if present						
G-6. Length of Sixth Point, if present						
G-7. Length of Seventh Point, if present						
H-1. Circumference at Smallest Place Between Burr and First Point						
H-2. Circumference at Smallest Place Between First and Second Points						
H-3. Circumference at Smallest Place Between Second and Third Points						
H-4. Circumference at Smallest Place between Third and Fourth Points (see back if G-4 is missing)						
TOTALS						

ADD	Column 1		Exact locality where killed
	Column 2		Date killed By whom killed
	Column 3		Present owner
	Total		Address
SUBTRACT Column 4			Guide's Name and Address
FINAL SCORE			Remarks: (Mention any abnormalities or unique qualities)

I certify that I have measured the above trophy on _____ 19_____
at (address) _____ State _____
                                              City   State
and that these measurements and data are, to the best of my knowledge and belief, made in accordance
with the instructions given.

Witness: _____ Signature: _____
                                                      OFFICIAL MEASURER [ ][ ][ ][ ]

INSTRUCTIONS FOR MEASURING WHITETAIL AND COUES' DEER

All measurements must be made with a ¼-inch flexible steel tape to the nearest one-eighth of an inch.
Wherever it is necessary to change direction of measurement, mark a control point and swing tape at
this point. Enter fractional figures in eighths, without reduction. Official measurements cannot
be taken for at least sixty days after the animal was killed.

A. Number of Points on Each Antler. To be counted a point, a projection must be at least one inch
long and its length must exceed the width of its base. All points are measured from tip of point to
nearest edge of beam as illustrated. Beam tip is counted as a point but not measured as a point.

B. Tip to Tip Spread is measured between tips of main beams.

C. Greatest Spread is measured between perpendiculars at a right angle to the center line of the
skull at widest part whether across main beams or points.

D. Inside Spread of Main Beams is measured at a right angle to the center line of the skull at widest point between main beams. Enter this measurement again in Spread Credit column if it is less
than or equal to the length of longer antler; if longer, enter longer antler length for Spread Credit.

E. Total of lengths of all Abnormal Points. Abnormal points are those nontypical in location (points
originating from points or from sides or bottom of main beam) or extra points beyond the normal pattern
of up to eight normal points, including beam tip, per antler. Measure in usual manner and enter in
appropriate blanks.

F. Length of Main Beam is measured from lowest outside edge of burr over outer curve to the most
distant point of what is, or appears to be, the main beam. The point of beginning is that point on
the burr where the center line along the outer curve of the beam intersects the burr, then following
generally the line of the illustration.

G-1-2-3-4-5-6-7. Length of Normal Points. Normal points project from the top of the main beam. They
are measured from nearest edge of main beam over outer curve to tip. Lay the tape along the outer
curve of the beam so that the top edge of the tape coincides with the top edge of the beam on both
sides of the point to determine baseline for point measurements. Record point lengths in appropriate
blanks.

H-1-2-3-4. Circumferences are taken as detailed for each measurement. If brow point is missing, take
H-1 and H-2 at smallest place between burr and G-2. If G-4 is missing, take H-4 halfway between G-3
and tip of main beam.

* * * * * * * * * * * *

FAIR CHASE STATEMENT FOR ALL HUNTER-TAKEN TROPHIES

To make use of the following methods shall be deemed as UNFAIR CHASE and unsportsmanlike, and any
trophy obtained by use of such means is disqualified from entry for Awards.

    I.   Spotting or herding game from the air, followed by landing in its vicinity
         for pursuit;
    II. Herding or pursuing game with motor-powered vehicles;
    III. Use of electronic communications for attracting, locating or observing
         game, or guiding the hunter to such game;
    IV. Hunting game confined by artificial barriers, including escape-proof fencing;
         or hunting game transplanted solely for the purpose of commercial shooting.
    ****

I certify that the trophy scored on this chart was not taken in UNFAIR CHASE as defined above by the
Boone and Crockett Club. I further certify that it was taken in full compliance with local game laws
of the state, province, or territory.

Date_____ Signature of Hunter _____
(Have signature notarized by a Notary Public)

OFFICIAL SCORING SYSTEM FOR NORTH AMERICAN BIG GAME TROPHIES

Records of North American Big Game	BOONE AND CROCKETT CLUB	205 South Patrick Street Alexandria, Virginia 22314

Minimum Score:
  mule   195
  blacktail 130

TYPICAL
MULE AND BLACKTAIL DEER

Kind of Deer _____

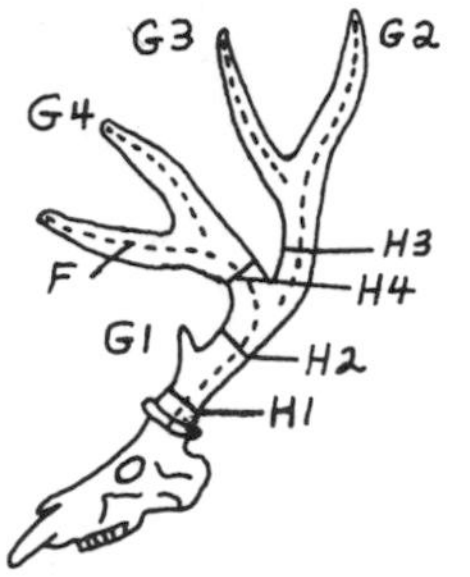

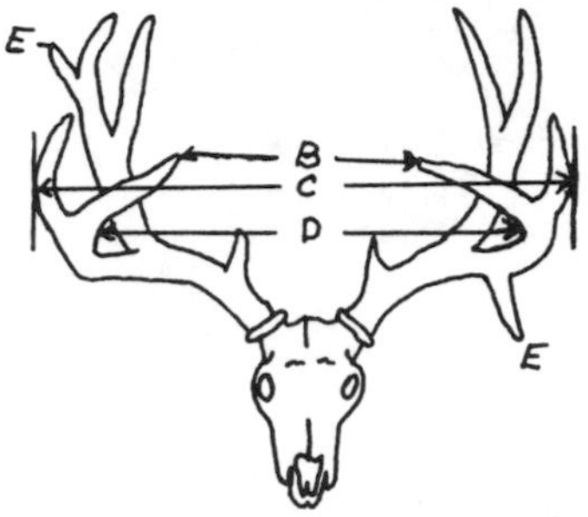

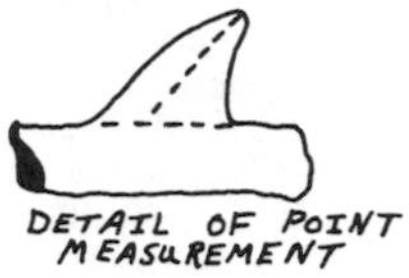

DETAIL OF POINT
MEASUREMENT

Abnormal Points	
Right	Left
Total to E	

SEE OTHER SIDE FOR INSTRUCTIONS		R.	L.	Column 1 Spread Credit	Column 2 Right Antler	Column 3 Left Antler	Column 4 Difference
A.	Number of points on Each Antler						
B.	Tip to Tip Spread						
C.	Greatest Spread						
D.	Inside Spread of Main Beams	Credit may equal but not exceed length of longer antler					
	IF Spread exceeds longer antler, enter difference						
E.	Total of Lengths of Abnormal Points						
F.	Length of Main Beam						
G-1.	Length of First Point, if present						
G-2.	Length of Second Point						
G-3.	Length of Third Point, if present						
G-4.	Length of Fourth Point, if present						
H-1.	Circumference at Smallest Place Between Burr and First Point						
H-2.	Circumference at Smallest Place Between First and Second Points						
H-3.	Circumference at Smallest Place Between Main Beam and Third Point						
H-4.	Circumference at Smallest Place Between Second and Fourth Points						
	TOTALS						

ADD	Column 1		Exact locality where killed
	Column 2		Date killed By whom killed
	Column 3		Present owner
	TOTAL		Address
SUBTRACT Column 4			Guide's Name and Address
FINAL SCORE			Remarks: (Mention any abnormalities or unique qualities)

I certify that I have measured the above trophy on _____ 19 _____
at (address) _____ City _____ State _____
and that these measurements and data are, to the best of my knowledge and belief, made in accordance
with the instructions given.

Witness: _____ Signature: _____

OFFICIAL MEASURER ☐ ☐ ☐ ☐

INSTRUCTIONS FOR MEASURING MULE AND BLACKTAIL DEER

All measurements must be made with a ¼-inch flexible steel tape to the nearest one-eighth of an inch.
Wherever it is necessary to change direction of measurement, mark a control point and swing tape at
this point. Enter fractional figures in eighths, without reduction. Official measurements cannot
be taken for at least sixty days after the animal was killed.

A. Number of Points on Each Antler. To be counted a point, a projection must be at least one inch
long and its length must exceed the width of its base. All points are measured from tip of point to
nearest edge of beam as illustrated. Beam tip is counted as a point but not measured as a point.

B. Tip to Tip Spread is measured between tips of main beams.

C. Greatest Spread is measured between perpendiculars at a right angle to the center line of the
skull at widest part whether across main beams or points.

D. Inside Spread of Main Beams is measured at a right angle to the center line of the skull at widest point between main beams. Enter this measurement again in Spread Credit column if it is less
than or equal to the length of longer antler; if longer, enter longer antler length for Spread Credit.

E. Total Lengths of all Abnormal Points. Abnormal points are those nontypical in location such as
points originating from a point (exception: G-3 originates from G-2 in perfectly normal fashion) or
from sides or bottom of main beam or any points beyond the normal pattern of five (including beam
tip) per antler. Measure each abnormal point in usual manner and enter in appropriate blanks.

F. Length of Main Beam is measured from lowest outside edge of burr over outer curve to the tip of
the main beam. The point of beginning is that point on the burr where the center line along the
outer curve of the beam intersects the burr, then following generally the line of the illustration.

G-1-2-3-4. Length of Normal Points. Normal points are the brow and the upper and lower forks as
shown in the illustration. They are measured from nearest edge of beam over outer curve to tip.
Lay the tape along the outer curve of the beam so that the top edge of the tape coincides with the
top edge of the beam on both sides of the point to determine baseline for point measurement. Record
point lengths in appropriate blanks.

H-1-2-3-4. Circumferences are taken as detailed for each measurement. If brow point is missing,
take H-1 and H-2 at smallest place between burr and G-2. If G-3 is missing, take H-3 halfway between
the base and tip of second point. If G-4 is missing, take H-4 halfway between the second point and
tip of main beam.   * * * * * * * * * * * *

FAIR CHASE STATEMENT FOR ALL HUNTER-TAKEN TROPHIES

To make use of the following methods shall be deemed as UNFAIR CHASE and unsportsmanlike, and any
trophy obtained by use of such means is disqualified from entry for Awards.

  I.   Spotting or herding game from the air, followed by landing in its vicinity
       for pursuit;
 II.   Herding or pursuing game with motor-powered vehicles;
III.   Use of electronic communications for attracting, locating or observing
       game, or guiding the hunter to such game;
 IV.   Hunting game confined by artificial barriers, including escape-proof fencing;
       or hunting game transplanted solely for the purpose of commercial shooting.
       ****

I certify that the trophy scored on this chart was not taken in UNFAIR CHASE as defined above by the
Boone and Crockett Club. I further certify that it was taken in full compliance with local game laws
of the state, province, or territory.

Date _____ Signature of Hunter _____

(Have signature notarized by a Notary Public)

OFFICIAL SCORING SYSTEM FOR NORTH AMERICAN BIG GAME TROPHIES

Records of North American
     Big Game

BOONE AND CROCKETT CLUB

205 South Patrick Street
Alexandria, Virginia 22314

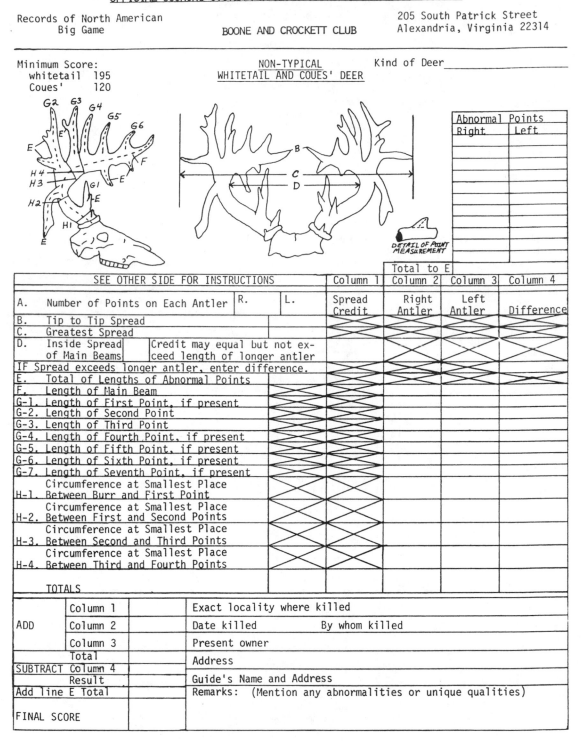

Minimum Score:
  whitetail 195
  Coues'   120

NON-TYPICAL
WHITETAIL AND COUES' DEER

Kind of Deer_____

| Abnormal Points | |
| Right | Left |

Total to E

SEE OTHER SIDE FOR INSTRUCTIONS		R.	L.	Column 1	Column 2	Column 3	Column 4
A.	Number of Points on Each Antler			Spread Credit	Right Antler	Left Antler	Difference
B.	Tip to Tip Spread						
C.	Greatest Spread						
D.	Inside Spread of Main Beams	Credit may equal but not exceed length of longer antler					
IF Spread exceeds longer antler, enter difference.							
E.	Total of Lengths of Abnormal Points						
F.	Length of Main Beam						
G-1.	Length of First Point, if present						
G-2.	Length of Second Point						
G-3.	Length of Third Point						
G-4.	Length of Fourth Point, if present						
G-5.	Length of Fifth Point, if present						
G-6.	Length of Sixth Point, if present						
G-7.	Length of Seventh Point, if present						
H-1.	Circumference at Smallest Place Between Burr and First Point						
H-2.	Circumference at Smallest Place Between First and Second Points						
H-3.	Circumference at Smallest Place Between Second and Third Points						
H-4.	Circumference at Smallest Place Between Third and Fourth Points						
	TOTALS						

ADD	Column 1		Exact locality where killed
	Column 2		Date killed By whom killed
	Column 3		Present owner
	Total		Address
SUBTRACT	Column 4		
	Result		Guide's Name and Address
Add line E Total			Remarks: (Mention any abnormalities or unique qualities)
FINAL SCORE			

I certify that I have measured the above trophy on _____ 19 _____ __
at (address) _____ City _____ State _____
and that these measurements and data are, to the best of my knowledge and belief, made in accordance
with the instructions given.

Witness: _____ Signature: _____

OFFICIAL MEASURER

INSTRUCTIONS FOR MEASURING NON-TYPICAL WHITETAIL AND COUES' DEER

All measurements must be made with a ¼-inch flexible steel tape to the nearest one-eighth of an inch.
Wherever it is necessary to change direction of measurement, mark a control point and swing tape at
this point. Enter fractional figures in eighths, without reduction. Official measurements cannot
be taken for at least sixty days after the animal was killed.

A. Number of Points on Each Antler. To be counted a point, a projection must be at least one inch
long and its length must exceed the width of its base. All points are measured from tip of point to
nearest edge of beam as illustrated. Beam tip is counted as a point but not measured as a point.

B. Tip to Tip Spread is measured between tips of main beams.

C. Greatest Spread is measured between perpendiculars at a right angle to the center line of the
skull at widest part whether across main beams or points.

D. Inside Spread of Main Beams is measured at a right angle to the center line of the skull at widest point between main beams. Enter this measurement again in Spread Credit column if it is less
than or equal to the length of longer antler; if longer, enter longer antler length for Spread Credit.

E. Total of Lengths of all Abnormal Points. Abnormal points are those nontypical in location (points
originating from points or from sides or bottom of main beam) or extra points beyond the normal pattern
of up to eight normal points, including beam tip, per antler. Measure in usual manner and enter in
appropriate blanks.

F. Length of Main Beam is measured from lowest outside edge of burr over outer curve to the most distant point of what is, or appears to be, the main beam. The point of beginning is that point on the
burr where the center line along the outer curve of the beam intersects the burr, then following generally the line of the illustration.

G-1-2-3-4-5-6-7. Length of Normal Points. Normal points project from the top of the main beam.
They are measured from nearest edge of main beam over outer curve to tip. Lay the tape along the
outer curve of the beam so that the top edge of the tape coincides with the beam on both sides of
the point to determine baseline for point measurement. Record point lengths in appropriate blanks.

H-1-2-3-4. Circumferences are taken as detailed for each measurement. If brow point is missing,
take H-1 and H-2 at smallest place between burr and G-2. If G-3 is missing, take H-3 halfway between
the base and tip of second point. If G-4 is missing, take H-4 halfway between the second point and
tip of main beam.
                          * * * * * * * * * * *
FAIR CHASE STATEMENT FOR ALL HUNTER-TAKEN TROPHIES
To make use of the following methods shall be deemed as UNFAIR CHASE and unsportsmanlike, and any
trophy obtained by use of such means is disqualified from entry for Awards.
    I.   Spotting or herding game from the air, followed by landing in its vicinity
         for pursuit;
    II. Herding or pursuing game with motor-powered vehicles;
    III. Use of electronic communications for attracting, locating or observing
         game, or guiding the hunter to such game;
    IV. Hunting game confined by artificial barriers, including escape-proof fencing;
         or hunting game transplanted solely for the purpose of commercial shooting.
         ****
I certify that the trophy scored on this chart was not taken in UNFAIR CHASE as defined above by the
Boone and Crockett Club. I further certify that it was taken in full compliance with local game laws
of the state, province, or territory.
Date_____Signature of Hunter_____
(Have signature notarized by a Notary Public)

OFFICIAL SCORING SYSTEM FOR NORTH AMERICAN BIG GAME TROPHIES

Records of North American Big Game	BOONE AND CROCKETT CLUB	205 South Patrick Street Alexandria, Virginia 22314

Minimum Score: 240

NON-TYPICAL MULE DEER

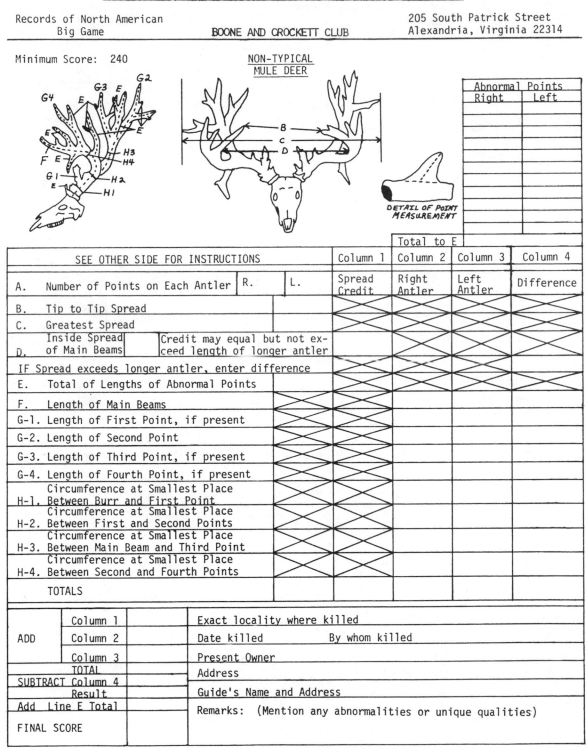

DETAIL OF POINT MEASUREMENT

Abnormal Points	
Right	Left
Total to E	

SEE OTHER SIDE FOR INSTRUCTIONS			Column 1	Column 2	Column 3	Column 4
	R.	L.	Spread Credit	Right Antler	Left Antler	Difference
A. Number of Points on Each Antler						
B. Tip to Tip Spread						
C. Greatest Spread						
D. Inside Spread of Main Beams — Credit may equal but not exceed length of longer antler						
IF Spread exceeds longer antler, enter difference						
E. Total of Lengths of Abnormal Points						
F. Length of Main Beams						
G-1. Length of First Point, if present						
G-2. Length of Second Point						
G-3. Length of Third Point, if present						
G-4. Length of Fourth Point, if present						
H-1. Circumference at Smallest Place Between Burr and First Point						
H-2. Circumference at Smallest Place Between First and Second Points						
H-3. Circumference at Smallest Place Between Main Beam and Third Point						
H-4. Circumference at Smallest Place Between Second and Fourth Points						
TOTALS						

ADD	Column 1		Exact locality where killed
	Column 2		Date killed By whom killed
	Column 3		Present Owner
TOTAL			Address
SUBTRACT Column 4			
Result			Guide's Name and Address
Add Line E Total			Remarks: (Mention any abnormalities or unique qualities)
FINAL SCORE			

I certify that I have measured the above trophy on _____ 19_____
at (address) _____ City _____ State _____
and that these measurements and data are, to the best of my knowledge and belief, made in accordance
with the instructions given.

Witness: _____ Signature: _____

OFFICIAL MEASURER				

INSTRUCTIONS FOR MEASURING NON-TYPICAL MULE DEER

All measurements must be made with a ¼-inch flexible steel tape to the nearest one-eighth of an inch. Wherever it is necessary to change direction of measurement, mark a control point and swing tape at this point. Enter fractional figures in eighths, without reduction. Official measurements cannot be taken for at least sixty days after the animal was killed.

A. Number of Points on Each Antler. To be counted a point, a projection must be at least one inch long and its length must exceed the width of its base. All points are measured from tip of point to nearest edge of beam as illustrated. Beam tip is counted as a point but not measured as a point.

B. Tip to Tip Spread is measured between tips of main beams.

C. Greatest Spread is measured between perpendiculars at a right angle to the center line of the skull at widest part whether across main beams or points.

D. Inside Spread of Main Beams is measured at a right angle to the center line of the skull at widest point between main beams. Enter this measurement again in Spread Credit column if it is less than or equal to the length of longer antler; if longer, enter longer antler length for Spread Credit.

E. Total of Lengths of all Abnormal Points. Abnormal points are those nontypical in location or points beyond the normal pattern of five (including beam tip) per antler. Mark the points that are normal, as defined below. All other points are considered abnormal and are entered in appropriate blanks, after measurement in usual manner.

F. Length of Main Beam is measured from lowest outside edge of burr over outer curve to the tip of the main beam. The point of beginning is that point on the burr where the center line along the outer curve of the beam intersects the burr, then following generally the line of the illustration.

G-1-2-3-4. Length of Normal Points. Normal points are the brow and the upper and lower forks, as shown in the illustration. They are measured from nearest edge of beam over outer curve to tip. Lay the tape along the outer curve of the beam so that the top edge of the tape coincides with the top edge of the beam on both sides of the point to determine baseline for point measurement. Record point lengths in appropriate blanks.

H-1-2-3-4. Circumferences are taken as detailed for each measurement. If brow point is missing, take H-1 and H-2 at smallest place between burr and G-2. If G-3 is missing, take H-3 halfway between the base and tip of second point. If G-4 is missing, take H-4 halfway between the second point and tip of main beam.   * * * * * * * * * * * *

FAIR CHASE STATEMENT FOR ALL HUNTER-TAKEN TROPHIES

To make use of the following methods shall be deemed as UNFAIR CHASE and unsportsmanlike and any trophy obtained by use of such means is disqualified from entry for Awards.

  I.   Spotting or herding game from the air, followed by landing in its vicinity
       for pursuit;
  II. Herding or pursuing game with motor-powered vehicles;
  III. Use of electronic communications for attracting, locating or observing
       game, or guiding the hunter to such game;
  IV. Hunting game confined by artificial barriers, including escape-proof fencing;
       or hunting game transplanted solely for the purpose of commercial shooting.
       ****

I certify that the trophy scored on this chart was not taken in UNFAIR CHASE as defined above by the Boone and Crockett Club. I further certify that it was taken in full compliance with local game laws of the state, province, or territory.

Date_____ Signature of Hunter_____
(Have signature notarized by a Notary Public)

The Mystery of Antlers

Antlers are one of nature's truly remarkable creations. They are found only on members of the deer family throughout the world. The smallest of the deer, the foot-high pudu of the South American Andes wears tiny antlers sometimes less than an inch long. I once spotted one of these little bucks standing on a log in the bushes as we floated by on a wilderness trout-fishing trip, and the somewhat fuzzy picture I snapped shows its thumb-sized antlers.

In early summer the bucks must feed heavily enough to provide for body maintenance plus the rapid growth of their heavy antlers.

At the other end of the antler spectrum stand the giant moose, elk, and caribou. The largest antlers the world ever knew were apparently those of the now extinct giant Irish elk that wore moose-like antlers sometimes reaching ten feet from tip to tip.

Among most of the deer, antlers are worn by the bucks only. The exceptions are the caribou and reindeer, among which both sexes are antlered, although the antlers of the female are smaller than those carried by the male. Antlers are shed each year, following the end of the breeding season. But spring is hardly underway again before the buck's new set of antlers begins to grow. They grow rapidly, providing food is in good supply.

While they are growing, the antlers are covered with velvet, a soft modified skin through which blood circulates, carrying nourishment to the growing parts.

Growing a new set of antlers takes from three to five months regardless of the size of the antlers. Larger antlers simply grow faster. By late summer the antlers are completing their growth, and as the buck goes into autumn his antlers harden, the blood circulation ceases, and the velvet dies. The bucks hurry the loss of velvet along by rubbing the antlers against saplings, frequently injuring the tree so severely that it dies. These saplings rubbed free of their bark are a sure sign of the presence of at least one breeding-age buck in the area.

Antlers are different from horns. Horns are not

Antlers are the mammal world's only example of regularly regenerated body parts. Different from horn, antlers are bone.

seasonal. They are not replaced. Instead of being bone, as in the case of antlers, horns are composed of keratin, the same material which comprises fingernails and hair. Keratin is a dead material while antlers are living, growing bone with their own blood supply. Antlers are unique in the world of animals because they are replaced each year. Scientists are interested in how antlers originate and grow because these are the only examples of regular regeneration of body parts by mammals. They may even hold clues that will someday help the human body replace lost parts.

The deer's antlers are a luxury. Bucks could have evolved without them, as did the males of most animal species. Growing this amount of new bone once a year, in preparation for the breeding season, makes heavy demands on the deer. Following the breeding season, the antlers drop off and for a few months the buck is free of his breeding duties while he rebuilds his strength, stores fat, and grows that next set of weapons.

The earliest stage of antler development starts before the buck is born when he develops the pedicels which are the permanent stumps, or bases on the skull, from which his antlers will grow. While the antlers that grow on them drop off every year, the pedicels remain. They carry the genetic code that determines the size and shape of the antlers.

The increasing hours of daylight, starting in late winter, trigger renewed glandular activity in the buck's body, and this brings on an increased flow of the male sex hormone, testosterone. The increasing supply of testosterone causes the antlers to resume growing.

Long-time deer hunters often complain that there are fewer trophy-sized bucks than there once were, and in some instances this is true. One explanation is that there are far more hunters today and not enough big bucks to go around. But closing the season on spike bucks may not be the answer. If there is an overpopulation of deer, and food supplies must stretch for the population, the energy a buck consumes first goes to regular body maintenance, depriving the antlers of the food needed for full development. Therefore, the buck that is going to grow impressive antlers needs abundant food, but he also needs to carry the genes for big antlers, and he gets these from having trophy-sized ancestors. Good nutrition only allows him to live up to his genetic potential.

This has been proved through solid research by Texas biologists. Hunters who believe that spike bucks should be left to grow so they become trophy-bearing bucks sometimes criticize biologists for advocating open seasons on spike bucks. In Texas, both spike bucks and bucks with trophy-sized antlers were kept in enclosures and fed identical rations. The biologists found that bucks with superior racks fathered offspring with big antlers when bred to does from families that also had heavily antlered males. Meanwhile, spike bucks tended to father more spike bucks whether food was plentiful or not. The conclusion by the Texas researchers, as well as those in other states, is that when good-quality deer foods are available spike bucks, instead of being protected, should be hunted heavily. Saving the spike bucks from hunting may actually be building up the percentage of spikes in the herd.

Antlers are no reliable indicator of the buck's age. When food supplies are abundant, the antlers

This Wyoming mule deer produced the kind of antlers that hunters hang on their walls.

Saving the spike bucks may not guarantee trophy heads. Some deer families are genetically restricted to growing spikes, regardless of age or nutrition. *Karl H. Maslowski*

gain in size each year up to about age six. In later years, they tend to grow smaller again. In areas overpopulated with deer, even the six-year-old may grow inferior antlers at an age when he should be at his finest. In one study in Pennsylvania, 61 percent of the bucks taken each year were one and a half years old and averaged 3.9 points, which is considered a fair set of antlers for deer of this age.

Young bucks in their first fall should be button bucks. They will show their first significant antlers in their second autumn when one and a half years old, and on good range may have from four to six points by this time. The eight pointer, with good heavy antler beams if he has lived well, may be three and a half years old. But antler condition is not a safe way to judge a deer's age.

Typically, the antlers are gracefully curved with matching points and the left and right antlers are mirror images of each other. But some deer grow non-typical antlers with strange shapes and points reaching out in various directions. These non-typicals are usually the result of genetics rather than injury. The pedicel, which gives rise to the new antlers, is "programmed" to produce the same kind of antlers year after year.

You might come across a high-scoring buck almost anywhere, but your chances for a big buck are better in some places than others. Although the wilderness was once the finest place to encounter a

trophy deer, some of the most impressive heads now come from farm country where woodland and cropland provide a mixture of quality food and cover. Some of the largest of all bucks are part-time cornfield residents, and this helps account for reports of giant bucks taken from Ohio and other Midwestern states. I know a typical southern Ohio hill farm community where one neighbor seldom gets his corn all harvested before spring. Deer beat trails to his standing corn all through the winter, as do raccoons, wild turkeys, and other wildlife. There is plenty of natural food in the area, but picking corn is easy living, and the deer make the most of it.

Favorite states for trophy whitetails include Ohio, Texas, Virginia, Maine, Missouri, Wisconsin, Michigan, and several others, along with the Canadian provinces of Manitoba, Saskatchewan, and Ontario.

Some of the top mule deer trophy heads have been coming from Wyoming, Colorado, Arizona, Idaho, and Utah.

But trophies are where you find them and even those regions not noted for championship antlers may have a few elusive old dominant bucks lurking around the best hiding and feeding areas.

Among hunters, the interest in big antlers continues to grow. Some of this is stimulated by the fact

The sika, or Japanese deer, is native to the Orient. It wears a dark brown winter coat and a summer coat that is reddish and lined with spots. The adult buck's antlers total eight points.

that collectors now comb the best deer country, tracking down clues they hope will lead them to the world's most spectacular sets of antlers. They collect antlers as some people collect beer cans or valuable old coins. In this secretive business a truly large rack of champion proportions may bring several thousand dollars from a collector.

Even more important in stimulating the interest in antlers may be the various state competitions in which successful trophy hunters assemble each year to compare antlers and receive recognition. Ohio, for example, has an annual day-long celebration of The Buckeye Big Bucks Club, Inc., ending with an awards banquet that draws hundreds of people. Georgia has its Buckarama, drawing thousands of visitors. At these and other such celebrations the big attraction is the display of antlers. Sometimes two hundred or more recently taken bucks score enough points to merit recognition at these special events. Consequently, hunters who take a heavily antlered buck during the open season ask themselves how it would compare with other big bucks.

Occasionally, a set of antlers appears that scores so high it seems no other set will ever top it. One such trophy came from Texas in 1892, a non-typical white-tailed deer that held the record for ninety years.

Then, one November day in 1981, near St. Louis, Missouri, Mike Helland and Dave Beckman came upon a giant buck already dead. While the Texas champion had scored 286 points, this newly discovered Missouri giant, which tooth rings showed to be five and a half years old, took over the championship spot with a score of 333⅞ points. Again, hunters said the new champion would never be beaten out of first place.

Then Dick Idol, research director for *North American Whitetail Magazine,* picked up a clue that led him to Kent, Ohio, to take a look at a very special whitetail whose trophy head was hanging on the barroom wall of a clubhouse. Idol took a close look and knew that it would score well.

This is the famous Hole In The Horn Buck and the astounding non-typical antlers that set him apart from all other whitetails. *Game and Fish Publications*

This buck, like the Missouri buck, was found already dead. The crew of a train spotted the animal beside the railroad tracks. Perhaps it was struck by a train. Nobody knows how it died. But for forty years the rack had hung on the barroom wall, unrecognized as championship material. After forty years of drying it still weighed eleven and a half pounds. It has a spread of 32⅝ inches and has forty-four scoreable points projecting from it in all directions.

Among its unusual features is a hole in one tine of the right antler, a hole that seems to have been made by a small-caliber bullet fired from a poorly aimed gun. This hole gave the buck its name—"The Hole In The Horn Buck."

Some say the spectacular Ohio deer will stand for all time as the world champion non-typical white-tailed buck. But who knows? Somewhere there may already be a set of antlers to edge it out of the top spot.

ELEVEN

LIFE OF A WHITETAIL BUCK

A buck lives from day to day. Some of his days are good. When foods are plentiful he has only to pick and choose. Other days are filled with uncertainties; wintertime brings dwindling food supplies. Some hours are filled with hazards. He must meet them with his sharp senses, speed, and cunning. If he survives disease, poachers, winter starvation, and the hunting seasons, he lives to become a monarch among his kind.

The herd is more important than the single male, but the life of an individual buck is important to that animal and to the hunter who pursues him.

As it is traced in these pictures the life story of the whitetail buck varies only slightly from that of the mule deer or the coastal blacktail. The differences are mostly those arising from geography. The great buck that crosses your sights began his life as a spotted fawn hiding in the grass and underbrush.

Nature equips the new fawn with the ability to lie quietly in one spot for long hours until the doe slips back to feed him. He is almost free of odors that might attract dogs or other animals. His spotted coat blends with his surroundings. *Maslowski & Goodpaster*

The fawn, usually one of twins, gains strength and boldness until he is increasingly able to escape predators, and soon begins to accompany his mother. *U.S. Fish and Wildlife Service*

When three and a half to four months old, he changes his spotted fawn's coat for one more like that of his mother's, and that is what he wears into his first autumn and his first hunting season. He already shows early evidence of antlers. *Karl H. Maslowski*

The following spring, when he is fourteen months old, soft spots erupt on his head and during the summer a set of small antlers grow from these spots. *Tennessee Wildlife Resources Agency, Robert Moore*

With the coming of autumn, when he is a year and a half old, the buck feels the restlessness known to all bucks in this season. But bigger bucks hold positions of dominance. The youngster must grow still-larger antlers. *Maine Department of Inland Fisheries and Wildlife, Ken Gray*

Just as many events in the world of nature follow cycles, so do the coming and going of the buck's antlers. A year later, a larger set of antlers begins to grow rapidly. These are lazy times for the vigorous buck. Food is plentiful and he has only to get out of bed and harvest it. *U.S. Forest Service*

By late summer he has grown fat and sleek, and autumn brings new treats. Apples drop from trees in abandoned orchards. Acorns can be harvested beneath the oak trees.
Karl H. Maslowski

In autumn, the strange restlessness fills him again. He wanders farther and farther through his territory, sorting out the trails of other deer and leaving his own trails for the does to track.

His neck grows big. His temper changes. He roams almost constantly and pays little attention to eating. In the mists of early morning, he encounters a buck of near-equal proportions and his challenge is accepted. With lowered antlers, they shove and push until the other buck, sensing defeat, leaves the woods to the dominant buck. Now he is king.

Men come into the woods with their rifles, just as they come every winter about this time. Evenings they sit around the stove and talk about the deer they have hunted. They recall the same stories they told the year before, and turn early to their bunks in anticipation of this new season's hunt. *Ontario Department of Travel and Publicity*

One of these hunters crosses the trail of the buck and follows it. He searches the underbrush ahead. The buck is moving slowly. The hunter works a zigzagging course across the trail and back. Then suddenly the buck comes out in the open where the hunter waits. *Ontario Department of Travel and Publicity*

In the pocket of his hunting coat he carries his deer tag which he attaches to the antlers of the big buck.

He waits for one of his friends to help drag the buck from the woods. Over the fresh snow the two men have little trouble sliding the buck back to camp. *Ontario Department of Travel and Publicity*

Other deer, some descended from the old buck himself, remain behind. Toward the end of winter they band up—does, fawns, and bucks without their antlers. They eat what they can find to survive the winter. By spring, with its warming days and fresh promise, the does once more will be heavy with fawn. The coming and the going of the buck and the coming and going of the hunter who took him were minor episodes in the centuries-long history of the deer in North America. *U.S. Forest Service*

TWELVE
SHOOTING YOUR DEER

Bill Mead and I were trying to figure out which side of the mountain to hunt when we spotted two big mule deer at the top of the ridge five hundred yards away and quartering toward us. They were running, but not fast, when they dropped down the edge of a rocky little canyon with a fringe of aspen along its floor.

The deer turned to go up the canyon. I was watching them in my scope when suddenly the lead one, a four-point buck, hit the ground an instant before I heard the crack of a rifle. The man who dropped the big deer was standing two hundred yards farther up the canyon. His shot had been skillfully accomplished. "That," said Bill, "is the way to do it."

This is the kind of shot that hunters like to recall later. The distance isn't the most important matter. You'll hear deer hunters tell of shots they made at forty and fifty yards and even less with considerable pride—as long as they were clean kills. But you won't hear much bragging from the man who gut shot his deer or the one who lost a cripple.

There are several reasons for misses or poor shots at deer. Among the common ones are inability to judge distance, shooting at a running deer, lack of knowledge of the deer's anatomy, lack of skill in gun handling, failure to understand the trajectory of your bullet, and nervousness or buck fever.

All the practice, scouting, and waiting finally pay off when the season opens and a buck comes into range.

Judging Distance

The most obvious reason why it is important to judge distance correctly is because you need to restrict yourself to shots within the effective killing range. You may be well equipped to bring down a mule deer at 250 yards, but how far is 250 yards? And, more specifically, is that deer 250 yards away or 450 yards away? The distance will help to determine how close your bullet comes to the point of

aim. If you're shooting a shotgun, your top effective range may be 75 yards. If you convince yourself that it's only 75 yards to a deer that is standing at a real distance of 125 yards, you may at best miss and at worst cripple the animal. With a 12-gauge shooting a 2¾-inch shell, the rifled slug will hit five inches lower at 100 yards than it does at 75. You may get a surprise if you lay off a measured course and find out what 75 yards or 150 yards really looks like in the brush and in the open.

Practice judging distances. Estimate the distance between common objects, then pace them off to see how close you come. Next study the ballistics tables in this book until you understand the trajectory of your bullet or slug. Then determine where your sights are zeroed in and you can figure out how you have to hold on a target to hit the point of aim at various distances. Most deer are shot at relatively short distances, usually fifty yards or less for whitetails. But it's when the shooter tries to extend his range that distances and gun capabilities become most important.

Know Your Gun

Probably the biggest reason of all for missing deer, especially among hunters with limited experience in deer hunting, is a lack of familiarity with their weapons.

Too often we read about today's fine weapons and high-powered ammunition, and figure that's all it takes. Then we wander forth into the deer woods with a new and untried gun or one that is dusty from lack of use. When a buck comes slipping through the brush, we aim and fire. The fine modern weapon and high-powered leads are expected to put venison on the table just as in the advertisements.

It's true that a deer in front of a modern firearm is in some danger, even if the hunter has never fired a round before. But many deer are missed every year by hunters who don't know their guns. A miss, however, is no tragedy. The deer that is hit, but not well enough, is a tragedy. Every deer hunter's aim should be to kill his deer with a single, well-placed shot. Bad shooting can cripple animals, cause suffering, lose deer, and spoil meat.

If you're buying a hunting license, deer tag, shells, gasoline, plus some other odds and ends and

essentials, you had better also set aside some time for gun-handling practice. You owe it to yourself, your companions, and the deer.

Especially if your gun is strange to you, practice offhand shooting until you can swing it into position smoothly and go through the actions you'll be called on to perform when a buck suddenly looms up in front of you. Do at least some practicing bundled in the clothes you'll be wearing when you go deer hunting.

Keep your eyes on the target as you automatically do everything else you must do. Learn to shift your feet automatically to a position of balance, raise your gun, release the safety, find the trigger, fit your cheek to the stock, line up the sights and, in the case of a moving target, swing your body. If you must get down to shoot beneath brush, don't bend at the belt, but drop to one knee instead.

If you're using a scope sight that is strange to you, dry-run practice is especially important. Work at it until you can find the image through the scope immediately.

With iron sights, learn to shoot with both eyes open. Two-eyed vision is natural and gives better depth perception and judgment of distance. Most

Most deer are taken when standing or moving slowly. A running deer, although tempting, often results in a poorly placed shot and an injured animal that is never found.

iron sights obscure part of the deer from the one-eyed shooter.

If possible, practice with a .22 carrying sights similar to those you will use in deer hunting. This can help you get the feel of shooting. The recoil isn't as likely to cause you to develop a flinch, the ammunition is inexpensive, and the muzzle blast is comparatively quiet. This .22 practice can be especially helpful on moving targets.

Most deer are shot when they are standing or just starting to move. Only a small percentage of hunters are good enough to make clean kills consistently on hard-running deer. The temptation is strong, however. In the western states the opportunities for a long shot at a running deer are much more frequent than they are in the East.

But before you commit yourself to one of these running shots, consider what you must accomplish.

Just as in bird shooting, there is the necessity to lead the game. Here's why.

A deer can get up a good head of steam. In 1951, a South Dakota biologist clocked a herd of eight mule deer by pressing them hard in his car for 1.4 miles. He passed the four fawns at twenty-four miles per hour. The adults reached a speed of twenty-nine miles per hour.

During the fall of 1956 a whitetail doe and her fawn were paced over an .8-mile course at a speed of thirty-seven miles per hour. So you can figure that a spooked deer is covering ground at about thirty miles per hour. How much you'll have to lead him depends partly on the angle at which he's running from you.

It also depends on the time it takes you to fire a shell, and how long the bullet takes to get there once you have fired it. At his thirty-mile-per-hour speed, the deer broadside to you is covering forty-four feet per second. If he's one hundred yards away, a high-powered bullet will take about .1 second to get there, and the average person needs an equal time to squeeze off the shot after he makes up his mind. In that fifth of a second the deer has traveled eight to nine feet, which gives you some idea of how much you would have to lead him to score. If he's running at an angle to you, the lead can be reduced.

There is a formula for figuring out how much to lead a running deer. First bear in mind that a deer walks briskly at about four miles per hour, trots at about ten, and runs full tilt at thirty. If the deer is going broadside to you, figure 17.6 times the speed of the deer in miles per hour times the range in yards divided by the average velocity of the bullet in yards per second. You may want to make up a chart in advance and memorize it to give you the lead at various distances for deer traveling at various speeds.

The mule deer, with his jumping gait, is especially difficult to hit while running at top speed. Largely it's a matter of practice in swinging with your target and timing your shot to reach home at the instant his feet touch the ground.

A lot of good hunters are quite willing to let the fast-running shot pass in the interest of good sports-

A responsible hunter wants only a clean kill, and waits until he has an unobstructed shot at a deer within reasonable range.

manship. On the other hand, I have seen riflemen, mostly in the West, who seldom seemed to miss on the fast-running shots. They weren't born with their shooting ability. It came from consistent gun use.

Buck Fever

One deer season my friend Denver Lease watched a buck coming at him. Denver decided to let him come close, but then the deer dipped down into a hollow. Denver expected the buck to come straight up over the edge, but instead he angled down the hollow.

The next thing Denver heard was a resounding shot. Someone had shot at his buck at close range. But the buck came lumbering over the edge of the depression untouched and hitting top speed. Denver waited no longer. He got off a quick sixty-yard shot that dropped the buck. Just then a hard-breathing hunter pulled himself over the edge of the rise behind the buck. Said Denver, without hesitation, "That's my buck."

"I—I know it," the shaking hunter mumbled. "I missed him clean, and at fifteen feet."

Buck fever is not the joke it is often considered. It's a very real barrier to good shooting and sometimes to any shooting. It is a malady usually reserved for the beginning deer hunter.

The attack often makes the hunter fumble until the buck is gone from sight. Sometimes it throws his aim so far off that the deer couldn't be safer if it were in the zoo.

Buck fever is closely related to that feeling of elation that comes to the successful hunter at the moment he bags his buck. If seeing a deer completely unnerves the hunter, the feeling is called "buck fever."

No one who hasn't shot a deer can be certain how he will react when he finds himself face to face with a buck. A few things, however, can help to prevent buck fever. One is familiarity with your weapon. This gives you confidence. Another is preseason scouting of your hunting territory. The more time you can spend in the woods, the more you get to feel at ease there. In the preseason scouting you may even see a deer or two, and the more deer you encounter the less likely you are to freeze when you see a legal one across your gun sights.

Be Sure It's a Deer

Alone in the woods the hunter can become the victim of his imagination. Every noise alerts him. The rustling of a ground squirrel in the leaves becomes the approach of a deer. The hunter may stare at the underbrush until his imagination manufactures a set of antlers. Even good woodsmen are guilty of these mistakes occasionally.

But this is the time for caution. Shooting at an inanimate object might do little more than embarrass you. But no hunter should shoot until absolutely certain of his game, and to shoot at sounds is inexcusable.

Unfortunately some hunters get into the deer woods every year without even having a very good idea of what a live deer looks like. Many objects, animate and inanimate, have, through the years, been shot for deer. One was a stuffed-deer form that an Illinois farmer with a sense of humor stood up in his field in order to see how many hunters would grind to a stop and take a shot. Several dozen did. Others have shot Jersey heifers and have even taken them into the deer-checking station tagged and ready for weighing.

Look twice before you lift your gun. Only when you're absolutely certain that there is a deer in front of you are you ready to shoot. A white handkerchief hanging from a fellow hunter's hip pocket should not be taken for a deer flag, and his gun sticking from behind a tree should not be regarded as the antler of a deer.

Deer hunting is a surprisingly safe sport, partly because of telescopic sights, which enable riflemen to get a closer look at what they see. Primarily, the sport is safe because of the general attitude of caution that most hunters take to the woods and field with them.

Where to Aim

Anytime you aim at a deer, you should aim at one of its vital sections. Knowing where they are isn't difficult to learn, and it's essential if you hope to score clean kills.

A head shot is a good one for a quick kill. But the head of a deer is a small target. Most deer hunters should not risk the head shot. If you hope to have a deer head mounted, you would, of course,

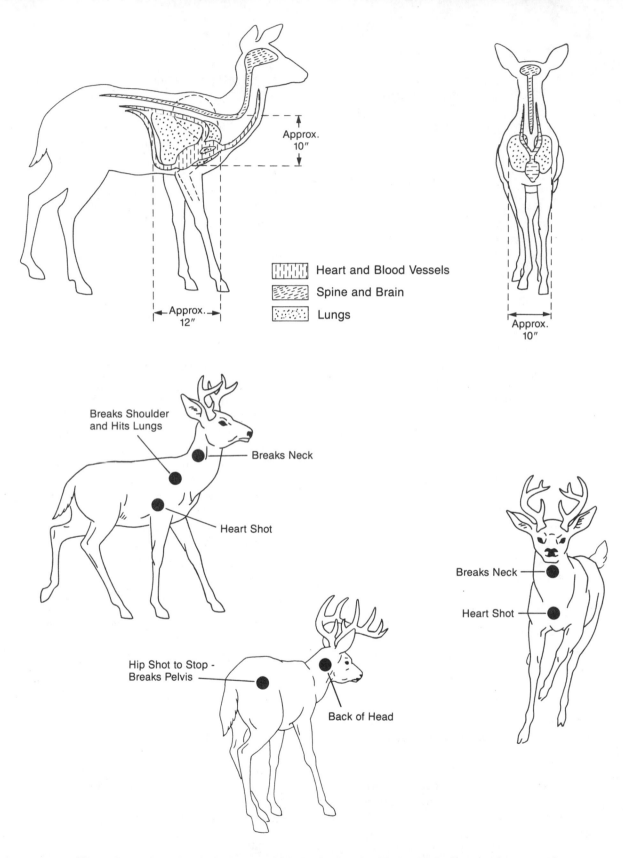

Heart and Blood Vessels

Spine and Brain

Lungs

Approx. 10″

Approx. 12″

Approx. 10″

Breaks Shoulder and Hits Lungs

Breaks Neck

Heart Shot

Breaks Neck

Heart Shot

Hip Shot to Stop - Breaks Pelvis

Back of Head

These charts show the vital areas at which the hunter should aim. If the hunter takes general aim at the entire deer he will probably wound it and it may then travel a long distance and die in a place where it will never be found. The best shot for most hunters is the heart and lung area in the lower front part of the body cavity, behind the shoulder, or above the elbow. *Charts courtesy New York Department of Environmental Conservation*

avoid the head shot. One of the best of all shots on a deer is the neck shot, either in the upper third or in the lower half of the neck. The upper part of the neck carries the spinal column. A high-powered exploding bullet will break it. The windpipe and jugular vein lie in the lower part of the deer's neck, and one bullet or arrow placed there severs them and usually drops the deer on the spot.

What if your shot is at a distance, where a neck shot may miss, or the deer is turned so that you can't get a clean shot at the neck? Then aim at the heart and lung region. For most deer hunters, this is the best bet, unless they're using a scope sight and can lay the cross hairs right on the mark and know from practice that the bullet will go there.

The deer carries his heart and lungs low and forward in the chest cavity. Aim at the rear edge of the shoulder above the foreleg, one third of the way up from the chest line. A few inches high or low will also kill the animal. Don't aim at the middle of the deer's body. A shot too far back may enable him to travel several miles before giving out.

The deer that comes toward you or quarters toward you wears a target in the white patch on his throat. If the deer bounds straight away from you, pass up a shot at the rump. If he stops to turn and stare back at you, that's another story and a welcome opportunity. But be ready to take advantage of it with a quick shot, because if he does stop he probably won't stand for long. If the deer isn't thoroughly spooked, you may be able to stop him with a low-pitched whistle. Sometimes it works.

Once you've shot a deer and you see he's down, keep your gun ready, with a second shell in the chamber, in case he is only stunned. You may or may not need to follow up with a second shot.

Trailing Your Deer

There will be times when you won't know whether or not you scored a hit on your target. If a buck escapes into thick cover the more seasoned hunter follows the deer a few hundred yards to see whether or not it was really as healthy as it appeared at last sight. Especially would they follow the deer that changed pace at the time of shooting or the one that dropped his tail.

The first question, once you've hit a deer or think

you have, is how soon to follow his trail. You will hear arguments on both sides. The injured deer, not thoroughly frightened, will probably lie down within a couple of hundred yards if there is good cover. When this happens you can often find him there half an hour later, dead. If you run after a deer, you will almost surely send him into high gear; that last frantic burst may enable him to cover two or three miles.

There are times, however, when you should not hesitate in following your deer. Somebody else may tag your deer before you go after him. Consider also the possibility that you may reach your crippled deer before he has time to recover from the first shock.

No deer hunter should ever leave a wounded deer without trailing it as far as is humanly possible, no matter how many hours the task might take. If darkness cuts off your search, you may be able to go back and pick up the trail the next morning.

Trailing a deer can be easy if there is snow on the ground. But finding the patch of hair the bullet knocked off, or following a blood trail through brown leaves, calls forth your skill and determination.

Move cautiously and search the cover ahead of you. Look especially closely in the thick cover, where a crippled deer will sometimes hide. If you lose the trail, backtrack until you pick it up once more, and try to work it out again. Two hunters often can trail better than one, providing they are in no hurry and are careful not to obliterate the trail.

You should find your deer within a couple of miles. He is a creature of habit and seldom wants to leave his home territory.

What Your Deer Weighs

Any hunter can be forgiven for overestimating the size of the deer he has just killed, especially if he had to drag it out of the woods by himself. Many a worker at a deer-checking station has had the accuracy of his scales questioned by hunters who couldn't quite believe that they really had overestimated their animal's weight by fifty pounds. But shake the scales as you will, inspect the seal and doubt the manufacturer, it's probably still right. A lot of people think of deer as bigger than they are.

Whitetails measure only thirty to thirty-six inches high at the shoulders, and mule deer a few inches higher.

Depending on where you hunt and the individual you bag, you can expect your adult whitetail to weigh from 75 to about 300 pounds. You'll sometimes hear of a deer that weighed 400 pounds, but that's a rare deer in any camp. Bucks of 250 pounds and more are not unusual through much of the whitetail range in the northeastern states.

In Nebraska, where whitetails come in magnificent proportions, one hunter hog-dressed one out at 310 pounds, or about 380 pounds live weight.

The New York Conservation Department owns the head of a buck killed near Mud Lake in 1890 that weighed 388 pounds.

The averages, however, run well below these figures. The average weight of bucks shot in Pennsylvania is said to run about 115 pounds. In Maine, bucks average out at about 150 pounds, and in New York they are about the same.

Hog-dressed Weight

If you know the hog-dressed weight of your deer (heart, liver, lungs, and all viscera removed)—to find how much it weighed on the hoof and/or how much edible meat you'll wind up with:

(1) Locate hog-dressed weight on left scale. *(Example:* 120 lbs.)
(2) Draw horizontal line to meet line A.
(3) Draw vertical line to meet bottom scale. Read live weight off bottom scale. *(Example:* 154 lbs.)
(4) Draw horizontal line from point where vertical line crosses line B to left scale. Read edible-meat weight from left scale. *(Example:* 87 lbs.)

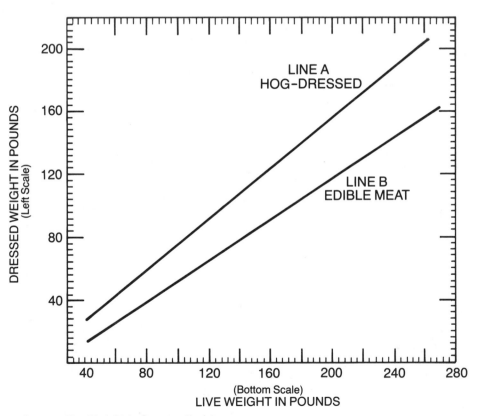

Courtesy New York State Conservationist.

Edible-Meat Weight

If you know the total dressed weight of edible meat from your deer—to find what the live and/or hog-dressed weight was:

(1) Locate edible-meat weight on left scale. *(Example:* 80 lbs.)
(2) Draw horizontal line to meet line B.
(3) Draw vertical line upward to line A. Draw horizontal line to left scale. Read hog-dressed weight from left scale. *(Example:* 111 lbs.)
(4) Draw from the point determined on line B a vertical line to meet bottom scale. Read live weight from bottom scale. *(Example:* 143 lbs.)

Live Weight

If you know the live weight—to find how much your deer will weigh hog-dressed and/or how much edible meat you will realize:

(1) Locate live weight on bottom scale. *(Example:* 120 lbs.)
(2) Draw vertical line to meet line A.
(3) Draw horizontal line to left scale. Read hog-dressed weight off left scale. *(Example:* 92 lbs.)
(4) Draw horizontal line from point where vertical line crosses line B to left scale. Read edible-meat weight from left scale. *(Example:* 66 lbs.)

Remember, dressed weights are read from left scale, live weight from bottom scale. Care should be used so that lines drawn are horizontally and vertically square with graph. Weights obtained by this method may vary by five lbs., high or low.

THIRTEEN
FIELD CARE OF DEER

All through the hunt and up to the moment he takes his deer into possession, the average hunter gives little thought to what he will do with the animal once he has it. A little advance study on the fine points of dressing out and handling a deer in the field can save a lot of venison and add the final reward to the hunt.

A major problem the successful deer hunter faces today is to convince his hamburger-oriented family that venison is really food. Properly handled, venison is among the finest of meats. Like any other meat, it can easily be spoiled, and for all the talk about that "wonderful wild taste" or "gamy flavor," the family collie still enjoys more than his rightful share of the venison dinner. More's the pity, and I have nothing against collies.

I am convinced, however, that there is little excuse for a reasonably youthful deer to be anything but excellent meat. Even the hunter who has never bagged a deer can do a fine job of handling his first one. Just how to go about this task should be part of his planning and study *before* he goes hunting.

Cleaning and taking care of a deer is not highly complicated, nor does it take a great amount of time.

The first step before cleaning your deer is to make sure he's dead. One acquaintance of mine decided to dress his deer at home, only a couple of

Field-dressing a deer, as these Ontario hunters are doing, reduces the animal's weight and, more importantly, allows it to cool quickly. *Ontario Department of Travel and Publicity*

miles from where he shot it. He dragged the animal to his car, stuffed it into the trunk, slammed the lid tight, and headed down the lane. Five minutes later he skidded to a stop in his driveway, jumped from the car, and yelled for his wife to come see. What she saw was soon the story of the week all over the neighborhood. When the trunk lid was opened, the buck, only momentarily stunned by the rifled slug, unfolded himself from his cramped quarters, scrambled out before his amazed captor could do a thing about it, and flew through the broom sedge toward the oak woods beyond.

The next day another deer hunter, six miles from where the buck escaped, brought down a fine animal. It carried a flesh wound in the shoulder plus a deer tag secured to the antler.

One Oregon hunter, who made the mistake of trying to stick his deer before determining that it was dead, fared considerably worse. His knife point revived the buck long enough for the dying deer to leap and strike the hunter in the head with an antler. They both died on the spot.

When you move in on a downed deer, keep your gun handy. Look at the animal's eyes to see if they're glazed over. Determine whether or not he's still breathing. Slashing hooves can deliver deep cuts. If there's any doubt about how dead he is, use another shell to make certain. The best place to deliver this shot is in the base of the neck, where the bullet will break the spinal column and cut major blood vessels to speed up the bleeding.

State laws vary as to when you may place your tag on a deer. Know your law on this point.

The deer that is shot in the heart or lung region will bleed so profusely there's no need to cut his throat. I've seen fine trophy bucks practically decapitated in the interest of bleeding them. If you're interested in having the head mounted, remember that a ragged field job can give the taxidermist trouble.

If you insist on sticking the deer in the neck, insert the blade of your knife to the hilt near the base on the underside of the neck and slash with it to cut arteries.

A word of warning is in order here: you're risking your game to leave it hanging in the woods unattended. Some hunters, rather than go home empty-handed, will relieve a fellow hunter of his game. If the bears haven't yet hibernated, they too can pose a threat to venison.

One of my friends recalls, with some bitterness, the high risk of trusting your deer to another's honesty. Hunting in the Mississippi lowlands, he shot a fine whitetail buck, and from nearby came a friendly stranger who congratulated him heartily and offered to stand guard while the successful hunter went for help. When my friend returned, the stranger was gone. So was the buck. In wilderness regions this is less of a risk because there are fewer people around.

To field-dress your deer the only tool you will really need is a hunting knife, which, of course, you will have sharpened before leaving home or camp. A relatively short hunting knife with a curved blade is better than a machete type. Some hunters rely on a good pocketknife and can do a neat, fast job of dressing the deer with the small blade.

Although some hunters hang their deer to field-dress it, the easier plan is to dress the animal on the ground. With the deer lying on its side, open up the entire body cavity by making an incision from the breastbone to a point between the hind legs. It is important not to run the blade so deep that you risk cutting into the intestines. You can make a neat, clean job of it by working with the cutting edge of the blade facing up while carefully using your other hand to lift the skin and guide the knife. The organs are held by the diaphragm, which you cut free.

Next, reach into the cavity and roll out the organs. Rescue the liver and heart and put them into a plastic bag that you tucked into your coat pocket earlier for this special job. In this manner they can be taken back to camp or home kitchen clean and ready for cooking.

Make a cut all the way around the vent area and work carefully to free the complete contents of the body cavity.

Now the animal is ready to drain completely. You have removed about twenty percent of the deer's weight and the task has taken perhaps a quarter of an hour. Roll the deer over on its belly to drain out the blood.

Do not leave the animal lying on the ground for lengthy periods after it is cleaned. It will cool faster hanging and fast cooling is important in retaining meat quality. Prop the body cavity open with a stick. Most hunters like to get the deer out of the woods immediately and hang it up back at camp.

One Colorado deer hunter whose method of cleaning a deer I admire is Ben Colarman, who does his hunting in the rocky canyons of the western slope. Ben no sooner has a deer down than he

Meat and hide can both suffer damage from dragging the deer over rough terrain. A layer of snow makes the job easier.

field-dresses the carcass and butchers it—all with a pocketknife and a hand ax.

He considers it especially important to get the hide off his deer. The hair has great insulation properties. Says Ben, "That's what nature put it there for—to keep the deer warm." To cool the deer fast, the hide must come off. This method is widely used through the West by deer hunters of long experience: the hide is removed, the carcass wrapped in cheesecloth, and the meat allowed to "case"; this means that the outside is air-dried so that a crust forms on it and gives it protection.

Ben skins the deer, then promptly cuts it into quarters. The loins have already been carefully cut out and spread to cool on some dried sagebrush (green sagebrush imparts a flavor) or on a clean rock. When he breaks camp he lashes the meat solidly on a pack board. Then he rolls the hide with the fur in and packs it to ride on top of the meat on his backpack board.

In the South, where deer seasons often come while the weather is still warm, flies and heat can be problems for hunters hanging deer up in the field. Texas whitetail hunters often whip the fly problem by hanging their deer in a screened box set up in the field for the purpose.

Most hunters prefer to leave the butchering for camp or home. In the eastern half of the country, at least, it's seldom more than a few hours from field to back porch. Properly field-dressed and transported, a deer carcass will make the trip in good shape if the weather is cool.

Getting a Deer Out of the Woods

Once the deer is field-dressed, you face the problem of moving it to camp, home, or your automobile parked out on the highway. Performing this task has challenged the deer hunter's ingenuity for decades. How you move your animal depends on

A friendly farmer with a handy garden tractor and cart can simplify the hunter's task when it is time to bring in the trophy.

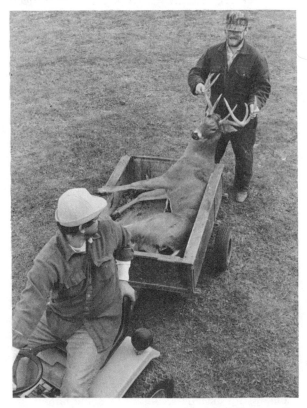

how far you have to carry or drag him, how many other hunters may be roaming the woods, and the state of your health.

The most obvious thing to do is to heave the deer over your shoulders and set forth. But this can be the deer hunter's Russian roulette. With the woods filled with hunters, you have a good chance of crossing the sights of someone who sees a deer but not the man under it.

"If you carry a deer on your shoulders," one Kentucky hunter told me, "you had better tie your blaze-orange jacket on his antlers and whistle 'Dixie' as you go."

Most of the time, you will prefer to drag, not carry, a deer out to the road. Take from your hunting coat a fifteen-foot length of stout, light-weight rope. Lay the deer's front legs alongside his head and neck and bind them tight to the neck by tying the rope behind the animal's ears. Now you are prepared to drag him out headfirst; this is the best fashion, because in this way you take advantage of his streamlined body shape. If he has a big rack, the antlers will reach out for each passing bush, and in thick cover you may have to work out a compromise plan for moving the buck.

Hunters sometimes lash the deer to two poles which they carry across their shoulders. It's possible to tie his feet together and sling him over a single pole, but it's not comfortable. He sways and swings and puts added strain on you.

Another method is to make an Indian-type sled from two poles to which you lash the deer. This will help keep fur and meat from being damaged by rough or rocky ground. If you're dragging him through snow, he will slide more easily and seldom get as bruised as on bare ground.

Some hunters equip themselves with carts on bicycle wheels and bring their deer out of the woods.

Through much of the western deer country, venison often comes out of the hills on horseback. The hunter who takes his horse along slings the deer across his saddle and ties the feet down. Horses never like this. The freshly killed meat makes them skittish. Some horses even have to be equipped with canvas blinders until the load is secured. And in no case should a hunter let the antlers hang free so that they spur the animal into a frenzy.

A lot of venison that gets out of the woods in good shape is promptly lashed to the hot hood of an automobile or piled into the stuffy trunk and ruined on the way home. Venison deserves better.

The best method is to use a cartop carrier that has a slatted or perforated platform to permit free movement of air around the animal. Don't cover the deer unless it's raining; if it's raining, tie a tarp over him.

If you have to transport him in the trunk of your car, it's highly important to prop the top open somewhat to permit circulation. If you put him in a station wagon, leave the windows down. Once you get your deer home, hang him up in a cool, dry place. If he can age for several days at 35 to 40 degrees, the meat improves noticeably.

If you haven't already skinned your deer, do so after you hang him up at home. It is not as difficult as you might expect. You're going to need a knife and a saw. First, make cuts between the tendons of the hind legs and the bone so you can hang the deer

A four-wheel-drive vehicle can often reduce the distance a deer must be dragged. Plan to keep the carcass cool all the way home.

An easy way to get a deer out of the woods is by horse or mule. Animals are skittish about having deer tied onto them and must sometimes be blindfolded. *Erwin A. Bauer*

head down from a hook, spike, or tree limb. If you have not already sawed the lower parts of the legs off, make a cut around one hind leg above the knee. Then make an incision on the inside of the leg from the pelvic area to this cut around the leg, and begin working the skin free of the meat.

Repeat this process on the other hind leg, pulling downward on the skin as you free it with short cuts between skin and muscle. The front legs are skinned in a manner similar to the hind legs and, with this done, you can free the skin from the entire body until it is hanging down around the animal's head. Finally, use knife and saw to cut through the neck and remove the skin and head.

Try to accomplish the skinning without slashing the hide if you plan to use it for clothing. Much of the job can be accomplished by pulling downward on the skin while working it free with the knife handle using short, deft cuts.

Texas hunters often hang deer in screened field boxes to protect meat from insects during the hunt. *Erwin A. Bauer*

How Old Is Your Deer?

Antlers are not accurate age indicators. They vary too much with different food supplies.

Teeth are the best indicators. A big-game biologist can look at the teeth of your deer and tell you its age, give or take a few months. Tooth condition in deer of known age has been checked so many

hundreds of times that this estimating technique has now become standard.

Some state conservation departments have worked up display boards of deer jaws at different ages. I have even seen them at deer-checking stations as a convenience for hunters. But, lacking such a board for comparison, you can still come up with a fairly accurate approximation of your deer's age.

Deer are born in the spring and hunted in the fall, so they are at the halfway mark between years when the season opens.

To arrive at the age of a deer, first count the teeth in the lower jaw. Count whole teeth, not points. If there are only four teeth to the side you have a fawn —about five months old. At six months the deer gets permanent incisors. There are six to the side. They will have eleven points on top. If the third tooth from the front has three cusps, the animal is sixteen to seventeen months old. If this third tooth has two cusps and is sharp and new-looking, the deer is eighteen months old. After the animal is one and a half years old its age is determined by judging the amount of wear on the teeth.

The permanent teeth begin to show wear (yellowish-brown dentine) at the age of two and a half years. The dentine is beginning to show on the third tooth, and the last cusp of the last molar in the jaw is beginning to wear off.

By the time the deer is eight and a half years old, only about one twelfth of an inch of tooth still shows above the gum line, and among deer he's an old-timer.

Get a Picture of Your Deer

A good picture of your deer will outlast the venison. If you carry your camera to the deer camp, as a lot of hunters do, you can improve upon the usual carcass snapshots by heeding the following suggestions.

1. Move in as close to your trophy as possible and still get it all in the picture. Too many pictures have too much unimportant detail.

2. Get people into the pictures. Have them look at the deer, not at the camera.

3. Shoot several pictures. Film isn't costly, and you may not get this opportunity again soon.

4. Unless your camera sets exposures automatically, use a light meter or follow the printed directions that come with film to get the best exposure. Then, for insurance, make two more exposures, one stop more and one stop less than the basic one.

5. Check the focus carefully. Too many pictures are unnecessarily fuzzy.

6. Use a flash to fill in shadows.

If you're in a deer camp for several days, work out a series of pictures. Show hunters arriving, on stand, cleaning guns, dragging deer, washing dishes, or swapping stories around the fireplace. Later, such pictures can mean a lot to you and your hunting companions.

Deer-hunting photographers can find a word of caution in the experience of one Missouri hunter. He brought down a fine buck, placed his rifle in the rack, stepped back to focus, and stared through his viewfinder in amazement as the buck recovered, bounded to his feet, and made off with the rifle, which never was found.

Have the Head Mounted

What do you do if you want to have a deer head mounted? It's best to have some of the answers in mind before you go hunting. You can't tell when you might collect a head of genuine trophy proportions.

There are good natural-looking mounts and many that are less skillfully done. And it's not the work of the taxidermist alone that determines how your mount will look completed. Part of it hinges on how skillfully you skin the head and how you handle it afterward.

I once asked my deer-hunting companion Woodrow Goodpaster, a crack commercial taxidermist in Cincinnati, what major fault he found with deer heads brought to him for mounting. "The taxidermist's job," Woody said, "would be a lot easier and the mounts a lot better if hunters made the cut up the top of the neck instead of the throat." When the mount is hanging on a wall, the throat is plainly visible; it is an extremely difficult area in which to conceal stitches in the skin.

To skin a deer head for mounting, start by making three major cuts. Cut first around the base of the neck. Next make the long cut up the top of the neck from the first cut to a point between the base of the antlers, cutting up from beneath the hide and not down into the hair. Then make a cut connecting with it and running between and just behind the antlers.

Work the skin free around the antlers with a screwdriver and carefully skin the entire head out with a sharp knife. Take special care around the eyes and lips. Leave the eyelids on the skin. Leave the lips, but cut slits in them from the inside so that you can work salt into them to help in preserving the skin while it is in shipment to the taxidermist. Cut the ear cartilage from the skull, but don't try to skin out the ears completely.

Remove the antlers by cutting away a section of the scalp to which they have grown. After you've skinned the head, saw off the top of the scalp by following a line through the center of the eyes.

Scrape or cut all meat away from the skin. Spread it over a log or rock and rub plenty of salt into every part of it on the inside, to prevent decay. Where the skin is folded, you may miss spots. These may decay and cause slippage of hair.

Once the skin is thoroughly salted, roll it and leave it for a few hours. Then unroll it and leave it in a shady, well-ventilated location until it begins to dry; roll it again with the hair inside and it's ready for shipping. Skins that are to be tanned or mounted should be shipped at the earliest possible moment.

According to the famous taxidermist establishment of Jonas Brothers in Denver, this is how to ship your trophy: "Treated scalps and hides should be wrapped in burlap or placed in a gunnysack tied to the skull or horns; then crated or boxed and your game license tacked on the outside. Ship by express or air." Double-check local game regulations to be sure you are within the law. Write your taxidermist, giving him directions at the time of shipping.

Deer hunters often use the deerskin for leather goods. A medium-sized deer hide will work up into about three pairs of gloves, and a jacket can be made from about three deerskins.

FOURTEEN

HOME CARE OF VENISON

There is one easy way to butcher your deer. I recommend it for most deer hunters, especially for those who aren't acquainted with the art of meat cutting. This is to have a butcher cut up the meat. In many areas there are butchers who specialize in butchering wild game and delivering it neatly wrapped and ready for the freezer. A standard requirement is that the deer tag accompany the carcass to the processor.

It is possible in some states to have wild game processed and shipped to your home in another state. This can work well for hunters who have traveled long distances, those who are flying and must avoid extra weight, or those traveling in large parties, when there is minimum space available for meat. But double-check the game laws.

One of my hunting companions hunts the same ranch every year in country over which he occasionally flies his own plane on business. He has equipped the ranch with an old but serviceable food freezer; the venison can be stored there and taken home as it becomes convenient. The plan works well, and the food freezer has long since paid for itself.

Experienced hunters like to cut up their own deer. If you want to do so, you can follow the directions of beef or veal butchering charts. Your county agricultural extension service can usually supply these.

Hang the carcass upside down. Cut the neck off, then cut out the tenderloins. Now cut the deer into halves by sawing it down the backbone.

Removing the hide helps the carcass lose heat. The job normally calls for a butcher's saw and skinning knife. Work carefully to avoid cutting hide or meat. Take special care around the head if planning to have it mounted.

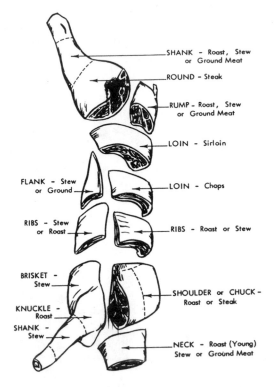

SHANK - Roast, Stew or Ground Meat
ROUND - Steak
RUMP - Roast, Stew or Ground Meat
LOIN - Sirloin
FLANK - Stew or Ground
LOIN - Chops
RIBS - Stew or Roast
RIBS - Roast or Stew
BRISKET - Stew
KNUCKLE - Roast
SHANK - Stew
SHOULDER or CHUCK - Roast or Steak
NECK - Roast (Young) Stew or Ground Meat

Before butchering, the deer must be skinned. If you plan to save the hide, salt down the flesh side, coating it thoroughly. Remove and renew the salt the next day. Fold the hide, flesh side in, to send to taxidermist for tanning.

Hang carcass by hocks and split it into halves by sawing down the backbone. To quarter, cut between ribs and loin and flank. Follow the diagram for butchering. Many experienced hunters go to the added trouble of boning all venison before packing it for the cooler because spoilage frequently begins around the bone. *Outdoor Indiana*

Next, lay the halves out on a large flat table, and make the cuts shown in the chart. Cut the deer into meal-size pieces. If you have a meat saw available, you may now cut the flank and loins into slices ready for cooking. This can also be done after they are frozen, but it's not easy. Wrap the pieces in heavy meat paper and freeze them.

More than likely, some of the meat will be torn where the deer was shot. It will be bloodshot, but this doesn't necessarily mean that it is wasted. If it's a small portion, trim it out and dispose of it. If there is considerable meat involved, soak it in a brine made by adding two tablespoons of salt to each quart of water. Soak these pieces for two days,

then trim off the bloody areas and use the meat for venisonburger or stew.

The deer hunter who has met all the challenges of finding, shooting, and butchering his deer often faces a still bigger challenge in getting his family to eat the meat.

The flavor of venison depends partly on the animal's diet. Through much of the country's agricultural lands, in addition to natural foods, deer often fatten on succulent crops snitched from the edges of farmers' fields. Deer doesn't taste like beef and shouldn't be compared with it. Venison tastes like venison. For me, one of the finest of meats, wild or domestic, is properly cooked venison. It is considered to be low in cholesterol for red meat.

Venison can be cooked like beef. It goes well in ground meat or as sausage, in stews, roasts, and steaks.

Every seasoned deer hunter eventually comes up with his favorite recipes for preparing venison, and usually they please the entire family. Those that follow come from a number of hunters of long experience.

Venison de Luxe

This recipe is offered by Mrs. Betty Bourne of Montana.

Make a sauce by simmering the following ingredients for about fifteen minutes.

1/4 cup chopped onion (more if you like)
1 tbs. drippings
2 1/2 cups tomatoes (or 2 cans tomato sauce)
1/2 cup cooked mushroom pieces
1/4 cup sliced pimiento slices (plus a little of the liquid)
1 bay leaf

While the sauce is simmering, brown enough venison round steak (cut into servings) for six or eight people. Add sauce, cover, and either bake at 350 degrees Fahrenheit for one hour or simmer on top of stove.

Deer Steak (or Elk or Moose, as the hunt may provide)

This one also comes from Betty Bourne's kitchen.

This Ohio buck grew big from years of plentiful food supplies until finally taken during the annual deer season for shotgunners. The big buck is hung in a cool place until the hunter is ready to butcher him.

time for cooking each side depends on your taste and the thickness of the meat.

If you like, you may brush each side with a mixture of oil and vinegar or with melted butter.

For pan broiling, get the frying pan sizzling hot, then melt a little butter or bacon fat in it. Brown the meat on both sides and turn it only once.

Venison Roast

From the deer-famous state of Michigan come these directions for roasting the round, loin, or shoulder.

Season the cut of meat with salt and pepper and place on a rack in uncovered pan, fat side up.

Do not add water and do not cover the pan.

Extra fat in the form of bacon strips or beef suet may be added.

Roast in slow oven (300 to 350 degrees Fahrenheit), allowing twenty to twenty-five minutes per pound. Turning the roast aids in uniform cooking.

1/2 cup onion chopped fine	1/2 cup sweet or sour cream
2 tbs. butter	2 tbs. flour
1 cup chopped mushrooms	4 to 6 steaks

Brown onions lightly in butter. Remove onions from fat. Slowly brown steaks on both sides in butter. Spread browned onions over steaks, cover, and cook very slowly for thirty minutes or until tender.

Meanwhile make smooth sauce of cream, flour, and mushrooms. Add to the meat while hot. Cover and let simmer for twenty minutes.

Tender Cut Steaks

With tender venison, especially steaks and loins from yearling animals, I broil the steaks as I would fine beefsteaks. Get the fire hot before putting steaks on to broil. You want them to sear fast. The steaks should not be overcooked, and the length of

Swiss Steak (for cooking tough round steaks)

1 1/2 lbs. round steak	1 cup tomatoes
3 large onions	2 tbs. Worcestershire sauce
1 medium stalk celery	salt and pepper
flour	

Steak should be about one and a half inches thick. Dredge with flour and season with salt and pepper, then brown in fat. When brown on both sides add other ingredients. Cover tightly. Cook in oven (350 degrees) or over low flame seventy-five minutes or until tender. Make gravy with drippings.

Venison Meat Loaf (use tough cuts)

1 lb. ground venison	1/2 tbs. chopped onion
1/2 lb. ground pork	
1 egg	1 1/2 tsp. salt
1/2 cup dried bread crumbs	1 cup milk

Beat egg, add milk and bread crumbs. Mix thoroughly with the meat and seasoning. Bake for one hour in greased pan in medium oven (350 degrees). Addition of pork may add flavor and tenderness to the loaf.

Venison Mincemeat

2 lbs. cooked ground venison
4 lbs. chopped apple
2 lbs. raisins
4 cups brown or white sugar
2 tsp. salt
3/4 lb. chopped suet or butter
1/2 tsp. cloves
1 tsp. mace
1/2 tsp. nutmeg
1½ tsp. cinnamon
apple cider

Mix ingredients thoroughly, then add enough apple cider to cover the mixture. Fruit juices may be substituted for cider. A mixture of six parts water to one part vinegar may also be substituted. Cook very slowly until fruits are tender (about an hour). Put into pies or store in fruit jars.

Meat Pie (tough cuts)

Use equal parts of diced vegetables and cooked meat. Season and cover with gravy thinned in water or gravy made with bouillon cube. Bake in covered casserole in medium oven (375 degrees) for one hour. Before serving, remove lid and cover meat with crust of mashed potato or biscuit dough, brown in hot (400 degree) oven, and serve.

Deer Liver

The liver of the deer is among the finest of foods. Deer hunters everywhere, especially those who hunt from camps, know the taste of fresh liver cooked within hours of the time it's taken.

The essential for serving good venison liver is to take it from a young animal, keep it clean, cool it rapidly, and cook it the same day. Slice liver in quarter-inch slices, dip in flour, and fry in clean (unused) frying oil. Onions go well with liver but should be cooked separately. It's better to undercook than overcook liver. Avoid frying liver until it looks like boot resoles.

Breaded Chops

If you're cooking steaks and chops, pound flour into them until they won't take any more. Have the frying fat smoking hot. Keep it that way by dropping only one piece of meat into it at a time. Allow three minutes on each side for the meat, then cut the heat down low for another fifteen minutes. The steaks will be cooked through and crusty brown on the outside. Good outdoor cooks say it's "sinful" to drop such meat into a frying pan that hasn't been preheated.

Venison Stew

Use about three pounds of rib meat cut into one-inch cubes. Use good solid red meat. No gristle, tendons, or tallow.

Sear the meat brown and drop it into an inch of briskly boiling water. Carrots, celery, and potatoes go in later so that they don't boil down to mush. From here on, season to taste with salt, pepper, celery, and onion powders.

Simmer on low heat for two to three hours, then let it stand with the lid off. After an hour or so give it another hour of simmering. It gets better all the time. Finally, about ten minutes before serving, stir in one-third cup of flour.

Of Wines and Marinades

An Idaho guide once told me his feelings about cooking venison with wine. "Good venison is very good," he said, "but when you try to make it taste like veal, or mutton, or some other darned thing, you ought to buy those meats in the first place and save all that disguising."

Venison Marinade

With this negative send-off, let us talk briefly of a marinade for venison. A marinade is a liquid concoction in which you can soak meat before cooking it. It helps to make the meat tender and changes the flavor.

One rather mild marinade can be made by starting with a pint of white vinegar and a bottle of good red wine. Mix them. The best container for this experiment is an earthenware crock, not a metal pan. Into the liquid goes a teaspoon of ground black pepper or a dozen bruised peppercorns, a tablespoon of salt, eighteen whole cloves, a cup and a half of chopped celery plus some of the leaves, two cups of sliced onions, a teaspoon of ground cinnamon, one-half teaspoon powdered thyme, a few bay leaves, and a pinch of sage.

Soak the meat in this for twelve to twenty-four hours. Then take it from the marinade, drain it, and cook. Even if you're a purist who prefers his venison without fancy fluids, dips, and dressings, this can offer something different in venison dishes.

FIFTEEN
DEER-HUNTING HAZARDS

The outdoors is a big, wonderful place where deer hunters seldom get into much trouble. But before you go, it's a good idea to review the possible hazards that could put a damper on your trip.

Those Aching Feet

Too often a hunter's feet give up hunting before his head does. Poor foot health is a by-product of the easy life we lead. Between one hunting season and the next we walk only as a last resort. Then we happily invade the wilderness on a week-long deer hunt.

One big-game-hunting friend of mine begins to condition himself for the hunt weeks ahead of opening day. Instead of having his wife drive him to the commuter train, he walks. Rather than take the elevators to his fourteenth-floor office, he climbs the stairs. The closer the hunting season comes, the more he increases his conditioning. He even rides his son's bike around the neighborhood.

The human foot is a fine bit of engineering. Its twenty-six bones are arranged into four arches that run lengthwise and crosswise. These are not rigid

Take it easy. Deer hunting should be fun, not heavy work that taxes your physical ability. These hunters have a long way to move their deer but there is plenty of daylight left. Hunters who lead sedentary lives should, ahead of the season's opening, get into good physical condition. *South Dakota Department of Game, Fish and Parks*

arches but flexible mechanisms, which enable the foot to absorb great shock.

When your feet begin to hurt it's time to stop and check them. Sometimes, on a long hike, you can rest your feet simply by varying your pace. Clean feet and socks are essential to foot health and comfortable walking. Soiled socks can neither breathe, as they should, nor insulate the foot properly. Many experienced woodsmen carry an extra pair of socks in pocket or pack and change at midday. The lunch stop may also provide an opportunity, if the weather is pleasant, to bathe your feet in the nearest stream or lake and relax them.

Carry some tape and cotton, or a foot patch, in case you should develop a blister during the day. Don't let a shoe salesman talk you into buying shoes larger than you need. The shoes you wear for deer hunting should be large enough to house your feet comfortably when you're wearing one or two pairs of medium-weight wool socks. Try on both shoes. Walk in them to learn how each one feels under your total weight. Forget the old idea that new shoes are supposed to hurt your feet until they're broken in. That's not true. But they should be worn for some weeks ahead of the season to form them to your feet.

The Old Heart

Deer hunters ordinarily bound to office desks, especially those hunters who have known many deer seasons, should take normal precautions against overtaxing their hearts. Every fall there are a few newspaper reports of hunters suffering heart attacks while in the woods and fields. Usually these victims pushed themselves too hard for their physical condition. Had they stayed home they might have been stricken while shoveling snow off the driveway.

If there is any question as to whether or not you can withstand the long, hard hiking, do your hunting from a deer stand close to the road. Tell a companion at what time to expect you out of the woods. Stay within sound of his gun and prearrange a set of signals. This is common sense.

When you bring a deer down, get help before trying to take it out of the woods. This is hard work, even for the rugged hunter.

Some deer-hunting trips are more strenuous than others, and before taking one of the more difficult ones, or going deep into wilderness country, many hunters would be wise to get their physician's opinion.

How Good Are Your Eyes?

There are hunters afield who should be wearing glasses but aren't. One widely known optometrist says that it would be wise legislation to require hunters to meet the same eye requirements for hunting as they must meet for passing a driver's test. If they wear glasses for driving, they should wear them for hunting.

There are a few things to keep in mind if you do wear glasses and you're planning a deer hunt. What would you do, for example, if your glasses fell off and broke? I asked this question of deer hunter Dr. Ralph Wick of Rapid City, South Dakota, then president of the American Academy of Optometry. He replied, "In many cases an extra pair of glasses would be more important than an extra gun on wilderness trips or long hunting expeditions. If a hunter is nearsighted his hunting trip could be ended by breaking a pair of glasses."

If you use corrective lenses, these are available in tinted shooting glasses. See your optometrist. Tinted shooting glasses are best in brush, where they bring out the contrasts between objects and help to "open up the woods" to you.

All types of eyeglasses can now be hardened for eye protection. "I have recommended hardened lenses for all hunters for years," said Dr. Wick. "There have been many records of eyes saved when hardened glasses were worn." Hardened glasses will often withstand a blow from a branch or rock fragment where ordinary lens would break. "This is the same type of lens," Dr. Wick added, "that is being used in industry in hazardous occupations."

If you want the best in sunglasses, start with a visit to your optometrist. If you engage in indoor work all the time, it will be an especially good idea to check with your optometrist about the kinds of glasses best suited to hunting.

As added protection for your glasses, keep them in a case when they're not in use. One of the elastic bands used by athletes to hold their glasses in place during rough play can be especially helpful in thick brush country.

Back Troubles

The human back is a complicated and sometimes easily injured collection of bones and tissues. Doctors tell us injuries to the lower back are on the increase, especially among men. Now, I am not going to offer advice on treatment of any reader's back troubles, but there are a couple of suggestions I would make to deer hunters with any history of back trouble.

Unless your back is in good shape at the time of the hunt, you would do well to take up a stand within easy calling distance of the road. Victims of back trouble have fallen and been unable to get up without aid.

If you are at a considerable distance from the road and you twist or strain your back enough to feel a pain of any severity, the most sensible plan is to start working your way out toward the road or camp immediately. Such injuries often get worse and can immobilize you within a few hours.

If you are no longer young, avoid overextending your physical capabilities by such youthful exuberances as crawling down cliffs, crossing creeks on fallen logs, or lifting heavy objects.

Often the person who exercises the least in his day-to-day work is the one most subject to back troubles and the one who should take the greatest precautions against such injuries.

Cold

The most common hazard the hunter faces from cold is frostbite. If you're hunting with a companion in bitter cold weather, you should inspect each other's ears, noses, and cheeks occasionally. Frostbitten areas show up grayish-white. The feet, too, may suffer frostbite and this can be serious.

When I was a boy we were told to thaw frozen hands or ears by rubbing them with snow. But, snow is frozen water; where would it get the heat that is said to thaw ears or feet or fingers? This dangerous theory is one to be dismissed along with stories about hoop snakes. The best thing for thawing frostbitten parts of the body is heat. Hold the frostbitten part, when possible, against another part of the body; cup your ear in your hand, or hold your foot against your thigh. It's a good plan to put the injured part into warm water, if this can be managed.

Never put a frostbitten area into cold gasoline or kerosene. Cold won't remove cold.

If you should step or fall into water, build a fire in as well-protected a spot as you can find and dry out your clothes.

Freezing to death is very rare. The hunter who takes a few precautions should manage to survive even the most severe weather. If caught out overnight, try to make a camp out of the wind. Build up a fuel supply for the night: get as comfortable as possible, and conserve your strength. It is usually wiser to wait out a heavy storm than to try finding your way through it, especially at night.

Prolonged cold can reduce body temperature below normal, and threaten life. This condition is known as hypothermia. Deer hunters, properly dressed in protective clothing, rarely have to worry about hypothermia unless they are caught out in a winter storm, or fall into icy water.

But cold does not have to be life threatening to ruin a day in the field. The clothing chosen is highly important if you want to enjoy the hunt despite foul weather. In recent times there have been highly effective new synthetics created for use in outdoor clothing—products that rival wool and goose down for warmth.

The old idea of layering your winter clothing remains sound. Wearing several thicknesses not only helps hold heat in but also permits you to remove garments for comfort. A windbreaker with hood is a good idea and the material used for this garment is typically either nylon or a blend of nylon and cotton.

Perhaps the most effective material for protecting an outdoorsman from rain or wet snow while permitting body moisture to escape is Gore-Tex, a synthetic membrane sandwiched between two layers of nylon. This remarkable product now widely used in outdoor clothing has advantages and disadvantages. Most importantly, it sheds water while "breathing." The manufacturer explains that Gore-Tex has "billions" of pores so small that water droplets cannot get through but still large enough for water vapor to escape, preventing condensation. Reported disadvantages are that it is costly, wears out in a few years, and may not allow all vapor to pass through under heavy use.

If You're Lost

Getting lost is no disgrace and usually it's not serious. But the lost person can easily make his situation serious by not knowing how to protect himself from various hazards.

Some people think it is impossible for them to become truly lost in the woods. They're wrong. Humans do not come equipped with homing devices. It is true that some excellent woodsmen almost never get lost, or at least never consider themselves lost, but that is only because they make a point of knowing constantly where they are, at least in a general sense.

If you are going into strange wilderness country, your best rule is to take a guide.

The most serious hazard the lost hunter faces is panic. Many a strong man, confronted by the certain knowledge that he hasn't the slightest idea where he is, has abandoned his horse sense completely and dashed off through the brush without reasoning. Eventually, unless he gets a grip on his senses, he can have his clothes torn by thorn bushes, maybe tumble over a cliff, or become exhausted and exposed to the elements.

There is nothing wrong with being afraid. Fear is a perfectly natural reaction to the unknown. But the lost person must fight his fears and not allow them to drive him into panic. Instead, he should force himself to begin giving serious thought to his dilemma.

I remember an autumn evening during an elk hunt in the mountains of northern Idaho when a member of our party wandered away from camp for an evening stroll in the forest. He probably was not paying too much attention to landmarks. Before long he realized that he was turned around, and he recalled that the wilderness area in which we were hunting was at least forty miles across in a straight line.

"I thought I knew which direction to go to get back to camp," he said later, "and probably could have walked right in, but all I had ever heard told me that this was the time to sit down and think." Sitting there beneath a giant tree, he began to look critically at the landscape and recall what he had done or seen to get to this spot. "I felt certain that following the little creek nearby would take me back toward camp. If this did not work I could always follow the creek back to this spot and try the next plan." He was lucky. The creek led him back to camp just as darkness settled over the wilderness.

He was not especially proud of himself, however, because he had made at least two serious mistakes. First, he should have told someone, or left a note, so others in the party would know the direction in which he set off. Furthermore, he should have taken a compass reading before leaving, even though he thought he was going to stay in the immediate area.

The reading on his pocket compass would have pointed him back easily enough if he had taken the reading properly. Too often deer hunters carry a compass but fail to use it, or use it improperly. Here is a simple plan to remember. Before leaving camp, hold the compass in your hand and turn it to align the zero with the compass hand pointing toward magnetic North.

Because there are 360 degrees on the face of the compass, the right half is now numbered 0 to 180 and the left half from 180 to 360. Note the direction you follow when leaving camp, or your car, and read the compass to see how many degrees from magnetic North you are heading. If you are starting off on a course of 25 degrees, you can later backtrack by adding 180 to 25 to give you the compass reading, which is the opposite direction from the direction traveled as you started out. If you start out on a course greater than 180 degrees, you can reverse your direction by taking a new reading when you start back and subtracting 180 degrees.

Trust your compass. It stands a far better chance of pointing north than you do.

Lost people trying to find their way through the wild places always face the possibility of traveling in a circle. Instead, you will want to straightline it and you can accomplish this by lining up trees well ahead of you. Follow the line established by two of these marker trees, and before reaching the first tree pick a third distant tree along the established line so you stay on course by repeating the process.

If you are operating without a compass and think you know the way back to car or camp but aren't certain, you can blaze a trail enabling you to backtrack for a fresh start. Knowing the time spent walking, and remembering landmarks, can help. Highway noises and trains may give you direction.

If you are hunting in the eastern part of North America, travel generally downstream; eventually you should come to a road, railroad, farm, or stream. The same rule usually works in the West, although you may have to hike forty miles instead of four. In the West there is also the possibility that a stream will lead you into a box canyon and not out of the wilderness.

Some days are more confusing than others. Snowstorms and fog can add to your confusion and sometimes make it inadvisable to keep walking.

Whatever the weather, if lost, *do not travel at night*. It makes sense for all members of a hunting party to agree that there will be no search mounted for a lost hunter the first night he is out. Everyone should instead get a good night's sleep, then take up the search at daylight.

Once you know you are lost, make camp well ahead of darkness. Pick a camp spot that is out of the wind, if possible, and get a fire going. Then you can begin to make a shelter of whatever you find at hand.

The wetter it is, the more difficult the fire starting will be. First, gather the materials. The inner bark of cedar trees or an old bird's nest may make good tinder. Cut small fuzz sticks that can be formed into a wigwam over the fine material before the fire is lighted. Then have larger pieces of fuel at hand to feed into the fire as it is able to handle them. Gun-

powder can help get the fire ignited. If you are carrying a pocket fire-starting kit, this is the time to use it.

When there is a chance that a search party will be out looking for you, make a smudge fire with green branches piled on your fire. Stay in one place. This way, the search party will have a far better chance of finding you. Three signals of any kind spell SOS wherever you are, whether they are three evenly spaced shots, or three fires visible to aircraft.

Even if you have never been lost in your life, it is wise to go prepared for the first time. A fanny pack, or large hunting-coat pocket should contain a few essentials, including waterproof matches, small flashlight, maps, compass, fire-starting tablets, extra pair of socks, possibly a lightweight plastic sheet, or space blanket, first-aid items, and a couple of candy or granola bars. A length of rope is also a handy item if you want to form the plastic into a shelter.

The fear of getting lost should not keep most of us from going deer hunting, birding, hiking, or whatever. Safety from the hazards of being lost in the outdoors is largely a matter of attitude. Most of us could be lost and still survive for many days—or weeks—if we possessed the right attitude.

SIXTEEN

WHERE THE DEER HUNTING IS BEST

In spite of the fact that deer live today in practically every part of the country, it is not always easy to find a place to hunt them. Farms and ranches are sometimes closed to hunters except for friends and relatives. Private hunting clubs hold sizable acreages in some regions, excluding the public. Highways, cities, and service stations cover ever-growing acreages with concrete.

But the picture is not nearly so drab as we sometimes think. There are vast acreages in public and private ownership alike where a man can go, in season, to take his deer, and this chapter will tell how to find these deer-hunting spots.

Many times there is more hunting territory open to the average deer hunter than he realizes. Consider, for example, the hunting areas in Florida. That state operates thirty-two wild-life-management areas. These are big units of land scattered around the state and covering some 3.5 million acres. All you need is a hunting license and one of the state's special permits, which sell at bargain prices.

Owners of these lands include the United States Forest Service, the Air Force, the Corps of Engineers, the Fish and Wildlife Service, a flood control district, the Florida Forest Service, the Florida Game and Fresh Water Fish Commission, and several private timber companies.

If you want to find out about public hunting areas in any state, all you have to do is write the game and fish agency at the address given for it in the following pages. The Florida Game and Fresh Wa-

ter Fish Commission, for example, can supply information on all these public hunting areas. Within your state the wildlife agency will almost invariably know where both private and public agencies have lands available for deer hunting.

How Many Acres?

The total land area of the United States is 2,273,000,000 acres and about a third of this is in forestlands. One third of the country's forests are in farm woodlots. Various government agencies hold title to about a fourth of all the forestlands in the country, and these public forestlands provide a wealth of hunting opportunity.

The first of our national forests was the Shoshone in Wyoming. It was established in 1905 and since that day 155 more national forests have been set aside. They cover 191 million acres in 44 states.

Millions of acres in the national forests have been set aside as wilderness areas in the belief that bits of America should be retained as they were before the white man carried civilization into the hinterlands.

One third of all the big game in the country lives in national forests, at least part of the year. More than half of all mule deer live on national forestlands.

Hunting is permitted in all national forests. The hunting regulations in these forests are the laws of the states in which the forestlands are located. State

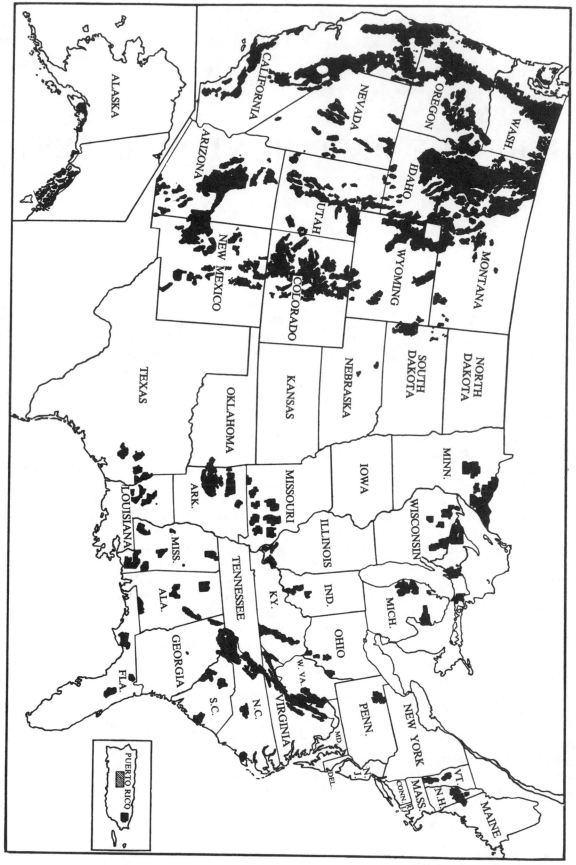

National forests of the United States. *U.S. Forest Service*

wildlife administrators work closely with the U.S. Forest Service in the management of wildlife resources.

Most of the national forest holdings are in the western half of the United States. Largely, they are in mountainous country, the wildest and most spectacular on the continent. But there are also national forests in the East—in the Carolinas, Virginia, Kentucky, Maine, New Hampshire, Vermont, Pennsylvania, Ohio, Missouri, and Arkansas. There are other national forestlands in Michigan, Minnesota, and Wisconsin. And some are in the deep South—Mississippi, Louisiana, and Florida.

Remember, however, that even within the boundaries of the national forests there are still private inholdings on which hunters must get permission to hunt.

Hunting on practically all national forestlands is free. The only exceptions are on those lands in a few eastern states where the U.S. Forest Service has cooperative agreements for managed state hunts.

The U.S. Forest Service operates its holdings on a multiple-use plan, to derive as much benefit from the lands as the welfare of the resources will permit. In summer, campers, hikers, animal watchers, and fishermen flock to the forests by the thousands. But during the hunting season the woods are left mostly to the rangers and the hunters. Some fourteen million fishing and hunting visits are made each year by sportsmen to the national forests.

If you want to set up a deer camp, the national forests offer a good opportunity. You can set up your tent in one of the campgrounds maintained in the national forests. There are some 4,700 camp and picnic areas in these forests. Although hunting is forbidden within recreation areas, the camps can be good headquarters for hunters seeking deer in the surrounding hills.

In some forest regions, visitors must obtain permits to build campfires. This is especially true through much of the national forestlands in the West Coast states. The danger of fire may result in posting any national forest area against fires and, on occasion, against all use. Such areas are usually conspicuously posted.

The U.S. Forest Service advances some guiding thoughts for outdoorsmen who would keep the outdoors in good, productive condition. They apply outside the national forests also:

1. Build campfires only in safe places and put them out before leaving.

2. Build fires only in designated places when using the regular camp and picnic areas.

3. Use the ashtray, not the car window, for disposing of cigarettes.

4. Leave a clean camp. Burn and bury your trash.

5. If packing into backcountry, take along reliable maps and let the rangers know where you're headed.

6. Carry shovel, ax, and water bucket in your car in case of fire.

7. Don't drink untested water.

There are several publications on the national forests. One, which you can obtain from the United States Government Printing Office, Washington 25, D.C., is called *National Forest Vacations* and contains a guide to the national forests.

For answers to questions about specific national forests, write Regional Office, United States Forest Service, at any of the following addresses:

Federal Building, P.O. Box 7669, Missoula, Mont. 59807

11177 W. 8th Avenue, Box 25127, Lakewood, Colo. 80225

Federal Building, 517 Gold Avenue, S.W., Albuquerque, N. Mex. 87102

Federal Office Building, 324 25th Street, Ogden, Ut. 84401

630 Sansome Street, San Francisco, Calif. 94111

319 S.W. Pine Street, Box 3623, Portland, Ore. 97208

Suite 800, 1720 Peachtree Road, N.W., Atlanta, Ga. 30367

310 W. Wisconsin Avenue, Milwaukee, Wis. 53203

Federal Office Building, Box 1628, Juneau, Ak. 99802

BLM Lands Are Open

When the country was young, most of the vast land areas belonged to the government. With homesteading laws and various other grants, lands were released to private owners over the years. Many of the areas, often those of least value, are still held by the government. Those not held by other government agencies for specific purposes are managed by the Bureau of Land Management (BLM). This bureau of the Department of Interior has some 447 million acres—more than twice the acreage held by the U.S. Forest Service. In spite of the fact that only a small percentage of BLM lands are in forests, their holdings still provide some of the country's best deer hunting. One good example of quality deer hunting on BLM lands is the mule deer hunting in the rugged Steens Mountain region of Oregon.

"With very few exceptions," says a BLM spokesman, "all of the national land reserve is open to hunting and fishing." These lands are put to a variety of uses. Grazing is a major use. But in recent times, with increasing pressure for outdoor recreational use of all lands, BLM administrators have emphasized that hunting is available on their lands. They have established campgrounds in some of the areas, and employed full-time wildlife biologists.

The BLM lands are scattered through eleven western states, including Alaska. Some areas are cut off from access because of private ownership of surrounding ranch lands. There is hope that through agreements more of these isolated regions will eventually be open to hunters and fishermen.

To get additional details on the deer hunting on BLM lands in the states that interest you, write to the State Director, United States Bureau of Land Management. Here are their addresses in the states where they manage public holdings.

702 C Street, Box 13, Anchorage, Ak. 99513

3707 N. 7th Street, Phoenix, Ariz. 85011

Federal Office Building, Rm. E-2841, 2800 Cottage Way, Sacramento, Calif. 95825

2020 Arapahoe Street, Denver, Colo. 80205

Federal Building, 550 W. Fort Street, Box 42, Boise, Id. 83724

222 N. 32nd Street, P.O. Box 30157, Billings, Mont. 59107

Federal Building, Rm. 3008, 300 Booth Street, Reno, Nev. 89520

U.S.P.O. and Federal Building, South Federal Place, P.O. Box 1449, Santa Fe, N. Mex. 87501

825 N.E. Multnomah Street, P.O. Box 2965, Portland, Ore. 97208

University Club Building, 136 E. South Temple, Salt Lake City, Ut. 84111

2515 Warren Avenue, P.O. Box 1828, Cheyenne, Wyo. 82001

350 South Pickett Street, Alexandria, Va. 22304 (eastern states)

Deer hunting is sometimes allowed on lands owned by the U.S. Army Corps of Engineers, the Fish and Wildlife Service, the Bureau of Reclamation, and various military agencies.

Across the country there are more than four hundred national wildlife refuges. Strangely enough, many of these offer hunting at times, some of it the finest hunting found anywhere. The refuge program operates largely for the conservation of waterfowl, but a big variety of other game occupies the areas. The hunting of species other than waterfowl on these refuges is done only as a management tool to keep populations within the limits of the carrying capacity. In one recent year forty-four national refuges were open at some time to big-game hunters. The refuge managers are the source of information on hunts. Usually these are special hunts, carefully controlled to insure the desired harvest of game. Bow hunters find some interesting deer hunting on the refuges from time to time. Examples include hunting the whitetail deer in the Aransas National Wildlife Refuge in Texas and hunting the abundant whitetails among the palmettos on Blackbeard Island off the coast of Georgia. National parks, as well as many state parks, are not open to deer hunting.

State Lands for Deer Hunters

About 4 percent of our forestland is in state ownership, and many of these areas offer deer hunters a place to hunt. Some holdings are in state forests, some in public hunting areas and a variety of other agencies. Here again, the best source of information is the state game and fish agency. Don't overlook the small state hunting areas. Even if they're established for hunting upland game species, they sometimes harbor deer or contain trails that deer may

Companies that own large acreages of timberlands normally welcome hunters to their lands during the regular state hunting seasons. *American Forest Products Industries*

follow when being pursued through surrounding farmlands.

Timber Companies Open Doors

There are thousands of companies that own timberland in the United States. They vary from relatively insignificant holdings to great wilderness areas. Such companies, in fact, own 12.8 percent of all our timberlands, and taken together, they provide a lot of good deer hunting.

Most of these companies crop timber to produce everything from beer barrels to plywood. The trend is toward opening more of these lands to deer hunting. This is good public relations, but it is also sound timber management because too many deer overbrowse the young growth on which the timber companies depend for future supplies.

Some companies send out hunting tips to deer hunters writing in for information. The Weyerhaeuser Company, operating out of Tacoma, Washington, says: "Local big-game hunters find the medium-sized rifles best for these areas. Conditions seldom permit a shot at more than two hundred yards, and most big game is killed on tree farms at one hundred yards or less. The exception might be the comparatively open areas of the Klamath Falls pine country, where mule deer are sometimes sighted at greater distances. A .30-30 is the most popular weapon, followed by a .30-06."

Deer hunting on most tree-farm lands is done under a permit system, because often the owners want to control the number of people there at any given time. They have to be especially careful during periods of high fire hazard.

"Posted"

Don't feel too sorry for yourself if, instead of invading the wilderness in search of a buck, you must limit your deer hunting to the farmlands and woodlands of the more heavily populated states.

Deer have adapted themselves amazingly well to farm living in recent decades, and hunters take hundreds of thousands of deer in agricultural areas.

This brings us face to face with the "No Hunt-

Land may be posted against deer hunting for various reasons. Most frequently mentioned cause of posting is abuse of the hunting privilege.

ing" signs that, in some neighborhoods, seem to crop up on every fence post when hunting season comes. A number of state game and fish departments have conducted studies to see how serious the land-posting situation really is. The general conclusion has been that much of the posted land is really not closed to hunters if they'll take the trouble to ask permission.

In Massachusetts, one of the most densely populated New England states, one study showed that 59 percent of the posted land was opened to hunters who sought permission. Posting was most often done because of property damage and shooting too close to buildings.

Backcountry Deer

How heavily deer country is hunted usually depends on how close it is to a highway. The percentage of hunters reluctant to get out of sight of public roads seems to be growing. But unless you're afraid

of getting lost or incapacitated, there's a real experience awaiting you once you decide to get off the road and into the wilderness. Solitude erases the pressures of civilization for a few days, and it's good for the soul to escape exhaust fumes, concrete, and television.

Even in the eastern part of the country there are choice hunting areas that can only be reached by foot or canoe. In such places the deer are seldom disturbed. Sometime in his life, the serious deer hunter deserves the opportunity to hunt in such country.

I recall a hunt on a West Virginia public hunting area some years ago that attracted more people than the county fair. The stand I chose turned out to be a people crossing. Every fifteen minutes during the morning other hunters stopped to chat about the weather and the shortage of deer.

Such crowding is not necessary. Before the season opens, survey the possible hunting places within convenient driving distance of home, and hunt out a place away from the beaten trail.

That Western Hunt

The dream of many an eastern deer hunter is to hunt in the wide-open country out west.

To fulfill that dream, you can take your equipment and set up camp on national forestland, or gain permission to hunt a privately owned ranch, or employ an outfitter.

Prices for pack-in hunts with outfitters and guides vary with length of the trip, distance into the wilderness from headquarters, services provided, and game hunted. Such an arrangement should be made early in the year. Most outfitters like to have their scheduled hunts filled up by early summer. A deposit is customary.

State game and fish departments sometimes have lists of outfitters. At least they know if the state has an association of outfitters. So will state chambers of commerce in the state capitals. Some western states with such associations screen their members.

Anyone going deer hunting should first make a careful study of the hunting regulations. He should do so even if he hunted in the same state the year before—the regulations might have changed. Determine whether all deer or bucks only are legal game and whether there is any legal restriction on

Eastern deer hunters often dream of a genuine, western-style deer hunt, complete with guide and pack animals, enabling them to spend the heart of autumn on a once-in-a-lifetime hunt in splendid mountain scenery. *Erwin & Peggy Bauer*

the antlers. Some states occasionally have a few days of antlerless deer season followed by a buck-only season. A few states require hunters, especially nonresidents, to be accompanied by a guide. What are the regulations on firearms and ammunition, bows and arrows, shooting hours, and transporting guns in your car? Are you required to wear clothing of any special color? Are you entitled to a camp deer?

You can get detailed copies of the regulations from the wildlife agency in the capital of the state in which you plan to hunt.

Who to Write or Call in Your State

Your local county conservation officer is an excellent source of information on deer-hunting regulations. You can locate the conservation officer by checking the telephone directory under the agency name in the following list, or by asking the county sheriff's office for the name and telephone number. Or you can contact any state wildlife agency central office at the following addresses.

Alabama Division of Game and Fish, 64 N. Union Street, Montgomery 36130

Alaska Department of Fish and Game, P.O. Box 3-2000, Juneau 99802

Arizona Game and Fish Department, 2222 W. Greenway Road, Phoenix 85023

Arkansas Game and Fish Commission, #2 Natural Resources Drive, Little Rock 72205

California Department of Fish and Game, 1416 Ninth Street, Sacramento 95814

Colorado Division of Wildlife, 6060 Broadway, Denver 80216

Connecticut Wildlife Bureau, State Office Building, 165 Capitol Avenue, Hartford 06115

Delaware Division of Fish and Wildlife, 89 Kings Highway, P.O. Box 1401, Dover 19903

Florida Game and Fresh Water Fish Commission, 620 S. Meridian Street, Tallahassee 32301

Georgia Game and Fish Division, 270 Washington Street SW, Atlanta 30334

Hawaii Division of Forestry and Wildlife, 1151 Punchbowl Street, Honolulu 96813

Idaho Fish and Game Department, 600 S. Walnut Street, Box 25, Boise 83707

Illinois Division of Fish and Wildlife Resources, Lincoln Tower Plaza, 524 S. Second Street, Springfield 62706

Indiana Division of Fish and Wildlife, 608 State Office Building, Indianapolis 46204

Iowa Fish and Game, Wallace State Office Building, Des Moines 50319

Kansas Fish and Game Commission, Box 54A, RR 2, Pratt 67124

Kentucky Department of Fish and Wildlife Resources, #1 Game Farm Road, Frankfort 40601

Louisiana Department of Wildlife and Fisheries, 400 Royal Street, New Orleans 70130

Maine Department of Inland Fisheries and Wildlife, 284 State Street Station #41, Augusta 04333

Maryland Forest, Park and Wildlife Services, Tawes State Office Building, Annapolis 21401

Massachusetts Division of Fisheries and Wildlife, 100 Cambridge Street, Boston 02202

Michigan Division of Wildlife, Box 30028, Lansing 48909

Minnesota Division of Fish and Wildlife, 300 Centennial Building, 658 Cedar Street, St. Paul 55155

Mississippi Department of Wildlife Conservation, Southport Mall, P.O. Box 451, Jackson 39205

Missouri Department of Conservation, P.O. Box 180, Jefferson City 65102

Montana Department of Fish, Wildlife and Parks, 1420 East Sixth Street, Helena 59620

Nebraska Game and Parks Commission, 2200 North 33rd Street, P.O. Box 30370, Lincoln 68503

Nevada Department of Wildlife, Box 10678, Reno 89520

New Hampshire Fish and Game Commission, 34 Bridge Street, Concord 03301

New Jersey Division of Fish, Game, and Wildlife, CN 400, Trenton 08625

New Mexico Game and Fish Department, Villagra Building, Santa Fe 87503

New York Division of Fish and Wildlife, 50 Wolf Road, Albany 12233

North Carolina Wildlife Resources Commission, Archdale Building, 512 North Salisbury Street, Raleigh 27611

North Dakota Game and Fish Department, 2121 Lovett Avenue, Bismark 58505

Ohio Division of Wildlife, Fountain Square, Columbus 43224

Oklahoma Department of Wildlife Conservation, 1801 North Lincoln, P.O. Box 53465, Oklahoma City 73152

Oregon Department of Fish and Wildlife, P.O. Box 3503, Portland 97208

Pennsylvania Game Commission, P.O. Box 1567, Harrisburg 17120

Rhode Island Division of Fish and Wildlife, 83 Park Street, Providence 02903

South Carolina Wildlife and Marine Resources Department, Rembert C. Dennis Building, P.O. Box 167, Columbia 29202

South Dakota Game, Fish and Parks Department, 445 East Capitol, Pierre 57501

Tennessee Wildlife Resources Agency, P.O. Box 40747, Ellington Agricultural Center, Nashville 37204

Texas Parks and Wildlife Department, 4200 Smith School Road, Austin 78744

Utah Division of Wildlife Resources, 1596 W. North Temple, Salt Lake City 84116

Vermont Division of Fish and Wildlife, Montpelier 05602

Virginia Game Division, 4010 West Broad Street, Box 11104, Richmond 23230

Washington Department of Game, 600 North Capitol Way, Olympia 98504

West Virginia Department of Natural Resources, 1800 Washington Street East, Charleston 25305

Wisconsin Department of Natural Resources, Box 7921, Madison 53707

Wyoming Game and Fish Department, Cheyenne 82002

SEVENTEEN
TOMORROW'S DEER

"Too many of us," a noted wildlife biologist once said, "worry about how good the hunting will be this fall, and never give a second thought to how good the hunting will be for Sonny when he's old enough to own a rifle."

The biologist had a point. Deer have been on this continent for twenty million years or more. But what of their future? What will deer hunting be like ten years from now, or twenty-five, or fifty? I've asked this question of many knowledgeable deer researchers, people who keep a critical eye on the entire deer picture and look far into the future. Taken together, their answers give us an interesting glance at what might be in store for deer and the people who hunt them.

For this year, and the next few years, the situation will probably go on about as it is now, the range supporting about the same number of deer we have. Habitat conditions over large areas tend to change gradually.

But there is another side to the picture: the number of deer hunters continues to grow. The more hunters there are, the further the deer supply must stretch. This has some authorities concerned because, as one wildlife professor explains, "The future of deer hunting anywhere depends on the interaction of three variables: deer population levels, deer habitat, and people."

The same professor points out that there has been a remarkable increase in whitetails since World War II, but that we cannot expect this growth to continue at the same rate indefinitely.

When deer population levels are below the carry-ing capacity of the land, deer increase. When they reach the capacity of the food supply, their numbers tend to stabilize. Because deer population size is, to a large extent, a function of the food available, there is a point beyond which it cannot increase. Deer populations throughout much of the country have reached levels where they are now a threat to their own food supplies or to commercial forestry and agriculture.

Deer numbers respond to changes in land use, especially farm and forestry practices. For some years, marginal farmland was being abandoned at a rapid rate through large sections of the country as agricultural production was shifted to big agribusiness-type operations and away from the small family-owned farms, especially those in less productive hill country. Deer prospered on these lands and the variety of second-growth vegetation that grew there. Then, as the trees matured, the available deer food supplies diminished and the deer herds leveled off.

Some timber harvesting is good for deer. As openings are created in woods, a variety of food plants move in within reach of the animals. Many corporate timberland owners now employ wildlife biologists and permit free access by deer hunters.

In the West, the populations of mule deer have fluctuated, sometimes mysteriously. High populations during the 1950s were followed by dwindling numbers of mule deer in the 1960s and on into the 1970s. Trends in the numbers of mule deer taken by hunters more or less followed the population trends, partly because states and provinces further

These Rocky Mountain mule deer are concentrated on a winter feeding ground during a period of food shortage. Properly designed hunting seasons help match deer numbers to carrying capacity of their range. *U.S. Forest Service*

restricted hunting as deer populations fell. There is widespread belief among wildlife scientists that mule deer population declines cannot be attributed to overhunting.

Numerous causes have been blamed, but, some biologists again note, the trouble stems from habitat changes. Guy E. Connolly, wildlife research biologist for the U.S. Fish and Wildlife Service, writing in the book *Mule and Black-tailed Deer of North America,* published by the Wildlife Management Institute, says, ". . . deer numbers ultimately are limited by habitat quantity and quality."

Following their low levels in many western states the mule deer began to increase again before 1980.

Holy Does

One of the most effective, if misleading, deer pictures ever taken was published in Michigan during the 1930s. The photographer came upon a dead doe in the woods, perhaps a deer shot out of season by a poacher who became frightened and left it rather than chance arrest. The photographer then found a spotted fawn still very much alive. To give his picture emphasis he posed the sad-eyed little fawn with the dead doe. To the public, here was dramatic evidence that shooting does—under any circumstances—was reprehensible and anticonservation. The fawn was innocent enough. He didn't belong to

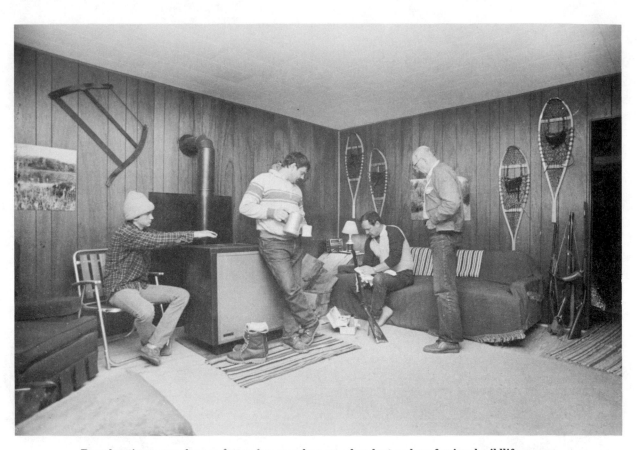

Deer-hunting camps have a future because deer are abundant and professional wildlife managers and research scientists work steadily to better understand deer and their needs.

the dead doe and, for that matter, probably was not even abandoned. But the picture did its work in helping perpetuate the legal shooting of bucks only.

Attitudes against shooting does cannot all be attributed to a single picture, but such pictures reflected a pattern of thinking that is still prevalent among hunters. However, Michigan wildlife biologists have calculated that, except for the bucks-only law, the state's hunters could have taken another one and a third million deer between 1930 and 1957 without harming the breeding herd in the least.

The buck law can be the right course while the deer herd is building toward the carrying capacity of the land. But once the herd reaches that level, a bucks-only law may allow deer to multiply to a level that threatens their food supply. This is especially true in northern states, famous for their whitetail hunting, and in much of the mule deer and blacktail-deer territory.

Deer are endowed by nature with amazing repro-

ductive potential. In 1928, four does and two bucks were released in a fenced 1,200-acre area on Michigan's George River Reserve. Until that time, the reserve had no deer. Five years later it had 160 whitetails.

How much of the annual deer production is taken by hunters varies from state to state. Overall, the annual harvest is believed to be around 10 percent of the population. A healthy deer herd, however, may be able to replace as much as a third of its numbers annually.

In general, hunters tend to want more restrictions on deer hunting as deer populations decrease, but this is not always a sound course in managing the deer herd. Instead, the final decision should be left to the professional wildlife managers, who spend their lives studying the animals. If the wildlife managers call for more or less hunting of does or more or fewer days of hunting, they normally have sound reasons. Permitting politicians to make

Modern high-speed highways are death traps for deer. Twin fawns were observed near where this doe was killed by a speeding vehicle. The danger of deer-vehicle collisions is greatest at night.

most fatal blow in their destruction. As the first tap of their death knell rings out . . . the hunter encases his smoking rifle and reflects upon the tragedy of 1919."

The Wisconsin citizens of 1908 and 1919 might well have saved their tears. But how were they to know that sixty-five years later Wisconsin hunters would be shooting not six thousand deer a year, but one hundred and sixty thousand, and all without harming the herd? That state alone estimates its whitetail herd today at eight hundred thousand deer.

Weeping for the Deer

game-management decisions is the worst possible answer. You do not necessarily increase the size of a deer herd by saving does. Poorly fed does drop fewer fawns than they would if they were well nourished. The more deer you crowd into an area, the less food there is to go around. Starvation becomes a fact of life.

Once does are on the protected list, reopening hunting of them is extremely difficult. One thing that amazes game and fish commissions is the ease with which they can shorten seasons and not be criticized by hunters, but if they suggest longer seasons, they are quickly and vigorously criticized.

A yellowing issue of the Mosinee, Wisconsin, *Times,* of November 6, 1908, says: "It has been estimated that last year [1907] over six thousand deer were killed in this state alone, and it is probable that the figures this year will reach nearly that amazing amount. And then people wonder why deer are getting scarcer."

But by 1919, the Wisconsin deer were still going strong. That year another Wisconsin publication carried this story: "When the tragic history of the extermination of the whitetail deer is finally written, the year 1919 will stand out as contributing the

On occasion the newspapers report that concerned "nature lovers" have stirred up a hullabaloo aimed at "saving" the deer they view as threatened by hunters and wildlife managers. Usually these deer live in a park or wildlife refuge where wildlife managers find their numbers increasing far in excess of the available food, and recommend a hunting season to bring the deer population more in line with the food supplies. Those who would "save" these deer believe that no deer should be killed by hunters, ever.

The humane activists have a point regarding national parks as well as most state or municipal parks because these are traditional non-hunting areas. But they extend their campaigns to include national wildlife refuges, which are highly managed areas. Their problem is myopia. While insisting that every individual animal be allowed to live until old age takes it, they lose sight of the fact that their aims endanger the whole population. Overpopulation of deer, or other species, can destroy habitat, then the deer die of starvation or become more susceptible to disease.

Sometimes they suggest capturing the excess deer and moving them to other areas. But any suitable area they could suggest already has its stock of

Numerous states now offer rewards and anonymity to citizens who turn in poachers.

deer. Dumping extra deer elsewhere might make the "protectionists" feel better, but it would accomplish little to benefit the deer.

No Deer for the Poachers

Poachers are not my favorite people. I don't warm up much to thieves, whether they steal money or wild deer. The law enforcement people have no way of knowing how many deer are taken illegally every year. Many states believe that the number equals or exceeds the total legal kill of deer during the hunting seasons. What they do know is that catching these outlaws is costly, difficult, and frustrating. I have ridden with game protectors trying to catch jacklighters, and the big problem is to

be on the scene and catch them before they can toss their gun and light in the ditch, or while they are actually working on a deer.

Some poachers are family meat hunters, others are professionals. Ohio had a poacher who eluded the wildlife law enforcement agents for years before finally being caught with the evidence. Once captured and convicted, he bragged that he had killed 389 deer out of season. He was infuriated when the judge gave him four months in jail. "You ain't seen nothing yet," he said. "Wait till I get out."

Occasionally, the officers will uncover a market operation involving a whole ring of professional poachers. In one such operation, in Michigan, 160 game agents, state and federal, captured fifty-three poachers in one roundup, breaking up a ring that had been supplying meat markets in Detroit and Jackson with wild game of wide variety.

In recent years, law-abiding citizens have begun to take a fresh look at poachers and have become more willing to turn them in. New Mexico set up a system to encourage people to feed the authorities tips on poachers' activities. They called their plan "Operation Game Thief," and provided a means for tipsters to remain anonymous. Furthermore, he or she could reap a reward for helping catch the poachers. The rewards for turning in deer poachers started at $250 and could go as high as $1,100, depending on the case.

As this plan began producing positive results for New Mexico, other states adapted it to their needs. In Ohio, after three years of anonymous rewards to tipsters, that state's TIP (Turn In A Poacher) plan had paid out $10,757 in rewards in deer-poaching cases and arrested eighty deer poachers. The fines collected totaled $24,000.

The promise of rewards doubtless accounts for much of the success of the TIP system and other such programs, but perhaps these poacher-fighting methods are making it socially acceptable to report poachers. The deer, and the law-abiding hunter, benefit. There remains much to accomplish, because annually deer poaching produces a multimillion-dollar loss of a valuable natural resource.

Law enforcement agents need the following information from those wanting to help bring deer poachers to justice: license number, description of vehicle, details on suspects, time of incident, place of incident, location of poached deer.

Biologists assure us that the future looks good for deer, and as long as the deer are there, hunters will look forward to the cool days of autumn when the new season opens.

Good Old Days

Deer hunting today is widely believed to be the best since the days of the settlers. There may be more deer, especially whitetails, than ever before. Furthermore, their numbers promise to remain high. Overall, the future of North American deer looks promising indeed. The adaptable whitetails, living around cornfields and superhighways, as well as in the remote woodlands, continue to prosper, and in many areas reach near-pest proportions. The future looks good for mule deer hunting and excellent for whitetails.

A Question of Manners

A big threat to deer hunting, or any hunting, is the growing conflict between hunters and those who believe that there should be no hunting. Hunters can strengthen their own case by sportsmanlike conduct in the outdoors.

We must understand that we owe more to the sport than the cost of a license and shells. We owe respect to the land and appreciation to the landowners permitting us to hunt. To the wild game we owe the restraint that keeps us from taking shots too long or too difficult for our level of skill with the gun or bow we carry. We owe it to the future of hunting everywhere and to our fellow humans to bring our best manners with us when we go into the outdoors.